D1570604

Proletarian Peasants

By the same author:

Gentry Politics on the Eve of Revolution:
The Russian Nationalist Party, 1905-1917

Proletarian Peasants

THE REVOLUTION OF 1905 IN RUSSIA'S SOUTHWEST

ROBERT EDELMAN

CORNELL UNIVERSITY PRESS

ITHACA AND LONDON

Copyright © 1987 by Cornell University

First published 1987 by Cornell University Press.

International Standard Book Number (cloth) 0-8014-2000-8
International Standard Book Number (paper) 0-8014-9473-7
Library of Congress Catalog Card Number 87-47544
Printed in the United States of America
Librarians: Library of Congress cataloging information
appears on the last page of the book.

The paper in this book is acid-free and meets the guidelines for
permanence and durability of the Committee on Production Guidelines
for Book Longevity of the Council on Library Resources.

This one's for Harry Scheiber, friend, fighter, and the only Giant fan I have ever truly forgiven.

Contents

Preface

This book examines the actions of peasants during the Russian Revolution of 1905. It concentrates on the right-bank Ukraine, an agriculturally advanced region known before 1917 as the southwestern borderland of the Russian Empire,[1] and is based on research conducted in regional Soviet archives little used by western historians. The work deals at the same time with the larger issues of rural revolution and peasant politics which activists and scholars throughout the world have debated for the last century and a half. Even today the majority of humanity is still peasant, and the difficulties of the developing world undermine global stability in such a way as to give these debates and issues continuing vitality.

The Russian experience is particularly germane to the understanding and resolution of these problems. At the time of the Revolution of 1917, three-quarters of the Russian population was rural. Events in the cities may have been decisive for the Bolshevik victory, but the revolution could not have succeeded without the mas-

---

[1]Throughout the text I have used "right-bank Ukraine" and "southwest" interchangeably simply in order to avoid repetition. Given the Ukraine's historical subjection to Russia, this rhetorical convenience might be taken to mask real differences in significance which are not intended here. To say "southwest" rather than "right-bank" could be construed as an acceptance of the idea of Russian domination, but such an impression of my position would be mistaken.

sive upheaval that swept the villages. Since then many historians of other nations have sought to understand the peasant world through theoretical approaches developed by Russian thinkers who survived the years of profound change in the countryside.

Because peasant revolution continues to be a matter for current concern, I have tried to make this investigation accessible to general readers as well as specialists. This choice has required that I write a work of manageable length, using nontechnical language. When two or three examples sufficiently demonstrate a phenomenon, I have restrained myself from including another eight. The first two chapters situate the case study in terms of the issues of rural revolution and peasant politics. Specialists will find original material primarily in chapters 3 and 4, which deal with the events of 1905.

The title of this work may seem an oxymoron. Proletarians and peasants have been, after all, very different kinds of laboring people. Rarely have they shared geography, economic activity, or cultural attitudes. More often than not, their political allegiances have diverged. My first concern is with the rural world. Peasants are my primary subject. "Proletarian," used as a modifier, merely describes certain characteristics of people who are otherwise fundamentally peasant.

This choice of words is deliberate. When a socialist revolution took place in Russia in 1917, it did so with the support of a politically conscious and militant revolutionary urban working class. Recent scholarship has located Bolshevik support among the most skilled and educated segments of the proletariat. This experience was unlike that of contemporary western Europe, where workers who had spent many years in the city took reformist rather than revolutionary paths. Scholars of Russia long sought to explain these differences by identifying the special characteristics of the Russian working class. Concentrating on Russia's backwardness, many emigré historians, representing the views of defeated candidates for power, argued that Russian workers were closer to their rural roots than their counterparts in the West. Illiterate Russian peasants were assumed to be unconsciously angry, rebellious, anarchic, and violent. Rebellious proletarians were then presumed to be peasants in worker disguise. The violence of the Russian worker could, in this fashion, be explained away.

Despite the new wave of scholarship, this theme remains alive, and there is still disagreement concerning the degree to which the Russian urban proletariat retained its rural roots.

In this book, I want to turn the tables and ask the opposite question: Under what circumstances might rural cultivators display the kind of rational, goal-directed behavior often ascribed to workers during strikes and revolutionary crises? Peasants acted in backward ways because they confronted conditions of backwardness. But was this phenomenon universal? In regions with modern, capitalistically organized agriculture, could one reasonably expect peasants also to react rationally and consciously at moments of political stress? The Ukrainian provinces of Kiev, Podol'e, and Volynia on the right bank of the Dniepr river comprised just such a modern region. During the revolutionary turmoil that began in 1905, these provinces witnessed thousands of strikes and disorders involving several million peasants and agricultural workers. Right-bank peasants demonstrated a capacity to formulate reasonable and realizable demands and to choose tactics and methods likely to achieve their goals. They were not especially violent, and their actions represented far more than the expression of elemental rage.

I am also attempting here to draw western scholars of Russia away from their search for the general and the typical. Those who have examined the history of other nations have produced a wide array of local and regional studies. Soviet specialists have done the same thing for the prerevolutionary Empire. Western historians of Russia, however, have not paid sufficient attention to the sharp regional variations in a vast territory. When they have focused on specific locales, they have until recently limited themselves to Moscow and Petersburg. Studies of rural Russia, when they have been focused at all, have tended to concentrate on the backward, but supposedly "typical," Central Black Earth and Mid-Volga regions. Assumptions about events and processes in significant peripheries have then been based on the picture of the center. Would a scholar of American agriculture claim that the findings of a work on farming in Iowa are typical for the rest of the United States? To gain a picture of what was truly universal, it is necessary to look outside the center of Russia.

For this reason, I have not sought to produce an account of the

Preface

Revolution of 1905 throughout rural Russia. In the course of broader works, Geroid T. Robinson, Teodor Shanin, Maureen Perrie, and Roberta Manning have provided clear and consistent pictures of rural Russia at that time. The highly empirical accounts of 1905 written by Soviet scholars in their own way support the approach of western historians. I have little quarrel with this prevailing view. My purpose, instead, has been to look closely at one analytically significant region, using local archival material to test concepts and theories relevant to the study not only of the Russian peasantry but of peasant revolution in general.

The reference to archives raises several thorny methodological points involved in research on the Russian peasantry. To paraphrase Marx, human beings write history but they do not write it under conditions of their own making. Ultimately historians are at the mercy of the sources available to them. Only Soviet scholars have produced detailed statistical treatments of the Russian peasant movement because only Soviet specialists have the unlimited access to archives and research time to produce such findings. Western scholars are granted limited stays in the Soviet Union. Once they are in the archives, they cannot see everything they wish to see. Catalogues can only rarely be consulted, and modern methods of photoreproduction have not been available. One may be shown but a portion of a large body of extant material. Extreme caution is required in the assessment of the typicality of those documents one does get to read.

Western scholars can make use of published statistical information available in Soviet and western libraries. Yet it is difficult if not impossible to correlate one's own archival data with Soviet statistics on peasant disturbances. Soviet and western analytical categories do not always correspond, and Soviet scholars are divided on the meaning of their own categories. I had hoped to correlate harvest statistics, available in the West, with archival information on strikes and disorders, but it proved impossible to obtain data that could be used alongside the published material. One is often limited to reproducing the work of Soviet historians. This information can then be combined with the more qualitative material found in the archives and elsewhere.

I make no claim to have resolved this methodological dilemma. I have sought to combine all sources, while pushing no claim beyond the limits of the available material. At times this method has required caution when boldness would be more satisfying to reader and author alike. Because of the difficulty of obtaining direct evidence, much western scholarship on rural Russia has concentrated on outsiders' perceptions of peasants. We know a great deal less about the peasants' own actions. Although I have paid attention to the rich Russian intellectual tradition concerning the peasant, my primary aim has been to describe what the peasants themselves actually did. Given the elusiveness of the peasant world, this has not always been an act of simple empiricism.

All dates in this work are in the Old Style Gregorian calendar used before the Revolution of 1917. The old calendar was thirteen days behind the new Julian calendar. This fact explains why, for example, the Revolution of October 25 is now celebrated on November 7.

There is no universally accepted system of transliteration used to render the Cyrillic alphabet into Latin letters. I have chosen to use the system known as Library of Congress, Type II.

This is a book about struggle, and it was written during several difficult years of professional and personal struggle. But though the period may have been a trial, it certainly was not a lonely one. I received much love, support, criticism, and comradeship during the years I was working on this book. My name may be on the cover, but the enterprise was truly a social one. For this, I am profoundly grateful.

David Macey and Maureen Perrie were my first mentors when I sought job retraining as a peasant specialist. They have read various drafts of the manuscript and have been constant sources of wisdom. Steve Hahn, Tom Dublin, and Esther Kingston-Mann carefully read the final product. Terry Emmons and Daniel Field criticized an earlier version. I have learned much from discussions with Tim Mixter, John Channon, Eric Van Young, Steve Wheatcroft, Bob Brenner, Judith Pallot, Bob Moeller, Frank Sysyn, and Rose Glickman. Ron Suny, Hans Rogger, Alexander Rabinowich, William Rosenberg, Reginald Zelnik, Loren Graham, Arno Mayer, Geoffrey Hosking, and Moshe Lewin provided crucial support when it was needed most. I owe a special debt to my colleagues in Kiev, Vladislav Verstiuk and Iurii Pavlovich Lavrov, for their hospitality and respect. I am especially grateful to the "history guys" of MARHO. Judith Evans, Jeannie Attie, Steve Brier, Josh Brown, Mike Wallace, Victoria diGrazia, Roy Rosenzweig, John Agnew, Harry Levine, and a host of others helped me reshape my sense of audience and regain my enthusiasm for the project and the profession. The Harvard Ukrainian Research Institute gave me the opportunity to learn the culture and history of the Ukraine. Jonathan Sanders provided ever-ready and jovial welcome at Columbia University's Harriman Institute for Advanced Russian Studies. Penny Waterstone helped assemble the tables in chapter 3. David Nasaw, Dinitia Smith, Steve Levitt, Manuella Dobos, Mary Malloy, Carol Becker, Jon Wiener, and Ruth Heifetz all contributed large ears and big hearts. At the end of the project Victoria Yablonsky appeared and gave the work its deepest possible meaning.

My greatest debt, however, is to Harry Scheiber. Without his faith, support, and very special effectiveness, I would never have been in a position to write this book.

I thank the Academic Senate of the University of California, San Diego; the National Endowment for the Humanties; the International Research and Exchanges Board; and the Kennan Institute for Advanced Russian Studies for generous financial assistance. The Academy of Sciences of the USSR in Moscow, Leningrad, and Kiev made possible a comfortable and efficient research stay in the Soviet Union.

I am grateful to the staffs of the Central State Archive of the October Revolution in Moscow, the Central State Historical Archive in Leningrad, the Central State Historical Archive of the Ukrainian SSR in Kiev, and the Zhitomir Region State Archive. I also thank the staffs of the Central University Library of University of California in San Diego (particularly Paul Zarins), the University of California Libraries in Los Angeles and Berkeley, the library of the Hoover Institution on War, Revolution and Peace at Stanford University, the University of Washington, Butler Library of Columbia University, the New York Public Library Slavonic Room, Widener Library of Harvard University, the Library of

Congress, the National Agricultural Library in Beltsville, Maryland, the British Library, the Baykov Library of Birmingham University, the Library of the University of London School of Slavic and East European Studies, the Institute for Historical Research, the Bibliothèque de Documentation Internationale Contemporaine, the Helsinki University Library, the Lenin Library in Moscow, and the Library of the Academy of Sciences in Leningrad.

ROBERT EDELMAN

Los Angeles, California

Proletarian Peasants

A Theoretical Debate,
a Political Struggle

On May 2, 1905, peasants in the province of Kiev withheld their labor from the large estate on which they had been working. Three years later, a correspondent of the semi-official Russian Imperial Free Economic Society, conducting a survey of the recent rural disorders, reported on the Kiev events:

> The earliest appearance of the movement occurred the second of May on the sugar plantation of A. Tereshchenko in Voitsovtsy [Skvir district]. According to the indictment, workers had received twenty-five kopecks a day since the early spring. In response to peasant demands, the wage was raised to forty kopecks. However, on the first of May, the administrators of the estate again lowered the wage to thirty kopecks. The peasants then demanded fifty to seventy kopecks and quit work on May 2. To replace them, peasants were invited from the neighboring villages of Verbovoi, Gorodishch, and Kharlievka. On May 10, a crowd of peasants from Voitsovtsy appeared on Tereshchenko's plantation with sticks and whips in their hands. They demanded that the peasants from the other villages cease work immediately. "Leave the fields," they said, "They didn't give us these kinds of wages. We don't need you here." When the outside workers did not stop, the peasants of Voitsovtsy threw themselves on the strikebreakers and, shouting loudly, drove them off. . . . Then the peasants headed for Tereshchenko's stables and

barns and pulled those working there off the job, threatening to "break their heads." The stablehands were warned not to return until the lord raised the daily wage. However, according to witnesses, the stablehands voluntarily stopped work and agreed not to come back until another ten kopecks a day had been "torn from the lord."[1]

Fifty-three years before the peasants of Voitsovtsy went on strike, Karl Marx sought to explain the politically conservative behavior of the French peasantry during the recent revolution and counterrevolution. In *The Eighteenth Brumaire* and *The Class Struggles in France,* Marx established the negative attitudes that urban-oriented socialists would bring to the analysis of the countryside. Rural votes had just swept Louis Napoleon into office. In the eyes of the left, peasants were individualistic, greedy, and ignorant, hardly the appropriate social base for revolution.

Long before 1852, Russian thinkers had been struggling to comprehend the character of their own peasantry. The celebrated debates between Slavophile and Westernizer intellectuals had been couched in moral and religious terms, but at their core, these arguments centered on the nature of what some outsiders chose to see as simple folk. Were peasants like other people, or was there something special and fundamentally different about their lives? The next question followed logically. Was Russia subject to the same laws of development as other nations, or was it exceptional?[2] Slavophiles rhapsodized over the purity and nobility of the only Russians untainted by foreign influence. These conservative intellectuals pictured harmonious and cohesive communities of mutually respectful village dwellers practicing traditional customs in peace and dignity. Liberal and radical Westernizers, on the other hand, felt the Russian countryside was a sea of ignorance, poverty, and exploitation. For them, peasants were as capable of selfishness

[1]*Agrarnoe dvizhenie v Rossii v 1905–1906 gg. (Trudy imperatorskago vol'nago ekonomicheskago obshchestva,* 1908, nos. 3, 4–5), 2 vols. (St. Petersburg, 1908), 2:173 (hereafter *AD*). (Translations are my own unless otherwise noted.)

[2]Martin Malia, *Alexander Herzen and the Birth of Russian Socialism* (New York, 1961), pp. 278–334. Andrzej Walicki, *The Slavophile Controversy* (Oxford, 1975), p. 531.

and brutality as anyone else. This debate was, in the most fundamental sense, about understanding the peasant world. Yet it was
also a political struggle about the future of Russian development.
Would Russia follow the historical path of the West, a path that
doomed the peasantry to extinction, or could that fate somehow be
avoided? These issues were not resolved in the 1840s and 1850s.
They have continued to reemerge throughout Russian and Soviet
history and have left an extremely ambiguous legacy even today.

In the 1880s and 1890s, populist and Marxist revolutionaries
asked precisely the same questions in the course of their extended
polemic about the socialist potential of the traditional repartitional
commune *(mir)* which periodically redivided the land among its
households. Was there, they asked, true equality in the *mir?* Russian Marxists doubted that such a state of affairs had ever existed,
but more important, they thought the commune, even if it had
functioned at one time, was now dying. As Russia's industrial base
and cities began to grow, a market emerged for an agrarian surplus
produced by the countryside. The subsistence economies of the
villages had permitted peasants to lead relatively hermetic exis-
tences. Their self-sufficiency was now undermined. As capitalism
came to the land, Marxists argued that the peasant could no longer
be considered exceptional. The same principles and categories that
explained the behavior of those in the towns could now be applied
to those living in rural Russia. The homogeneous traditional peasantry was to be replaced by rural counterparts of those classes
found in the cities. In response, populists denied the profundity of
these changes and maintained that Russia did not have to pass
through the modes of production that Marxists thought all societies passed through. They thought it possible to avoid the hor-
rors of capitalism by passing directly from a traditional to a socialist society. In this process, a crucial example was to be provided
by the long-standing cooperative practices of the commune. Populists did not deny the demonstrable evidence of inequality in the
countryside. Rather, they understood its sources and consequences
differently than Marxists.[3] As in the 1850s, the argument centered

[3]Esther Kingston-Mann, "Marxism and Russian Rural Development: Problems
of Evidence, Experience, and Culture," *American Historical Review* 86 (October
1981), 734.

on the usefulness of certain universal schema for understanding life in the Russian countryside. Again, the stakes in the debate were not simply theoretical but also political. Both groups were seeking to overthrow tsarism, and their arguments concerned the fitness of the peasantry as the social basis of a possible revolution.

Before and after 1917, the populist Socialist Revolutionary party continued these arguments with the Marxist Social Democrats. Among Social Democrats, the Bolshevik and Menshevik wings of the party continually differed on the role of rural cultivators in the socialist movement. Mensheviks tended to ignore the countryside, while Lenin and some of his colleagues had positive views about the peasantry's revolutionary potential. After the revolution, the question of understanding rural society was at the center of the great theoretical and political struggles of the 1920s. Among agricultural specialists, Alexander V. Chaianov and his Organization and Production school were attacked as "neo-populists" by their opponents, L. N. Kritsman and the Agrarian Marxist group, who offered an analytical approach closer to that advanced before the revolution by Lenin. Debates between the left and right wings of the Bolshevik party also centered, in large measure, around the "peasant question." This extremely rich and continuing tradition contributed much theory to the study of peasants not only in Russia but throughout the world.[4] Neither camp could claim to have vanquished the other intellectually. Both sides had able representatives capable of making strong cases. It was only with Stalin's forced collectivization that many of these issues were rendered moot.

In the 1930s and 1940s, the once-raging controversy seemed meaningless, given Stalin's unilateral termination and resolution of the debate. The success of the Chinese, Vietnamese, and Cuban revolutions, however, revived interest in peasant politics and changed many attitudes about the revolutionary potential of rural cultivators. The preponderance of peasants among the population of the Third World gave the old arguments new immediacy. The poor of the countryside were no longer considered politically retro-

[4]Terry Cox, "Class Analysis of the Russian Peasantry: The Research of Kritsman and His School," *Journal of Peasant Studies* 11 (January 1984), 11–60.

grade. Marx's characterization of the mid-nineteenth-century French peasantry as politically conservative was challenged by peasant participation in modern revolutions in the developing countries. To explain these unexpected phenomena, new attention was focused on the "moral economy" of village life. Cultural considerations, rather than economic decision making, were invoked to explain patterns of behavior that seemed otherwise irrational. To understand the peasant world, one had to view it on its own terms, not the terms of the city. This new approach was strikingly similar to the old Slavophile concept of peasant uniqueness. The universal assumptions of classical economics, shared by Marxists and non-Marxists alike, were now thought to be inappropriate to the rural world. Peasants were not seen as petty entrepreneurs concerned with maximizing profits. Their first priority was simply survival. A new emphasis was placed on the internal workings of the village itself. The retention of custom was no longer dismissed as mere superstition. In response, other writers reemphasized the political economy of the peasant world and noted the rationality of peasant decision making. A wide variety of Marxist writers, having abandoned many older orthodoxies, rejoined the debate as well, stressing the relationships of the village to such external forces as markets, landlords, and governments.

As in the 1890s and the 1920s, the more recent debates recall those between the Slavophiles and Westernizers. Could peasants be understood according to principles that had proved useful in analyzing the lives of many millions of other people, or is it necessary to invent a whole new approach that emphasizes the special qualities of the peasant world? The present debate is perhaps more theoretical than earlier versions, but, in many ways, it revives the older political struggles. Many of the same questions posed about past events are again being asked: How homogeneous was the village? Was there significant stratification? What kinds of social and economic choices did the peasants make? Was culture a meaningful force in the countryside? Copious quantities of Russian ink and blood have been spilled trying to find workable answers to these questions. Progress has surely been made as others have joined the debate, but it should be clear that the old arguments still have meaning.

Because of its prevailing illiteracy, the peasant world does not reveal itself easily to the historian. When the timeless equilibrium of village life is left to run its own course, one cannot learn all one needs to know. For that reason, moments of instability, disturbances of one sort or another, provide opportunities to break through peasants' necessarily self-preserving secrecy. When they were forced to confront the forces acting upon them, peasants exposed the internal workings of their communities. Their political activity was, however, not the same as the involvement of the city dweller. Parties and other organizations were few, and their rural networks were tenuous at best. But fires, crop stealing, destruction of property, and agrarian strikes were political acts nonetheless. This book is concerned, first and foremost, with one of these atypical but telling moments of instability. The character of the disturbances speaks to the character of peasant life.

Political activists and scholars have always wanted to know which elements within the village have taken the lead, who has participated, who has stood aside. All these outsiders, whether states or revolutionaries, have looked to the countryside for political support of one sort or another. Their analyses of rural life were, therefore, undertaken with the goal of identifying likely allies.

The various political groups contending for peasant loyalty "wagered," to borrow the phrase of one Russian prime minister, on particular elements within the countryside. The tsarist government went so far as to foster the creation of an authentic rural bourgeoisie. This book seeks to evaluate the success of a different sort of political "bet." Politicians and historians, both Marxist and non-Marxist, have been affected in fundamental ways by the revolutionary example of propertyless industrial workers in the cities. In following this logic, considerable attention has been paid to landless, wage-earning laborers as a potentially revolutionary force in the countryside. Some have even referred to these men and women as a "rural proletariat" and viewed them as an especially militant force for change in the village. The actions of this segment of the rural population cannot be separated from the actions of others who worked the land, but their special position provides an analytical starting point for an examination of the broader peasant movement. I intend to evaluate the political potential of what were called "agricultural workers," by looking at their actions in a part of the world in which agrarian wage work was quite common (the Ukrainian provinces of Kiev, Podol'e, and Volynia on the right bank of the Dniepr, the southwestern region of the Russian Empire). I examine their actions at a moment of extreme political agitation and social unrest (the Revolution of 1905–7). This region, where commercial agriculture had made great strides in the late nineteenth century, was engulfed by a wave of strikes and disturbances involving millions of peasants between the spring of 1905 and the summer of 1907.

In an investigation of this sort, it is necessary to devote special attention to the specific forms chosen by rural cultivators to express their resistance. Peasant aims and tactics were not superficial phenomena. Rather, they express deeper truths about the character of all peasant societies and the nature of their politics. In making these choices, were peasants motivated by the forces they confronted outside the village or did they act according to the customs, norms, and traditions of their own communities? Did they respond, as Marxists have argued, to phenomena external to their world, or were their actions rooted, as culturalists claim, in the timeless internal structures of peasant life?

In looking at Russia's southwest during 1905, I concentrate on these two sets of questions. Events in this distinctive region require both schools of thought to examine their assumptions and expectations concerning peasant behavior at moments of crisis. It is not simply that each of the prevailing explanations is only partly successful in explaining events in these provinces. Rather, an investigation of this sort can suggest ways in which both schools can revise their thinking.

Views of the Rural Proletariat

Russian revolutionaries of the late nineteenth century continually analyzed the social structure of the countryside. In doing this, they hoped to pinpoint those groups that would support the struggle against the tsarist state. The swift industrialization which began in the 1880s threatened the populist belief that the repartitional commune, with its periodic redivisions of the land, contained the kernel of a future socialist society. Marxist intellectuals believed the growth of Russian capitalism spelled doom for the traditional organizations of the peasantry. V. I. Lenin was but one of several contributors to this controversy. His subsequent political success meant that his works on the subject became the basis of current Soviet historiographical orthodoxy on peasants. Lenin's views on rural Russia still represent a starting point for most subsequent Marxist and much non-Marxist thought on agrarian economics in general and the Russian experience in particular. Along with many in the revolutionary movement and the tsarist government, Lenin argued that the growth of Russian capitalism was extensive and irreversible and that this shift had changed social and economic relations on the land. The cohesion of the commune would now be undermined. Instead of cooperating, Russian peasants were now thought to be competing with each other. The accumulated advantages and disadvantages in this competition led over time to class differentiation in the village. A relatively homogeneous peasantry would now be replaced by a "rural bourgeoisie" of rich peasants and a "rural proletariat" of the poor and landless. The group of traditional peasants, whose level of wealth fell in the middle of these expanding extremes, was thought to be ever diminishing. Under the impact of capitalism, social relations on the land were now supposed to resemble those of the city.[5]

Russian Marxists had fixed on the urban proletariat as the social force that would lead an eventual socialist revolution. Yet the working class of the cities was still a small fraction of the entire population. To be politically effective, workers had to seek allies. In the countryside, the most logical choice was that group of workers described by Lenin as the rural proletariat.[6] It was expected that this group would become the most militant and active revolutionary force on the land. Although he was well aware of the unclear relationship of the rural proletariat to the poorer elements of the peasantry, Lenin maintained a faith throughout his career in

[5]V. I. Lenin, *The Development of Capitalism in Russia*, in *Collected Works*, 4th ed., 12 vols. (Moscow, 1972), 3:175.
[6]Ibid., p. 179.

what he often simply called the "rural poor."[7] Accordingly, subsequent Soviet studies have assigned a paramount role to what they have called a rural proletariat. In attributing revolutionary potential, if not socialist consciousness, to this group, Lenin went beyond the pessimistic expectations of Marx and Engels. In *The Eighteenth Brumaire* and elsewhere, Marx was hardly optimistic about the revolutionary potential of the peasantry. Later in his career, in correspondence with early Russian populists, he showed some willingness to see potential in the commune. More generally, Marx held some hope that a segment of the rural population, ruined by the growth of capitalism, might then ally with the industrial working class.[8] Engels, writing after many Prussian peasants had already been rendered landless, harbored a similar belief, despite his essential pessimism about a social group he considered to be doomed by the advance of history:

> The agricultural proletariat . . . is the class which, thanks to universal suffrage, sends into parliament the numerous feudal lords and Junkers; but it is also the class nearest to the industrial workers of the towns, which shares their living conditions and is steeped in misery even more than they. To galvanize and draw into the movement this class, important because split and scattered, is the immediate task of the German labor movement.[9]

By 1900, many educated Russians (inside and outside the government) shared the belief that an inevitable advance toward capitalism had already begun.[10] Later historical accounts contributed

---

[7]Lenin, "To the Rural Poor," *The Alliance of the Working Class and the Peasantry* (Moscow, 1959), pp. 43, 71, and 86. See also "The Agrarian Program of Social-Democracy in the First Russian Revolution," *Collected Works*, 13:241.

[8]Karl Marx, *The Eighteenth Brumaire of Louis Bonaparte* (New York, 1963); *Capital*, 3 vols. (New York, 1967), 3:123–24, 334–35. See also Gavin Lewis, "Conservative Agrarianism in Lower Austria," *Past and Present*, no. 62 (November 1978), 120.

[9]Frederick Engels, *The Peasant War in Germany* (Moscow, 1974), p. 16.

[10]Teodor Shanin, *The Awkward Class: Political Sociology of Peasantry in a Developing Society* (Oxford, 1972), p. 1. Anita Baker, "Deterioration or Development? The Peasant Economy of Moscow Province prior to 1914," *Russian History* 5 (January 1978), 1–2.

to a strange but not altogether surprising consensus among Marxist revolutionaries, tsarist officials, and Western scholars, most of whom shared assumptions concerning the "rationality" of the peasant as the market economy came to the countryside.[11] Most scholars held the view that various forms of capitalism were widespread features of rural life right up to the moment of forced collectivization in 1930 and 1931. As competitive production for the market replaced the traditional peasant goal of subsistence, clearly defined social classes with antagonistic interests were supposed to emerge. It was also believed (by Leninists in particular) that people in the countryside could readily perceive those social divisions and that they acted politically according to a precise understanding of class tensions in the village. The emergence of clearly defined social classes necessarily led to the growth of a true class struggle on the land.

Since the 1960s, these older views have been challenged by a number of writers from several disciplines. Today one would be hard pressed (even in the Soviet Union) to find a thoroughgoing defense of the orthodox Leninist position on the rural proletariat. The idea that landless wage earners played a universally vanguard role in agrarian disturbances is not widely accepted. Divisions among Western students of peasantries now center on two questions: first, whether landless laborers may be included at all among those who play crucial roles in rural disorders and, second, whether landholding peasants, under certain circumstances, may behave much like urban workers.

In comparative works, which made extensive reference to the

[11]E. H. Carr and R. W. Davies, *Foundations of a Planned Economy*, 2 vols. (London, 1969), vol. 1. Sylvain Bensidoun, *L'Agitation paysanne en Russie de 1880 à 1902* (Paris, 1975). Maurice Dobb, *Soviet Economic Development since 1917* (New York, 1966). Lazar Volin, *A Century of Russian Agriculture* (Cambridge, 1970). Naum Jasny, *The Socialized Agriculture of the U.S.S.R.* (Stanford, 1949). G. P. Pavlovsky, *Russian Agriculture on the Eve of the Revolution*, (New York, 1968). Exceptions to this consensus, more by virtue of caution than by an elaborated counterexplanation, are the classic account of Geroid T. Robinson, *Rural Russia under the Old Regime* (Berkeley, 1932), the more impressionistic work of John Maynard, *The Russian Peasant and Other Studies* (New York, 1942), and Lancelot Owen, *The Russian Peasant Movement, 1906–1917* (London, 1937).

Russian case, Eric Wolf and Hamza Alavi were among the first to argue that the so-called middle peasant (the group least affected by rural capitalism) was the most active supporter of rebellion.[12] Wolf went so far as to exclude landless laborers from his definition of peasant because the landless could not make "autonomous" decisions concerning the process of cultivation and because they did not possess the tactical mobility of the middle peasant who could revert to subsistence farming in times of trouble. Landless laborers were dependent on their wage for survival, and without it, they were literally left with nothing.[13] Instead of militance, rural proletarians exhibited political paralysis. Teodor Shanin also defined the landless laborer as "analytically marginal," but rather than focusing on a particular element of peasant society as a special repository of militance, he described the entire village as a politically, socially, and culturally cohesive unit acting in opposition to all outsiders be they landlords, bureaucrats, priests, commissars, or merchants.[14] Shanin had less, if anything, to say about peasant attitudes toward their counterparts in other villages.

Writing at roughly the same time, Barrington Moore agreed that assigning a leading role to the rural proletariat was not possible. He refused to rule out this group as a significant participant in agrarian unrest, however.[15] Henry Landsberger saw strong similarities between rural protests and labor agitations, the differences being less of kind than of degree. He refused to exclude the landless from the category of peasant and insisted that this group could be active in a broad variety of disturbances. The specific role assumed by these kinds of workers was to be determined by empirical research on specific historical situations.[16] Sidney Mintz, however, noted that studies of this sort could not always identify and isolate

[12]Eric Wolf, *Peasant Wars of the Twentieth Century* (New York, 1969), pp. 291–92. Hamza Alavi, "Peasants and Revolution," *The Socialist Register* (1965), 241–77.

[13]Wolf, 1969, p. 290.

[14]Shanin, 1972, pp. 203–18.

[15]Barrington Moore, *The Social Origins of Dictatorship and Democracy* (Boston, 1966), p. 455.

[16]Henry Landsberger, "Peasant Unrest: Themes and Variations," in Henry Landsberger, ed., *Rural Protest: Peasant Movements and Social Change* (London, 1974), p. 14.

landless wage earners with the precision one might desire. Rural proletarians were not the same as urban proletarians, and their presence could be concealed by many of the structures and practices of the communities of which they may have been a part.[17]

Empirical studies, conducted since these differing views were published, have demonstrated the difficulty of arriving at a clear picture even when they have confirmed the participation of landless laborers in agrarian unrest. Recent work on modern Europe has shown that those fitting a strict definition of rural proletarian were far from invisible at moments of turmoil. It should come as no surprise that so orthodox a Marxist as Albert Soboul found evidence of militance on the part of the landless in nineteenth-century France.[18] Maurice Agulhon and Ted Margadant have described similar phenomena.[19] J. A. Perkins and Robert Moeller have offered documentation for a rural proletarian presence in eastern Germany.[20] Not one of these writers has tried to demonstrate a vanguard role for this segment of the rural population, however.

The debate about the most militant segment of the village population raises many broader questions. It was and is a conflict about the nature of the countryside in moments of stability as well as instability. Differences about the role of a rural proletariat are tied to larger arguments about how best to understand rural society and politics in general. As such, a discussion of Lenin's specific concern for the landless raises definitional problems which require an examination of the varying opinions on the peasant and rural life.

[17]Sidney Mintz, "The Rural Proletariat and the Problem of Rural Proletarian Consciousness," *Journal of Peasant Studies* 2 (October 1974), 305.

[18]Albert Soboul, *Problèmes paysannes de la revolution (1789–1848)* (Paris, 1976), p. 117.

[19]Maurice Agulhon, Gabriel Desert, and Robert Specklin, *Apogée et crise de la civilisation paysanne*, vol. 3 of Georges Duby, ed., *L'Histoire de la France rurale*, 4 vols. (Paris, 1976), p. 46. Ted Margadant, *French Peasants in Revolt: The Insurrection of 1851* (Princeton, 1979), p. 79.

[20]J. A. Perkins, "The German Agricultural Worker, 1815–1914," *Journal of Peasant Studies* 11 (April 1984), 3–27. Robert Moeller, *German Peasants and Agrarian Politics, 1914–1924, The Rhineland and Westphalia* (Chapel Hill, N.C., 1986), pp. 18–19.

A Theoretical Debate, a Political Struggle

Schools of Thought on Peasantries

The challenge to what was once the prevailing consensus on the peasantry came both from those concerned with Russian and Soviet history and from those who adopted a more comparative and conceptual approach. A crucial element of these new interpretations has been the attempt to reestablish the analytical usefulness of the concept of "peasant." This project touched off renewed debate, and in the course of the discussion, it became possible to arrive at more specific understandings of the concepts of "peasant" and "rural proletarian."

In a sense these two terms for rural cultivators may seem incompatible with each other. Each term is rooted in a different political and scholarly tradition, and each reflects an emphasis on different factors as central to understanding social and political relations on the land. Marxists have long denied that the term "peasant" possesses any particular analytical meaning. They have argued that it is too broad and therefore useless for distinguishing the wide variety of groups one confronts on the land.[21] Wolf, Shanin, and others contended that there was such a thing as a universal peasant type and that peasant societies were homogeneous and cohesive.[22] In their view, not all those on the land could be called peasants; although the majority of agrarian working people could be placed in this broad category.

Social and cultural homogeneity explained political cohesion. The idea of the village as a working unit was inspired by such anthropological pioneers as Robert Redfield and A. L. Kroeber.[23] As a result, it became common for opponents of this new school to brand its representatives as "culturalists." I will also be using this

[21]Judith Enew, Paul Hirst, and Keith Tribe, "Peasantry as an Economic Category," *Journal of Peasant Studies* 4 (July 1977), 295. Mark Harrison, "Resource Allocation and Social Mobility among Russian Peasant Households, 1880–1930," *Journal of Peasant Studies* 4 (January 1977), 128.

[22]Shanin, 1972, p. 204. See also Teodor Shanin, "The Nature and Logic of the Peasant Economy," *Journal of Peasant Studies* 1 (October 1973), 63–80. Eric Wolf, *Peasants* (Englewood Cliffs, N.J., 1966), p. 2, and Wolf, 1969, pp. xii–xv.

[23] Robert Redfield, *Peasant Society and Culture* (Chicago, 1956), p. 23. A. L. Kroeber, *Anthropology* (New York, 1948), p. 284.

term primarily because it is brief enough and broad enough to encompass what is by no means a monolithic approach. Cultural considerations were also central to the views of Alexander Chaianov, who offered the most influential explanation of the economy of the peasant household and community. Chaianov, a Soviet agricultural economist, published both before and after the Revolution. He argued for the specificity of peasant production, and his views have influenced Shanin and many others.[24] Shanin's own definition of a peasant owes much to Chaianov. He highlights four elements: (1) a family farm; (2) land husbandry; (3) a specific traditional culture; (4) multidirectional subjection to powerful outsiders.[25]

Barrington Moore, despite sharp differences with the culturalist approach, offered a strikingly similar definition.[26] It included: (1) legal subordination to a landed class; (2) sharp cultural distinctions (distinct from landlords); (3) de facto possession of land. The ownership or control of land is crucial to both definitions. This consideration has led many to exclude agricultural laborers from the peasantry. According to Mintz, rural proletarians are landless, wage earning, and store buying. They may not be part of the self-sufficient community of peasants, but they may constitute communities on their own.[27] They are, in Eric Hobsbawm's words, part of the "agrarian problem" but not part of the "peasant problem."[28]

The distinction between the landless and the poor who possess some land is often blurred in the analysis of concrete historical situations. A rural proletariat is by no means the same as an urban proletariat. It might be expected that the surplus population in the countryside would be forced to migrate to the towns. If, however, the cities had not yet reached a stage of development sufficient to absorb people with no holdings, then the landless had little choice but to remain in the countryside. In this sense, a rural proletariat

[24]Alexander Chaianov, *The Theory of the Peasant Economy* (Homewood, Ill., 1966), p. xiv.
[25] Shanin, 1973, pt. 1, p. 64.
[26]Moore, p. 111.
[27]Mintz, 1974, p. 236.
[28]Eric Hobsbawm, "Peasants and Politics," *Journal of Peasant Studies* 1 (October 1973), 4.

may be considered a transitional phenomenon that emerges during what may be the lengthy period between the first signs of agrarian change and the full maturation of the urban industrial sector.

Nevertheless, the image of the propertyless city worker has profoundly affected subsequent thought (both Soviet and Western) on peasant societies and peasant disturbances. As a result, it may be surprising that Lenin's own use of the term was consciously ambiguous. He included both the landless (by his own estimate a relatively small group in Russia) and the poor landholding peasantry in the category of rural proletarians.[29] All those within this group were expected to behave in much the same manner. It was no accident Lenin lumped these two groups together. This analytical step reflected his sensitivity to the ambiguous character of Russian agriculture in the immediate prerevolutionary period:

> Our literature frequently contains too stereotyped an understanding of the theoretical position that capitalism requires the free, landless worker. This proposition is quite correct in indicating the main trend, but capitalism penetrates into agriculture particularly slowly and in extremely varied forms. The allotment of the rural workers is very often to the interests of the rural employers themselves, and that is why the allotment-holding rural worker is a type to be found in all capitalist countries.[30]

Whether he defined it broadly or narrowly, Lenin expected this group to be the element in the village most eager to take action against landlords and the state.

This less-than-orthodox approach to class categories led Lenin to describe poor peasants with some land as "semi-proletarians." He included in this sizable group those who could survive only by working for others or by renting their lands.[31] Thus, their situations were mixed. Wage-earning allotment holders exhibited some characteristics ascribed by Mintz to rural proletarians and other patterns ascribed by Shanin to peasants. One could, of course,

[29]Esther Kingston-Mann, *Lenin and the Problem of Marxist Peasant Revolution* (Oxford, 1983), p. 50.
[30]Lenin, *The Development of Capitalism in Russia*, p. 178.
[31]Kingston-Mann, 1983, p. 63.

argue that Lenin's use of the term "semi-proletarian" was just an analytically imprecise way to impute proletarian consciousness and revolutionary politics to what were simply peasants. Yet Phillip Huang's 1985 work on prerevolutionary China has demonstrated that under specific circumstances "semi-proletarian" can be a rigorous category. It may be used, he says: "to characterize a process of social change distinctive of a peasant society and economy under the combined pressures of social differentiation and intense population pressure without the outlet and relief provided by dynamic capitalist development."[32] As shall be seen in greater detail later, the state of affairs described by Huang pertained to the rural cultivators of Russia's southwest. These men and women earned wages on large, noble-owned capitalist estates. Landlord success, in turn, closed agrarian modernization as a possibility for the region's allotment holders. Migration to the cities was possible but still far from free. In this sense, the term "semi-proletarian" accurately describes their situations. If one speaks of peasants throughout the Russian Empire, it is possible to dismiss Lenin's use of this category as more a political wish than an economic reality. In the right-bank Ukraine, however, the term precisely described the region's rural cultivators. In this sense, it would not be incorrect to call them "proletarian peasants."

Culturalist criticism of the Leninist approach has sought to direct attention to two crucial structures of peasant life, the family farm and the commune. This school has stressed the internal elements of the community rather than the external forces impinging on the village. Shanin, in particular, relied heavily on Chaianov and his associates in the Organization and Production school of early Soviet rural economists who sought to integrate Marxist discourse with a respect for the characteristics of peasant life. Since the mid-1960s, Chaianov has become fashionable among historians of the rural world. Emmanuel Le Roy Ladurie found Chaianov's *Theory of the Peasant Economy* compatible with the behavior of the thirteenth-century peasants described in *Montaillou*.[33]

[32]Phillip Huang, *The Peasant Economy and Social Change in North China* (Stanford, 1985), p. 17.
[33]Emmanuel Le Roy Ladurie, *Montaillou* (Paris, 1978), p. 354.

Scholars of the medieval and early modern English peasantry have
made extensive use of this theory.[34] Conversely, the Marxist art
critic and observer of rural life John Berger has taken pains to
stress Chaianov's emphasis on the peasants' commitment to
survival.[35]

Chaianov centered his analysis of rural society and economy on
the peasant family farm. Concentrating on the individual unit of
the system, rather than the forces and relations surrounding it, he
advanced the concept of an unchanging "peasant mode of production" which was supposed to be as analytically useful and historically meaningful a guide to understanding rural life as the familiar
Marxist concepts of the ancient, feudal, and capitalist modes of
production, all of which followed one after the other.[36] This peasant mode of production had existed within the larger framework
of very different historical epochs. One could even speculate that
Chaianov was implicitly rejecting this essential element of the
Marxist approach to the course of history. Calling this static peasant way of life a "mode of production" may have been a politically
necessary way (in the Soviet Union of the 1920s) of putting a
Marxist veneer on a concept that challenged the basic historicity of
Marxism. It was no surprise that Chaianov's opponents attacked
him as a "neo-populist."[37] This claim was not without some basis.
His *Land of Peasant Utopia*, published pseudonymously in 1920,
was in some ways even neo-Slavophile. Although it was not overtly
politically conservative, Chaianov's book expressed skepticism
about the fate of the peasantry at the hands of an essentially urban
party.[38]

[34]Examples of tests of Chaianov's theories can be found in Richard Smith, ed.,
Land, Kinship, and Life Cycle (Cambridge, 1984).

[35]John Berger, *Pig Earth* (New York, 1979), p. 197.

[36]Chaianov, pp. 41–42.

[37]For a full treatment of the debate see Susan Solomon, *The Soviet Agrarian
Debate* (Boulder, Colo., 1977).

[38]Ivan Kremnev (pseudonym of Chaianov), *The Journey of My Brother Alexei
to the Land of Peasant Utopia*, in R. E. F. Smith, ed., *The Russian Peasant, 1920
and 1984* (London, 1977), pp. 63–106. On Chaianov's neo-Slavophilism see Ka-
terina Clark, "The City versus the Countryside in Soviet Peasant Literature of the
Twenties: A Duel of Utopias," in Abbot Gleason, Richard Stites, and Peter Kenez,
eds., *Bolshevik Culture* (Bloomington, Ind., 1985), p. 179.

The peasant farm operated with the labor of the members of the household. They received no wages for their work. For Chaianov, this concept was central. Without monetary wages, costs and profits could not be calculated according to capitalist criteria.[39] The peasant farm was not an enterprise concerned with maximizing profits. Rather, the household's primary goal was survival. Risk taking was not encouraged. The peasant farm operated according to what Chaianov called a "labor-consumer balance" between the satisfaction of family needs and the drudgery of farm labor. The continued existence of the household, rather than the search for all possible revenues, determined the peasant's economic choices.[40] By the criteria of classical economics those choices were often irrational, but by the peasants' own standard they might have been perfectly logical. With wages a minimal factor, the labor force of the Russian household was more or less fixed by family size. The growth of family income depended on the growth of the family. Large families, with many members of working age, were wealthy, while small families were poor. As a result, the demonstrable inequality among peasants had to be interpreted as the result of demographic factors which might vary sharply from generation to generation. Differences of wealth in the eyes of Chaianov and his colleagues were not caused by advantages and disadvantages accumulated over years. Therefore, because they did not regenerate, these were not differences of class, in the Marxist sense. If the various groups on the land could not properly be called social classes, then the Leninist political strategy, based on class struggle in the village, was without meaning. Accordingly, it should be clear that the stakes of this debate about the countryside were far from purely theoretical.

In the late 1960s, Chaianov's analysis was extended by the Polish rural sociologist Boguslaw Galeski, who reemphasized the inappropriateness of considering the peasant farm as a modern business enterprise.[41] He too stressed the survival of the family as the

[39]Chaianov, p. 87.
[40]Ibid., p. 92.
[41]Boguslaw Galeski, *Basic Concepts of Rural Sociology* (Manchester, England, 1972), p. 11.

first goal of the peasant. As the family is not exclusively an economic structure, one must then grant that social and cultural considerations assume decisive importance in the peasant's life. Shanin combined this approach with Robert Redfield's understanding of the peasant community as a closely knit network of interpersonal relationships and kinship patterns. For Redfield, the peasant village was a halfway step between the complete isolation of the primitive tribe and what he called "the extensive integration" of the modern industrial city.[42] The continuing vitality of the community was supposed to bind peasants to each other in opposition to the outside forces of landlords, governments, markets, and (one should add) other villages. This last view dominated Shanin's conception of the political sociology of the peasantry. With its strong emphasis on the centripetal forces in the village, Shanin's approach left little room for the formation of true social classes in general and a rural proletariat in particular. The dominant struggle on the land then became one of united insiders versus outsiders rather than of rich against poor within the village.

Marxist responses to the culturalist approach have acknowledged the need for some revision of orthodoxy. Hobsbawm agreed with Shanin that, in general, the peasantry is a "class of low classness."[43] Referring specifically to Russia, Mark Harrison accepted both the slowness of capitalist development and the absence of unambiguous class barriers in the village.[44] Instead, Marxist criticism of the culturalist approach has centered on the problem of definition. Judith Enew and her collaborators, along with Harrison, Hobsbawm, Mintz, and others, remain convinced of the the heterogeneity of rural populations.[45] Many recent historical studies have confirmed the presence of a wide variety of groups in the

---

[42]Redfield, p. 23.

[43]Hobsbawm, 1973, p. 5.

[44]Mark Harrison, "Chayanov and the Economics of the Russian Peasantry," *Journal of Peasant Studies* 1 (April 1974), 409.

[45]Enew et al., p. 297. Hobsbawm, 1973, p. 18. Mintz, "A Note on the Definition of Peasantries," *Journal of Peasant Studies* 1 (October 1973), 91. Mark Harrison, "The Peasant Mode of Production in the Work of A. V. Chayanov," *Journal of Peasant Studies* 4 (July 1977), 324.

countryside.[46] Marxists have continued to emphasize the decisive importance of external forces on the peasant world as the crucial consideration in understanding the process of differentiation. Chaianov was, accordingly, criticized for attempting to base the description of an entire mode of production on the internal characteristics of its individual unit.[47] Even the least orthodox Marxist writers have continued to emphasize the enveloping totality of relations in order to determine the particular mode of production of which the peasant community may be just a part. Culturalists, Eric Wolf in particular, have hardly been blind to this outside world. Nevertheless, they have based their search for explanations on the *internal* mechanisms of cohesion within the village rather than on the disruptive forces *external* to it.

Harrison, in particular, criticized Chaianov's emphasis on the goal of subsistence as an explanation for the apparent timeless equilibrium of peasant society. Harrison argued that Chaianov derived the requirements for subsistence, post facto, from already achieved levels of consumption. This step meant that Chaianov inadvertently accepted a state of affairs that included malnutrition, poverty, disease, and ignorance as unchanging aspects of daily life.[48] All populist and Marxist writers and activists were politically committed to eradicating these conditions. Marxists saw capitalism, despite its enormous human costs, as a force for progress in the countryside. By contrast, the source of change in Chaianov's system was not clear. The idea of a timeless peasant mode of production was necessarily static and ahistorical. As a result, Marxists, then and now, argued that Chaianov's approach led to the political acceptance of the centuries-old poverty of the Russian peasant.

The culturalist emphasis on the role of patriarchy and kinship has also been challenged by Marxists. The expectation that each male should have his own houschold and farm assigned decisive importance to the ways relations among families distributed wom-

---

[46]Margadant, p. 79. Moeller, p. 19. Florencia Mallon, *The Defense of Community in Peru's Central Highlands* (Princeton, 1983). Temma Kaplan, *Anarchists of Andalusia* (Princeton, 1977).

[47]Enew et al., p. 307.

[48]Harrison, 1974, p. 414.

en among men. Status and blood ties were significant considerations under such circumstances. The continuing importance of patriarchy in the village necessitated an analysis of kinship patterns in order to determine real power in the village. This, in turn, influenced demographic processes which also worked against the emergence of clear class differences in the village. Harrison, however, contended that the concept of patriarchy could not adequately explain the leveling tendencies of the Russian commune, in particular. Patriarchy had, after all, existed in all times and places. Peasant communes, both Russian and non-Russian, were, on the other hand, historically and geographically limited phenomena. Even if patriarchy was a significant element of village life, and it certainly was, it was necessary to characterize the particular nature of patriarchy in a given situation.[49] The French anthropologist Claude Meillassoux argued that kinship patterns themselves reflected, in imprecise ways, relations of production. Similarly, demographic trends could not be seen as autonomous factors. These too were influenced by the changing character of a mode of production.[50] The population explosion in the Russian countryside after the emancipation of 1861 would seem to be an example of such a pattern. Sidney Mintz contended that the use of culture as an explanation of peasant homogeneity left open important questions about the concept of culture itself. Were the norms and values of peasant societies necessarily autonomous or were they influenced by a variety of factors, some of which might have been economic?[51] Finally, Harrison, in a different context, showed a number of ways in which the increased specialization of agriculture transformed the character of the traditional village without completely destroying it.[52]

In the mid-1970s, several American social scientists gave further

[49]Harrison, "Resource Allocation," p. 148.
[50]Claude Meillassoux, "The Social Organization of the Peasantry: The Economic Basis of Kinship," *Journal of Peasant Studies* 1 (October 1973), 85, and Claude Meillassoux, "The Economic Basis of Demographic Reproduction: From the Domestic Mode of Production to Wage-earning," *Journal of Peasant Studies* 11 (April 1984), 50–61.
[51]Mintz, 1973, p. 96.
[52]Harrison, "Resource Allocation," p. 147.

Proletarian Peasants

impetus to the old debates about peasant society. Their research centered on Third World countries that had been colonized, but their theoretical concerns evoked echoes of familiar arguments. Jeffrey Paige offered a number of theories of rural class conflict. As part of a broader approach to agrarian revolution, he specified the kinds of circumstances in which true rural proletarians could play active roles. He also sought to revive the idea that landownership or control of land could make peasants resistant, rather than receptive, to revolutionary movements. In order to explain these phenomena, Paige placed the relations between cultivators and non-cultivators at the center of his analysis.[53]

At the same time, a culturalist approach to the question of peasant rebellion was offered by James Scott. Peasants were part of a distinctive "moral economy" in which their subsistence ethic was the central motivating force. Disorder would occur when the traditional understandings between cohesive villages and powerful outsiders were broken. New demands could trigger unrest. For this reason peasant aims were seen as restorative, even backward-looking. It was common for peasants to hark back to a mythical earlier time when there were no lords and the land was theirs. For Scott, the relationship between lord and peasant was as much psychic as economic, and it was the breaking of the psychic bonds that was thought to be destabilizing. Culture was central to Scott's analysis. For him, peasants were concerned with the consumption needs of their families, first and foremost. They made decisions according to criteria that were theirs alone. This emphasis placed Scott squarely, though surely not consciously, in the tradition of the Slavophiles and the populists.[54]

Scott and other culturalists were criticized by Samuel Popkin who offered a non-Marxist reaffirmation of the importance of classical economics to an understanding of peasant decision making. Arguing that peasants made "rational" economic and political decisions, Popkin criticized the "moral economy" school for "romanticizing" peasant life. Like Scott, he gave his attention to the

[53]Jeffrey Paige, *Agrarian Revolution: Social Movements and Export Agriculture in the Underdeveloped World* (New York, 1975), p. 16.
[54]James Scott, *The Moral Economy of the Peasant: Rebellion and Subsistence in Southeast Asia* (New Haven, Conn., 1976), pp. 8–10, 157, 188–203.

22

relatively recent history of Vietnam where the colonial market had transformed self-sufficient villages. Popkin demonstrated that individual peasants were capable of risk taking and innovation, that they were able to view the world according to the criteria of capitalism.[55]

Peasant actions that might have seemed backward-looking and even irrational could have had their own logic. Peasants might want to return to a mythical past, but in voicing their demands, they limited themselves to the more appealing aspects of that past. They might ask that certain lands that they had used for centuries be returned to them, but they never expressed much nostalgia for corporal punishment, conscription, or severe taxation. Popkin's approach, while not Marxist, did place emphasis on many of the same outside forces that Marxists stressed. In this limited sense, his work could be seen as an extension of that old consensus which stressed the usefulness of classical economics for an analysis of rural society. The debate between Popkin and Scott, while basically scholarly, retraced many of the paths outlined earlier by Russian thinkers of the nineteenth century.

In a certain sense, the sides in these debates are not that far apart. If one examines both Marxist and culturalist expectations about peasant disturbances, it becomes clear that the two schools have most often talked about very different things. Each side has tended to choose as objects of study situations likely to provide information that supports their views and expectations. Rural cultivators tended to follow Marxist scenarios when they found themselves in situations that could properly be called capitalist. Thus, most Marxists (Hobsbawm and Rodney Hilton are exceptions) have preferred to look at the modern world.[56] By contrast, traditional societies have fostered the kinds of activities predicted by the culturalists as normal peasant behavior. Such observers as Shanin have concentrated on historical situations that were, in his words, "pre-industrial."[57] When peasants have been integrated into market economies, they have proven capable of making what

[55]Samuel Popkin, *The Rational Peasant* (Berkeley, 1979), p. 3.
[56]Eric Hobsbawm, *Primitive Rebels* (New York, 1959), pp. 57–107.
[57]Shanin, 1972, p. 207.

Marxists and classical economists would call "rational" economic and political decisions. When their lives have been more hermetic and self-sufficient, their actions often have assumed what might be considered exotic forms. Thus, this long-standing and often-renewed debate does not revolve around the clear-cut universal superiority of either school of thought. Rather, it is concerned with the specific applicability of either of the schema to the particular concrete historical situation being studied. If that situation is basically capitalist, then Marxist, Leninist, or political economy conceptions can, in fact, be useful. If, on the other hand, one is describing a society or community that is more backward, then the culturalist approach may be more fruitful.

Since the late 1970s, the divisions between the two schools have blurred somewhat. Along with John Berger, Durrenberger and Tannenbaum have urged Marxists to take a more sympathetic approach to Chaianov.[58] Other Marxists have talked about the utility of a "household mode of production" for understanding early America.[59] David Goodman and Michael Redclift, writing from what they call a Marxist perspective, have also shown an openness to other schools.[60] On the other hand, Eric Wolf's 1982 book places far greater emphasis on history in general and the surrounding mode of production in particular. In addition, Wolf's own conception of a mode of production fits quite comfortably into the Marxist camp.[61] Not to be outdone, Shanin has invoked Marx in defense of his own views, citing the famous letters to Vera Zasulich (who was a populist in the 1870s at the time the letters were written) as proof of "the master's" own openness to the socialist potential of the commune.[62] Elsewhere, Shanin has

[58]E. Paul Durrenberger and Nicola Tannenbaum, "A Reassessment of Chayanov and his Recent Critics," *Peasant Studies* 3 (Winter 1979), 48–67.

[59]Mike Merill, "So What's Wrong with the 'Household Mode of Production'?" *Radical History Review*, no. 22 (Winter 1979), 141–46.

[60]David Goodman and Michael Redclift, *From Peasant to Proletarian: Capitalist Development and Agrarian Transitions* (Oxford, 1981). For a Marxist critique see Tom Brass, "Peasant Transition or Permanent Revolution: Peasants, Proletarians, and Politics," *Journal of Peasant Studies* 11 (April 1984), 108–17.

[61]Eric Wolf, *Europe and the People without History* (Berkeley, 1982), p. 263.

[62]Teodor Shanin, "Marx and the Peasant Commune," *History Workshop*, no. 12 (Fall 1981), 108–28.

stressed that the primary task of any analysis is measuring the level of agrarian capitalism in order to determine the particular theories that may be relevant. In doing this, he has suggested criteria that were originally raised by the Soviet agricultural economists of the 1920s.[63]

Richard Smith's recent survey of scholarship on the medieval and early modern English peasantry confirmed this trend. He found neither Chaianovian nor Leninist models to be universally applicable. Instead, some villages were organized around the concerns of kinship, culture, and demography, whereas other settlements exhibited high levels of stratification and responsiveness to the market. Given this state of affairs, it would seem that the two prevailing theories can aid in identifying the nature of a particular object of study. Yet they cannot make unnecessary the meticulous reconstruction of historical reality.[64]

This coming together of the two major schools reflects an understanding that the disputants have not always been talking about the same things. One group's "peasants" have often been the other's "rural proletarians." Attempts to advance the theoretical debate have stalled in recent years. Instead, the task has fallen to historians, sociologists, and anthropologists to uncover the peasants' well-hidden world and to describe their lives and actions as precisely as can be done.

Schools of Thought on Russian Peasant Society

Culturalist analyses of rural Russia have devoted much attention to the resurrection of a number of fundamental ideas of the populist movement. They have stressed the absence of politically meaningful stratification in the countryside and have sought to demonstrate the continued vitality of the village commune. In the

[63]Teodor Shanin, "Measuring Peasant Capitalism: The Operationalization of Concepts of Political Economy: Russia's 1920's–India's 1970's," in Eric Hobsbawm et al., eds., *Peasants in History: Essays in Honour of Daniel Thorner* (Oxford, 1980), pp. 83–104.

[64]Richard Smith, "Some Issues Concerning Families, and Their Property in Rural England, 1250–1800," in Richard Smith 1984, pp. 1–86.

mid-1960s Moshe Lewin demonstrated the ambiguity of the standard class categories of landless *(batrak)*, poor *(bedniak)*, middle *(seredniak)*, and rich *(kulak)* into which Lenin, and later Soviet analysts, divided the rural working population. It was difficult in the 1920s to find meaningful criteria for assigning peasants to one of these categories, and it proved extremely hard for those actually in the countryside to determine which individual peasants fit into which group. The postrevolutionary Bolshevik aim of entering a village in order to foment class warfare became problematic when one accepted the fact that the character of particular households was difficult to determine with any accuracy.[65]

Whereas Lewin limited his discussion to the 1920s, Shanin studied the period between 1910 and 1925. His central aim was to explain the failure of modern social classes to appear in the Russian village. Shanin did not deny the existence of different levels of wealth among the peasantry, nor did he claim that the formal repartitional mechanism of the commune was an effective force guaranteeing equality. Instead he noted, as have observers of other peasant societies, a positive correlation between family size and wealth. This meant that the stratification Lenin was able to demonstrate in *The Development of Capitalism in Russia* was not economic. Rather, it was demographic, or more precisely, biological. Shanin argued that peasant households combined and divided constantly, a process he called "substantive changes."[66] Given the decisive predominance of partible succession, the largest and wealthiest peasants would divide their holdings among several sons in the next generation. Each man had to have, for the strongest of social and cultural reasons, a household and a farm. He was not considered a true man unless he had these things, nor could he participate in the traditional assembly of heads of households in which the crucial decisions of village life were made. At the opposite end of the spectrum, poor families, who might even be

---

[65]Moshe Lewin, *Russian Peasants and Soviet Power* (London, 1968), pp. 41–80
[66]Shanin, 1972, pp. 81–85. Shanin later focused on the peasant during 1905 as part of a broader treatment of the revolutionary period. His conclusions, based on secondary material, confirmed the consensus as to the continued vitality of traditional forms. See Teodor Shanin, *Russia 1905–1907: Revolution as a Moment of Truth* (London, 1985), pp. 138–80.

unrelated, found clear economic advantages in combining their households and allotments, given the relationship of family size to wealth. Thus, Shanin argued, although social mobility did exist, changes in peasant social status were cyclical. Households rose and fell from generation to generation, as members entered and left their prime working years. Because neither wealth nor poverty were passed on, true social classes could not emerge.[67] Because each man had to have a wife, kinship patterns, not economic relations, were supposed to be the best guide to an understanding of the social structure of the village.

In very different ways, Lewin and Shanin forced a reappraisal of Russian and Soviet rural history. They were able to show that the peasants themselves did not describe the social structure of the village in the same ways as did Lenin and other Marxists. In the absence of clear peasant awareness of class differences, it was impossible for them to act politically according to Bolshevik scenarios. Before and after the revolution, peasants appear to have spent little time fighting each other. Instead, they displayed considerable political cohesion in combating a variety of outside forces that undermined the traditional equilibrium of what was a relatively self-sufficient way of life.

Soviet specialists who work on the prerevolutionary period have not sought to contradict this view. They have ascribed the absence of class tension in the village to overriding emnity for the landlords in particular and to the still-traditional character of rural life in general. If peasants acted in precapitalist ways, then it was because they lived under precapitalist conditions. To understand peasant behavior, it was necessary to determine how extensive was, to borrow a phrase from an obvious source, the development of capitalism in Russia. For decades such orthodox historians as S. M. Dubrovskii and P. N. Pershin stressed a fairly high level of rural capitalism but maintained an awareness of "semi-feudal" forms.[68]

---

[67]Ibid., pp. 76–80.

[68]S. M. Dubrovskii, "K voprosu ob urovne razvitiia kapitalizma v sel'skom khoziaistve Rossii i kharaktere klassovoi borby v period imperializma (dve sotsial'nye voiny)," in *Osobennosti agrarnogo stroia Rossii v period imperializma* (Moscow, 1962), pp. 5–44. P. N. Pershin, *Agrarnaia revoliutsiia v Rossii*, 2 vols., (Moscow, 1966), vol. 1.

More recently, A. M. Anfimov argued for a view of the countryside that emphasized its backwardness.[69] In the 1970s and 1980s, I. D. Kovalchenko led a team of computer-equipped quantifiers in an attempt to specify the level of capitalist development in the various regions of the empire.[70] Their research has led Anfimov to revise some of his views and accept the existence of a higher level of agrarian capitalism than he had earlier thought.

Kovalchenko and his collaborators have placed regional differences at the heart of their discussion. For too long, both Western and Soviet scholars have suffered from a kind of analytical centralism that forced them to offer conclusions which were supposed to apply to all of Russia. In particular, this led to a distorting emphasis on conditions in central Russia. Although one may question the usefulness of the kinds of criteria employed by Kovalchenko and his team, it is at least clear that they are in the process of providing answers to the kinds of questions that must be asked before one can gain any understanding of what Soviet historians call "the peasant movement."

Schools of Thought on Russian Peasant Politics

In recent discussions of the Russian peasantry, political issues have been of secondary concern. Yet, here too, the utility of either of the two main schools is largely a function of the concrete situation that must be explained. Shanin, as noted, has described the political attitudes of peasants as "pre-industrial." Accordingly, he has preferred to cite the activities of rural cultivators in regions relatively untouched by the market economy. Those attitudes and activities bear a striking resemblance to the disorganized, spontaneous, backward-looking, violent, and even millenarian behavior of English medieval peasants described by Hilton, early modern

[69] A. M. Anfimov, "Krestianstvo v 1907–1914 gg.," paper presented to annual meeting of the American Historical Association, December 1971, New York City.

[70] I. D. Kovalchenko, N. B. Selunskaia, B. M. Litvakov, *Sotsial'no-ekonomicheskii stroi pomeshchich'ego khoziaistva evropeiskoi Rossii v epokhu kapitalizma* (Moscow, 1982).

French peasants discussed by Le Roy Ladurie, and eighteenth-century Russian peasants studied by Michael Confino.[71] Shanin, Alavi, and to a lesser extent Wolf, have written about groups that were relatively unaffected by the growth of commercial agriculture and wage labor. Their situations were precapitalist, and we can describe the forms assumed by their actions as "traditional." Random violence, arson, pillage, crop stealing, and murder were the ways peasants expressed their discontent in those times and places. Their goals were rarely achievable, and their actions often seemed injurious to their short-term interests. For these reasons, many outsiders characterized peasant rebellion as irrational. More properly, traditional peasants had their own logic, and the tactical conditions were appropriate to the conditions they confronted. Yet that logic was not a capitalist logic.

By contrast, both orthodox and newer Marxists have chosen to concentrate on those segments of the rural population whose lives were significantly altered by phenomena that could properly be called agrarian capitalism. Marxists had expected the city, not the countryside, to be the center of revolutionary activity. Urban proletarians, in Europe and elsewhere, had not manifested their discontent in the atavistic and expressive ways of the peasant. Instead, city workers primarily used the strike weapon. They made a variety of explicit political and economic demands, some of which had to be winnable. When they engaged in violence, their actions were usually defensive, directed at strikebreakers, police, or soldiers. For Marxists, this "proletarian" form of struggle was instrumental and rational. If "backward" peasants manifested one approach to rebellion while "advanced" proletarians demonstrated another, it would then follow that the forms of struggle adopted by those who were "semi-proletarian" would likely be similarly mixed. This turned out to be the case in Russia's southwest during 1905.

Since the revolution, Soviet scholars have produced extensive and detailed studies of what they call "the peasant movement." They have not ignored the largely spontaneous and poorly orga-

[71]Rodney Hilton, "Peasant Society, Peasant Movements, and Feudalism," in Landsberger, pp. 84–89. E. Le Roy Ladurie, *Carnaval de Romans* (Paris, 1979), pp. 175–96. Michael Confino, *Systèmes agraires et progrès agricole* (Paris, 1969), p. 326.

nized character of most rural disorders, but they have always stressed a leading role for the poor and the landless, the proletariat and the semi-proletariat.[72] Despite their necessarily Leninist emphasis, Soviet historians have been able to integrate a variety of phenomena into their approach. A flood of studies on the peasant movement were published in the mid-1950s during the fiftieth anniversary of the Revolution of 1905. Most of these works accepted a dominant role for what they called the "middle peasantry" and what Shanin would call simply "the peasantry."[73] On the other hand, the leading Ukrainian specialist M. N. Leshchenko, writing at the same time, kept the familiar emphasis on the agrarian proletariat as the most militant segment of the rural population, at least, in his particular part of the empire.[74]

More recently, M. S. Simonova summarized the Soviet literature on 1905 and reasserted the special "avidity" of those without land.[75] Soviet views on peasant politics are, therefore, not monolithic. Differences of opinion exist. Though the emphasis on the rural proletariat has not been discarded, this has not prevented Soviet scholars from describing events with considerable accuracy.

[72]N. Mirza-Avakiants, *Selianskii rozrukhi na Ukraini 1905–1907 roku* (Kharkov, 1925). E. A. Morokhovets, *Krestianskoe dvizhenie i sotsial'-demokratiia v epokhu pervoi russkoi revoliutsii* (Moscow-Leningrad, 1926). A Shestakov, *Borba sel'skikh rabochikh v revoliutsii 1905–1907 gg.* (Moscow-Leningrad, 1930).

[73]Dubrovskii, *Krestianskoe dvizhenie v revoliutsii 1905–1907* (Moscow, 1956). A. Shestakov, *Krestianskaia revoliutsiia 1905–1907 gg. v Rossii* (Moscow, 1926). I. U. Kharitonova and D. Shcherbako, *Krestianskoe dvizhenie v Kaluzhskoi gubernii 1861–1917 gg.* (Kaluga, 1961). K. I. Shabunia, *Agrarnyi vopros i krestianskoe dvizhenie v Belorussii v revoliutsii 1905–1907 gg.* (Minsk, 1962). V. I. Popov, "Krestianskoe dvizhenie v Riazanskoi gubernii 1905–1907 gg.," *Istoricheskie zapiski* 49 (1954), 136–64. A. G. Mikhailiuk, "Krestianskoe dvizhenie na levoberezhnoi Ukraine v 1905–1907 gg.," *Istoricheskie zapiski* 49 (1954), 165–201. V. M. Gokhlerner, "Krestianskoe dvizhenie v Saratovskoi gubernii v gody pervoi russkoi revoliutsii," *Istoricheskie zapiski* 52 (1955), 186–234. P. N. Abramov, "Iz istorii krestianskogo dvizhenia 1905–1906 gg. v tsentral'no-chernozemnykh guberniakh," *Istoricheskie zapiski* 57 (1956), 293–311.

[74]M. N. Leshchenko, *Selianskii rukh na pravoberezhnii Ukraini v period revoliutsii 1905–1907 rr.* (Kiev, 1955).

[75]M. S. Simonova, "Krestianskoe dvizhenie 1905–1907 gg. v sovetskoi istoriografii," *Istoricheskie zapiski* 95 (1975), 204–53. For a more recent but similar view, see L. T. Senchakova, *RSDRP i krestianstvo v revoliutsii 1905–1907 gg.* (Moscow, 1984).

Recent Western research on peasant politics has been comparatively limited. Much social history has been written about Russian peasants, but political issues have, with few exceptions, been avoided in favor of economic, social, and institutional questions.[76] Shanin's specific discussion of peasant political behavior imputed more than it demonstrated, and the majority of his examples were drawn from the postrevolutionary period when the decisive power of the landlords was no longer a factor. His 1985 book on the 1905 revolution throughout Russia affirmed the international consensus on the dominant role of the middle peasant. Nevertheless, Shanin's approach has been corroborated by some modern Western scholarship. Graeme Gill's book on the provisional government in 1917 and Eugene Vinogradoff's essay on the elections of 1912 both confirm, for central Russia, strong patterns of political cohesion, relative indifference to the outside world, and still-vital traditional practices and attitudes. Marc Ferro and John Keep have favored similar approaches in their discussions of peasant activity in 1917.[77]

The most suggestive research on peasant politics has been carried out by Maureen Perrie, who studied the massive disturbances throughout the countryside during the Revolution of 1905-7. Perrie's approach was more cautious than that of other writers, but, by and large, her work confirmed the contentions of Wolf, Alavi, and Shanin that the leading role in 1905 was played by the middle peasantry.[78] Perrie, however, gave special emphasis to the forms assumed by peasant struggles in order to draw conclusions about

[76]Moshe Lewin, "Rural Society in Twentieth Century Russia: An Introduction," *Social History* 9 (May 1984), 171, 180. Dorothy Atkinson, *The End of the Russian Land Commune, 1905-1930* (Stanford, 1983).

[77]Graeme Gill, *Peasant and Revolution in 1917* (London, 1979). Eugene Vinogradoff, "The Russian Peasantry and the Elections to the Fourth State Duma," in L. Haimson, ed., *The Politics of Rural Russia* (Bloomington, Ind., 1979), pp. 219-60. John Keep, *The Russian Revolution: A Study in Mass Mobilization* (New York, 1976), pp. 383-463. Marc Ferro, *October, 1917: A Social History of the Russian Revolution* (London, 1980), pp. 112-39. See also Shanin, 1985, pp. 130-83.

[78]Maureen Perrie, "The Russian Peasant Movement of 1905-1907: Its Social Composition and Revolutionary Significance," *Past and Present*, no. 81 (November 1972), 123-55. See also Roberta Manning, *The Crisis of the Old Order in Russia: Gentry and Government* (Princeton, 1982), pp. 138-76.

political practices and attitudes. Here, she was able to demonstrate that the character of the economy of a particular region strongly affected the specific kinds of actions taken by peasants. Behavior that other scholars have described as traditional was most prevalent in those parts of the empire where agriculture was most traditional. In more advanced regions, peasants acted differently.

There is now a broad consensus, Soviet and Western, culturalist and Marxist, that the middle peasant, not the rural proletariat, was the most active force in the Russian countryside between 1905 and 1907. Despite their special attention to tensions within the peasantry, Soviet scholars have accepted the fact that peasants acted cohesively in 1905. To explain this, they have advanced the idea of two "social wars," the first pitting the entire peasantry against the landlords and the second pitting the poor peasantry against the rich.[79] The events of 1905–7 represent a case of the first type of social war. Historians in the Soviet Union differ, as do their colleagues in the West, on whether the second phase of the struggle ever began. It should, however, be clear that they have not sought to make an extended case for sharp intravillage tensions during 1905.

Nevertheless, the international consensus on 1905 cannot, as Perrie has noted, be sustained for all parts of the empire. Regional variations allow one to raise, in a different way, the possible roles played by landless laborers, narrowly defined rural proletarians. Cohesion characterized the movement in the provinces of central Russia, especially the famous Central Black Earth region (the provinces of Kursk, Orel, Tula, Riazan, Tambov, and Voronezh). There, agriculture was still practiced in primitive and traditional ways. The three-field system predominated, and the repartitional commune continued to function. The kinds of "preindustrial" behavior noted by Shanin, Wolf, Gill, and Vinogradoff are consistent with and supported by the traditional economic and social structures that were still vital in central Russia in 1905. Class differentiation among the peasantry of central Russia was not of such an order as to foster sharp struggles within the village. Instead, peasants united to face the outside world.

[79]Dubrovskii, 1962, p. 17.

Finally, as Perrie demonstrated, the forms of peasant agitation in these provinces during 1905 were disorganized, spontaneous, violent, and in most cases backward-looking in their aims. They followed patterns that have often been called "irrational," whether or not they had their own internal logic. The universal cause of the disorders of 1905 was simply lack of land, and the peasants' characteristic solution to the crisis was the immediate confiscation of all gentry, state, and church land, without compensation. At the time, this goal seemed completely utopian. Yet it should not be forgotten that what seemed impossible in 1905 would, in fact, be realized in 1917. Between the two revolutions, conditions changed drastically. The destruction of the autocracy meant the collapse of all authority in the countryside. During 1905, the state's loss of control was only partial and temporary. The first Russian revolution, in this sense, was no "dress rehearsal." In 1905, peasants throughout the empire were expressing their rage. Twelve years later, they were able to settle age-old scores.

The Southwest as a Test Case

The relationship between the manifestation of peasant solidarity and the persistence of traditional practices was close. Accordingly, it would be important to learn whether the forms of the movement manifested in central Russia were duplicated in areas where agrarian capitalism was well advanced. Shanin's claim for the universality of his approach is not fully proven, and, as Perrie has suggested, further research on specific regions could reveal important variations. If it could be demonstrated that the kinds of political behavior described by culturalists were also encountered in advanced regions, then this school would have greatly strengthened its case in terms of the Russian experience. If, on the other hand, one could identify a true rural proletariat (landless wage earners) in these capitalist regions and demonstrate its important role in rural protest, then one would have to conclude that certain Leninist and Marxist approaches could still be considered applicable to parts of the empire.

The validity of the two approaches can be tested by selecting a region of extensive agrarian capitalism and studying the peasant movement there during a moment of extreme agitation. The Revolution of 1905–7 was just such a time. The thousands of disturbances of those years were a decisive turning point in the history of Russia. The autocracy's faith in the basic conservatism and loyalty of the peasantry was shattered, and the state then added its weight to the forces seeking to destroy the village commune.

Several agriculturally advanced regions suggest themselves for comparison with central Russia, but the southwestern provinces of Kiev, Podol'e, and Volynia in the right-bank Ukraine provide several useful analytical possibilities. Noble landlords in this region practiced profit-oriented agriculture on their plantations and employed many thousands of wage workers. At the same time, the communal institutions of the village were still alive although they did not practice repartitional tenure. Instead, allotments throughout the Ukraine and in much of western Russia were held hereditarily. As a result, the right bank was different from central Russia. Yet it was not so thoroughly different as to make comparisons meaningless. The provinces of Kiev, Podol'e, and Volynia take on added importance for the historian of the peasant movement in the light of two other crucial facts:

1. The "per capita" incidence of disturbances in the right bank between 1905 and 1907 was higher than in any other region.
2. This agitation was sharply different in form from similar events in central Russia. Peasants in the right bank demonstrated the ability to organize themselves coherently and make appropriate tactical choices for the attainment of realizable goals.

The exceptional character of the right bank allows one to test the validity of certain universal rules. Accordingly, any investigation of events in this part of the world leads immediately back to the same questions scholars and political activists have been asking for more than a century. How best to comprehend the peasantry?

2

Economy and Society
in the Southwest

The southwest (after 1917, the right-bank Ukraine) comprised the prerevolutionary provinces of Kiev, Volynia, and Podol'e, all of which became part of the Russian Empire after the third partition of Poland in 1795.[1] Most of the region was in the northern reaches of the "black earth" zone, in the fertile open steppe. The northern half of Volynia (the westernmost province), however, was in the forested steppe, which is geographically more like central Russia than the rest of the southwest.[2] Podol'e was south of Kiev and Volynia. Situated between Russian Poland and the west bank of the Dnieper, these three provinces were highly fertile. Their climate was milder than that of central Russia, with an average temperature of -3.3 degrees centigrade in January and $+20$ degrees in July.[3] As a result, the growing season in the right bank was usually a month longer than in the Central Black Earth region.[4] Rainfall was often insufficient in Russia's fertile provinces, but the south-

---

[1]*Istoria selianstva Ukrainskoi RSR* (Kiev, 1970), 1:300 (hereafter *Istoria selianstva*).

[2]K. Voblyi, *Ekonomichna geografiia ukraini* (Kiev, 1925), p. 60.

[3]A. I. Skvortsov, *Khoziaistvennye raiony evropeiskoi Rossii*, vyp. I (St. Petersburg, 1914), p. 84.

[4]F. L. Liubanskii, *Kratkii obzor 12-tiletnei deiatel'nosti Podol'skogo obshchestva sel'skogo khoziaistva* (Vinnitsa, 1911), p. 4.

west had extensive precipitation. This combination of fertility and good rainfall was rare. It meant that a lot more than grain could be raised in the region. Specifically, the southwest was also well suited for the production of sugar beets, an important cash crop that played little role in the peasant diet. Instead, landlords, following the example of Prussian Junkers, organized and profited from sugar beet production and refining.

The flat, fertile plains of the right bank covered nearly 150,000 square kilometers. The three provinces contained 36 districts *(uezdy)*, more than 500 cantons, and over 20,000 villages.[5] In all the southwest, there were more than 13 million *desiatiny* (one *desiatin* = 2.7 acres) of forest and arable land. By virtue of its size, fertility, location, and climate, this region was a significant, productive, and distinctive center of agricultural activity.

Population

After the emancipation of 1861, the population of Russia began to increase dramatically. Although the new institutional and economic structures constituted only partial steps toward the emergence of capitalist relations of production, peasant expectations about the future changed. So too did their needs. Under new conditions peasants made different decisions about expanding their families. These new attitudes, combined with limited but significant improvements in the quality and availability of health care, produced the same kind of population boom that western European nations had experienced earlier. Between 1858 and the first universal census in 1897, the peasant population of the empire increased from 50 million to 79 million, about 60 percent. This growth placed an obvious strain on available resources, most significantly the land itself. The resulting land hunger has been well documented. On the eve of the Revolution of 1905, these profound demographic changes were undermining all of Russia's social, political, and economic relationships.

As swift as the growth of population had been throughout Rus-

[5]N. P. Oganovskii, *Sel'skoe khoziaistvo Rossii v xx veke* (Moscow, 1923), p. 12.

Table 1. Increase in Southwest Peasant
Population, 1858–1897

Province	1858	1897
Kiev	1,474,437	2,768,542
Podol'e	1,360,503	2,437,736
Volynia	1,045,732	2,241,062
Total	3,880,672	7,447,340

Source: Compiled from 1897 census and D. P.
Poida, *Krestianskoe dvizhenie na pravoberezhnoi
ukraine v poreformennoi period (1866–1900)*
(Dnepropetrovsk, 1960), p. 65.

sia, the increase was even faster in the southwest. In 1897, 9.6
million people lived in Kiev, Podol'e, and Volynia.[6] By 1905 the
Ministry of Interior would estimate the figure had grown to over
11 million. At the time of the 1897 census, almost 7.5 million of
the residents of the right bank were members of the peasant estate
(soslovie).[7] That figure had increased nearly 90 percent since 1858
(see Table 1).

Of all the regions of Russia, only the Ukrainian steppe, known
earlier as Novorossiia, increased at a faster pace.[8] Population den-
sity in the southwest was greater than anywhere else in Russia.[9]

Population growth in the right bank did not result from large-
scale migration. Not many people moved away from Kiev, Podol'e,
and Volynia (only 76,300 between 1863 and 1897).[10] Some peasants from the left bank and the Central Black Earth region had
moved into the southwest, but the overwhelming majority of residents of the region lived where they had been born. Over 95 per-

[6]P. P. Telichuk, *Ekonomichni osnovi agrarnoi revoliutsii na Ukraini* (Kiev,
1971), p. 39.

[7]Tsentral'nyi statisticheskii komitet Ministerstva vnutrennykh del, *Pervaia
vseobshchaia perepis' naseleniia rossiskoi imperii 1897 g.* (hereafter 1897 census)
(St. Petersburg, 1904), Kiev, p. iv, Podol'e, p. 111, Volynia, p. 1.

[8]Tsentral'nyi statisticheskii komitet Ministerstva vnutrennykh del, *Urozhai na
1905 g.* (St. Petersburg, 1906), p. xxvi.

[9]A. M. Anfimov, *Krestianskoe khoziaistvo evropeiskoi Rossii, 1881–1904 gg.*
(Moscow, 1980), p. 22.

[10]1897 census, Kiev, p. iv.

cent of right-bank peasants lived in the province of their birth, and 90 percent lived in the district in which they had been born.[11]

Almost 150,000 nobles dominated the lives of the region's 7,447,340 peasants.[12] There were nearly 25,000 merchants *(kuptsy)* along with 1,806,253 members of that social estate known as the *meshchanstvo* (best understood as the petty bourgeoisie).[13] The city of Kiev dominated the entire area. In 1897, it had 247,723 residents. By 1905, estimates would place the population of the city above 400,000.

Yet the growth of Kiev did not change the overwhelmingly agricultural character of these three provinces. As in the rest of the Russian Empire, nearly the entire peasantry engaged in agricultural pursuits. In Kiev, 2,495,673 persons were so engaged; in Podol'e, 2,255,491, and in Volynia, 2,219,097, according to the 1897 census. The same census counted 377,157 individuals engaged in what was called "industrial work of a supplementary character."[14] This category included a variety of activities, ranging from handicrafts to sugar refinery work. In no case did any of this work tear peasants completely away from the countryside. Kiev may have been growing rapidly, but much of its expansion came with industries such as railroads and food processing which were closely tied to agriculture. The economy of the southwest was in a rapid state of flux, but in 1905, the region was still overwhelmingly rural.

Peasants in the southwest were not especially mobile. Some did go to Novorossiia for seasonal labor, while others would sign contracts to work several months in the region's sugar refineries. Most peasants, however, remained in their native villages. The kind of seasonal oscillations that Robert Johnson and others have noted for Moscow were not characteristic of the southwest.[15] This situation meant that the traditional structures of the village showed continuing strength. The growth of commercial agriculture in Kiev,

[12]1897 census, Kiev, p. xi, Podol'e, p. 42, Volynia, p. xvi.
[13]1897 census, Kiev, p. 2, Podol'e, p. 2, Volynia, p. 81.
[14]1897 census, Kiev, p. 2, Podol'e, p. 2, Volynia, p. xi.
[15]Robert Johnson, *Peasant and Proletarian* (New Brunswick, N.J., 1979). Joseph Bradley, *Muzhik and Muscovite: Urbanization in Late Imperial Russia* (Berkeley, 1985), pp. 103–40.

Podol'e, and somewhat less so in Volynia obviously affected the region's communal structures. Nevertheless, traditional patterns persisted. Marriage was every bit as universal in the countryside of the southwest as it was in the rest of Russia. Both men and women began marrying at the age of fifteen.[16] As elsewhere, a man did not consider himself complete until he had an allotment and a family. Kinship, therefore, was still an essential element of the intravillage power structure.

The persistence of traditional family structures meant that the villages of the right-bank Ukraine were as patriarchal as those of central Russia. Differences in the literacy rates of men and women indirectly reflected the position of females in the village. With 20 percent of men and 7 percent of women able to read some language, the level of literacy was roughly the same in the southwest as in the rest of Russia. Similarly, the rural parts of Kiev province were little different from central Russia, but it is worth noting that 40 percent of women in the city of Kiev could read.[17]

Literacy among young men between twenty and twenty-nine was fairly high (about 35 percent) in the right bank. During the disturbances, these men, the most mobile element of the rural population, would play highly visible and militant roles. Yet, for the most part, the figures on marriage and literacy reveal that for all the changes the southwest was undergoing, it remained primarily a rural region in which the village and the household were still significant forces.

National divisions in the right bank corresponded closely to class divisions. Nearly the entire peasantry was Ukrainian. According to the 1897 census, the population included 7,357,543 Ukrainians, along with 413,000 Great Russians, 322,108 Poles, and 1,194,569 Jews. There were also smaller numbers of Czechs and Germans. Landlords were usually Polish or Russian, but fully a third of those the census described as nobles listed Ukrainian as their native language (the official indicator of nationality).[18] Nev-

[16] 1897 census, Kiev, p. 246, Podol'e, p. 240, Volynia, p. 156.
[17] 1897 census, Kiev, p. ix, Podol'e, p. 32, Volynia, p. 28.
[18] 1897 census, Kiev, p. ix, Podol'e, p. viii, Volynia, p. ix.

ertheless, there was no sense of national solidarity between the Ukrainian peasantry and that segment of the gentry that spoke Ukrainian. Landlords with Ukrainian names publicly described themselves as Russian and identified with the Russian elite. For decades, the most powerful landowners had been Polish, but by 1905 Russians were approaching Poles in wealth. During the disturbances, however, national distinctions proved meaningless to the peasants who attacked all large landowners (and large-scale renters) regardless of nationality, political persuasion, or personal qualities.

Jews, who comprised about 12 percent of the population of the right bank, were, for the most part, confined to the towns. Their contact with peasants was limited, and their ownership of large blocs of land was rare. Some very few Jews did own sugar refineries and as a result rented large amounts of land. They did not escape the peasants' wrath, nor were they singled out.[19] Right-bank peasants demonstrated comparatively less open anti-Semitic feeling than Ukrainians and Russians in the towns, but this attitude was the result of lack of contact with Jews rather than enlightenment. Peasants might attack a Jewish trader they felt had cheated them. At the same time, many of the political agitators welcomed into the villages were Jewish, and Ukrainian peasants proved willing to listen to and work with these outsiders. As we shall see later, pogroms, a common part of the urban scene in southern and western Russia, occurred relatively infrequently in the countryside of the southwest.

Noble Landholding and Commercial Agriculture

As late as 1800, a considerable portion of the Ukraine was still virgin land. Even at that late date, agriculture in many of its regions could still be quite primitive. By comparison, the right bank was a more developed region dominated by educated and agriculturally

[19]1897 census, Kiev, p. 1. On the presence of Jews in the countryside, see Hans Rogger, *Jewish Policies and Right-Wing Politics in Imperial Russia* (Berkeley, 1985), pp. 113–75.

sophisticated Polish landlords whose families had been engaged in farming for many years.[20] Before the peasant emancipation, many landlords throughout the Ukraine tried to adapt their estates to the production of grain surpluses for an expanding European market. Right-bank nobles also experienced some success in responding to the new circumstances, but a more profound transformation of agriculture had to await tsar Alexander II's edicts of 1861 and 1863, which dictated the ways the newly emancipated serfs would receive land. These reforms were not intended to allow the complete capitalist transformation of the Russian and Ukrainian countrysides. Nevertheless, significant possibilities were created, and in the last decades of the century, change was swift.

By 1905, the Ukraine had attained its well-known status as the breadbasket of Europe. Ninety percent of its arable land was devoted to winter and summer grains which were exported in massive quantities along Russia's quickly expanding railroad network and through the thriving port cities on the Black Sea.[21] The steppe provinces of Kherson and Ekaterinoslav were the main suppliers of this trade. Chernigov, Poltava, and Kharkov, on the left bank of the Dniepr, also produced extensively for export. Of the three regions of the Ukraine, the right bank, in fact, was the least oriented toward the raising of grain for the external market. Rather, the combination of soil and climate found in the southwest created possibilities for more diversified agriculture. Cash crops, which were of little use to peasants but which were raised by landlords, became increasingly significant.

These trends toward specialization should not obscure the immense importance of the raising of grain for the agrarian life of these provinces. The right bank may have trailed the rest of the Ukraine as an exporter of grain, but most of the energies of the region's cultivators were still devoted to meeting the basic nutritional needs of local peasants, the city of Kiev, and the internal

[20]Tsentral'nyi gosudarstvennyi istoricheskii arkhiv Ukrainskoi SSR (hereafter TsGIAU), fond 442, opis 855, delo 109, list 83 (hereafter abbreviated f., o., d., and l.).

[21]Lewis Siegelbaum, "The Odessa Grain Trade: A Case Study in Urban Growth and Development in Tsarist Russia," *Journal of European Economic History* 9 (Spring 1980), 113–51. Telichuk, p. 15.

Regions and provinces of European Russia. Reproduced from Maureen Perrie, *The Agrarian Policy of the Russian Socialist-Revolutionary Party* (Cambridge, 1976), by permission of Cambridge University Press.

market. Winter grains were far more common than summer grains in the southwest. Winter rye and wheat, in particular, occupied 45 percent of the region's sown area as of 1900.[22] In 1905, almost 1 million *desiatiny* were sown with winter rye and more than 450,000 *desiatiny* were under winter wheat.[23] Little summer wheat, the most desirable export crop, was raised in the southwest. The raising of grain was in no way specific to the right bank. Nevertheless, its significance must be stressed. The distinctive characteristics of this region played a crucial role in explaining the peasant movement in these provinces. Yet it is essential to make clear the considerable concern still devoted there to the most common and familiar agrarian activities.

Landlords and peasants of the southwest also raised specialized crops. Tobacco was farmed in Podol'e, as it was throughout Novorossiia.[24] Hops were raised in Volynia, and many noble landowners in Podol'e and Volynia enjoyed some success with dairy farming.[25] In addition, the right bank experienced an enormous increase in the production of potatoes, output tripling between 1861 and 1905.[26] As a result, many distilleries were built on gentry estates as landlords sought to exploit their holdings in new and profitable ways.[27] These sorts of small factories were characteristic of the southwest. Heavy manufacturing, even in the city of Kiev, was not extensive. Food processing firms were the most significant enterprises in the right bank's largest urban center. Kiev also became a major transit point, with railroading playing a major role in the life of the city. By 1900 over 10,000 *versts* (one *verst* = 1.06 kilometers) of railroad crisscrossed the southwest.

None of these activities gave the southwest its special dynamism. The raising and refining of sugar beets was the distinctive characteristic of agriculture in the right bank Ukraine. Kiev and Podol'e, in particular, were the centers of the Russian sugar industry, ac-

[22]Confino, p. 254.
[23]O. M. Kolomiets, *Polozhenie krestian i krestianskoe dvizhenie na pravoberezhnoi Ukraine v nachale xx veka*, avtoreferat dissertatsii (Kiev, 1969), p. 9.
[24]Anfimov, 1980, 180.
[25]Leshchenko, 1955, p. 28.
[26]Telichuk, p. 12.
[27]D. P. Poida, *Krestianskoe dvizhenie na pravoberezhnoi Ukraine v poreformennoi period, 1866–1900* (Dnepropetrovsk, 1960), p. 53.

counting for almost 90 percent of national production in 1900. Although some sugar beets were raised in the left-bank Ukraine and in the central Russian province of Kursk, no region could compete with the southwest. In large measure the importance of sugar in the right bank was the result of fortuitous natural circumstances. But the particular attitudes and experiences of the region's landlords also made them able to adapt to the demands and opportunities posed by this new kind of crop.

Absenteeism was one of the chronic problems caused by the demands of state service on the Russian landowning nobility. Polish landlords were under no such service obligation. Until the turn of the century, they dominated gentry agriculture in the southwest. In the 1880s and 1890s, as Russian landlords came to retire from bureaucratic and military careers, they found a ready model in their Polish counterparts. With the burgeoning of both the internal and external markets, Russian nobles saw opportunities in returning to this fertile region to try to become gentleman farmers. By 1905, Russian landlords owned more land than Polish landlords, and both groups were engaged in the exploitation of their holdings through the active pursuit of commercial agriculture. Large landholders in Kiev, Podol'e, and Volynia had ceased to view their estates as static sources of relatively fixed rents and instead came to think of them as expanding producers of profit.

Faced with the necessity of adapting to the modern world, right-bank landlords were taking what Lenin and subsequent historians have come to call the "Prussian path" to capitalism.[28] Their conscious model was the East Prussian Junker who had adapted his ancestral lands to production for the market. These erstwhile soldiers had forsaken their traditional social and economic roles in order to maintain their political dominance in a swiftly changing Germany. Significantly, one of the most important crops on the Junker estates was sugar beets. The cultivation of sugar beets was organized by landlords with the labor of massive numbers of wage workers who were often peasants unable to draw a sufficient living from their own lands. This politically conservative approach to the

[28]M. N. Leshchenko, *Ukrains'ke selo v revoliutsii 1905–1907 rr.* (Kiev, 1977), p. 45.

problem of the transition to capitalism was contrasted with what Lenin and others called the "American path."[29] In that particular situation, peasants, not lords, adapted their lands to changed conditions and worked as profit-oriented family farmers producing for a commodity market. This small-scale agrarian capitalism was often difficult to detect, and it differed sharply from landlord capitalism. Nevertheless, there is evidence that this particular path toward modern agriculture had emerged in the left-bank Ukraine and Novorossiia where peasants had acquired large amounts of land and were producing for the market.[30] Right-bank peasants, by contrast, had made little such progress.

The weakness of peasant agriculture in Kiev, Podol'e, and Volynia was the direct result of landlord success. The combination of high fertility, natural circumstances, and institutional peculiarities gave the nobles of the southwest special opportunities. They capitalized on these advantages despite certain initial handicaps. At the time of the 1861 emancipation, the autocracy sought to penalize Polish landlords and aid what the government chose to call Russian peasants.[31] Throughout Russia, peasants received less land than they had previously tilled, and they were forced to compensate the gentry for it at rates above the market value. In the southwest, just the opposite occurred. Peasants were given generous allotments at reasonable rates.

These advantages soon disappeared under the impact of agrarian progress and demographic expansion. In most parts of Russia, the emancipation marked the beginning of the steady decline of noble landowning. By 1905, members of the nobility (*dvoriantsvo*) had lost half their lands. This pattern of failure was not repeated in the southwest. Between the two universal land surveys of 1877 and 1905, aristocrats throughout Russia lost 30 percent of their lands. In the southwest, nobles relinquished just 16 percent of what they owned.[32] In the left-bank Ukraine and the steppe region, moreover, noble land loss was nearly twice as high as in the right

[29]Lenin, "The Agrarian Program of Social-Democracy," *Collected Works*, 13:239.
[30]Kingston-Mann, 1983, pp. 50–53.
[31]Skvortsov, p. 120. Telichuk, p. 27.
[32]Pershin, 1:14. Robinson, p. 88. Leshchenko, 1955, p. 20.

bank.[33] Peasants acquired most of the land given up by the nobility. This was especially true in the left bank and Novorossiia. Yet, in Kiev, Podol'e, and Volynia, peasants were unable to purchase or rent even the limited amounts of land made available by nobles. Merchants and members of the *meshchantsvo* proved better equipped to compete in the land market of the southwest.[34]

By 1905, nobles possessed almost 75 percent of the privately owned land in the right bank (this does not include allotment lands). Southwest peasants had only 13 percent of such lands. The contrast between the right bank and the rest of the Ukraine was stark. In the left bank, nobles owned 50 percent of private land, close to the national average of 52 percent.[35] In Novorossiia, nobles owned only 40 percent of private land. Right-bank nobles also possessed far greater portions of the available arable and forest land than did their counterparts in the rest of Russia.[36]

Soviet scholars are fond of contrasting the sharp size differences of landlord and peasant holdings. This practice has usually been considered a crude way of demonstrating the character of what all observers knew was a thoroughly exploitive relationship. Nevertheless, the difference in the right bank is worth noting precisely because the contrast was so stark. In Kiev, Podol'e, and Volynia, 8,535 landlord estates averaged nearly 900 *desiatiny,* while 452,417 peasant households occupied an average of almost 9 *desiatiny.*[37] In Kiev, the most advanced of the three *gubernii* (provinces), the contrast was even sharper.[38] In other parts of the empire, both nobles and peasants had been able to take advantage of changing conditions in the countryside. In the southwest, agricultural advancement was almost exclusively a noble enterprise.

[33]Leshchenko, 1955, p. 38.

[34]M. Rubach, "Sotsial'naia struktura agrarnykh otnoshenii i rassloenie krestianstva v ukrainskoi derevne v 1917g.," in *Osobennosti agrarnogo stroia Rossi v period imperializma*, p. 47.

[35]V. P. Teplytskii, *Reforma 1861 roku i agrarni vidnosini na Ukraini* (Kiev, 1959), p. 159. Skvortsov, p. 120.

[36]Teplytskii, p. 159. Skvortsov, p. 116.

[37]Anfimov, 1980, p. 93. Poida, 1960, p. 20.

[38]A. K. Butsik, "Agrarnye otnosheniia na Kievshchine nakanune revoliutsii 1905–1907 gg.," *Naukovi zapiski Kiivskogo Derzhavnogo Universitetu*, vol. 8, vyp. I (1949), p. 78.

There can be little question that the right bank was the scene of extensive agrarian development. The amount of land under cultivation had grown steadily over the course of the nineteenth century. Grains and potatoes were planted in increasingly larger amounts during these decades, and productivity rose steadily. Peasants played some role in this expansion but, cash crops, such as winter wheat and sugar beets, were produced almost entirely by landlords or by large agricultural firms, renting from landlords.

By the turn of the century the gentry estates of the right-bank Ukraine were evolving into capitalist enterprises. The traditional lord-peasant relationship with its paternalism and mutual obligations, was becoming a dead letter. Landlords in the southwest were coming to treat those who worked their lands as employees. Responding to the growing internal and external markets required a new set of organizational practices. This did not involve the massive introduction of agricultural machinery. As late as the 1890s, sophisticated farm tools were still relatively rare in the southwest.[39] Mechanical innovations were far more common in Kherson and Ekaterinoslav. Instead, right-bank landlords came to produce cash crops for expanding markets through the increasing use of wage labor, especially day labor. Estate owners abandoned old obligations. As elsewhere, estate owners took away common pastureland from peasants and restricted the use of forests and water supplies. In the southwest, unlike the rest of Russia, peasants did not confront a class in decline. Landlords in the right bank were not leaving their lands, nor were they selling their estates to peasants. Gentry success made peasant lives all the more difficult in this region.

Beyond these economic handicaps, peasants were also victimized by the major institutional peculiarity of the southwest. In 1864, tsar Alexander II created a network of local government bodies on the provincial and district levels. These semi-autonomous organs, called *zemstvos,* were given the task of performing such important services as health care, primary education, road building, insur-

[39]R. Munting, "Mechanisation and Dualism in Russian Agriculture," *Journal of European Economic History* 9 (January 1980), 743. M. N. Leshchenko, *Klasova borot'ba v ukrainskomu seli v epokhu domonopolistichnogo kapitalizmu* (Kiev, 1970), p. 50.

ance, and agronomic assistance. The *zemstvos* were given their own powers of taxation but were subject to a number of controls from the central government. During the late nineteenth century, the *zemstvos* undoubtedly improved the lives of peasants throughout Russia, but these bodies did not exist in the southwest until 1911.[40]

Membership in the *zemstvos* was elective, but participation was based on a series of property requirements that gave large landholders dominance. Noble landlords came to see the service they performed for the *zemstvo* as an important part of their own adaptation to the modern world, but this process could not go on in the southwest. There, the majority of landlords in 1864 were Polish. In the wake of the Polish rebellion of 1863, the Russian autocracy was not about to deliver local government in a borderland into the hands of those it deemed unreliable. As a result, peasants in Kiev, Podol'e, and Volynia were denied a number of social services that their central Russian counterparts had long taken for granted. At no time during the disturbances of 1905–7 did the peasants express a desire for *zemstvos*. Yet there can be little doubt that the absence of these institutions made their lives more difficult.

Circumstances of soil and climate plus the weakness of state and *zemstvo* service traditions combined to create special opportunities for right-bank landlords. Large numbers of them adapted their estates to changing conditions, using modern agronomic techniques, sophisticated multifield systems of crop rotation, and rigorous business practices. This change occurred throughout the region and was not restricted to the larger and more efficient sugar plantations. Many middle-sized estates (500 to 5,000 *desiatiny*) planted the more familiar crops. Landlords usually ran these holdings themselves, utilizing multifield rotations for a wide variety of grains, fruits, and vegetables. Nevertheless, grains in general, and winter wheat and rye in particular, occupied most of the area of these estates. Landlords raised a variety of grasses for fodder, and planted potatoes, most of which were distilled in small factories

[40]Terence Emmons and Wayne S. Vucinich, eds., *The Zemstvo in Russia* (Cambridge, 1982), pp. 423–45.

48

built by landlords on the estates.[41] Even on the nonsugar estates, less land was left fallow than under the three-field system, and those areas that were not planted received extensive natural and chemical fertilization.

As was common on most modernized estates, a comparatively small skilled regular staff worked on an annual basis.[42] Unskilled and semi-skilled laborers then supplemented their efforts. These laborers usually came from among the local peasant population. Goliaki, the Podol'e farm of Count Alexander Feodorovich Geiden, was in many ways typical of the right bank's nonsugar-producing estates. Geiden owned 1,200 *desiatiny* in Vinnitsa district. Of his land, 850 *desiatiny* were planted with a wide variety of crops in a nine-field system. Most attention was devoted to potatoes which were converted to alchohol in a distillery on the premises.[43] Atypically, the count lived in Petersburg and hired a Danish administrator who was paid 1,200 rubles a year plus 6 percent of the profits.[44] Between fifteen and twenty yearly *(godovye)* workers were hired for forty rubles a year (in 1905) plus sixty *pudy* (one *pud* = 36.11 pounds) of grain, the use of a house *(izba),* and sufficient feed for one cow. Day laborers, both men and women, were taken on, when needed, at whatever the going rate might have been. Geiden's estate was successful. Between 1894 and 1907 he averaged a profit of over 9,000 rubles a year.[45] Compared to sugar plantation owners, however, Geiden's profits were modest. Labor comprised almost half of his total costs, and his outlays per *desiatin* were considerably higher than those on the estates producing sugar beets.[46]

Wide varieties of crops were raised in the right bank. Even those

[41]Ministerstvo zemledeliia i gosudarstvennykh imushchestv, *Kratkie spravochnye svedeniia o nekotorykh russkikh khoziaistvakh* (St. Petersburg, 1897), pp. 170–71 (hereafter *KS*).

[42]Kievskoe Agronomicheskoe Obshchestvo, *Trudy komissii po izucheniia khoziaistv iugo-zapadnogo kraia* (hereafter *Trudy*), vyp. II (Kiev, 1913), p. 39.

[43]Liubanskii, 1911, p. 20.

[44]Ibid., p. 3.

[45]Ibid., p. 23.

[46]Ibid., p. 16.

who had not converted to raising sugar beets could easily be successful. But it was the southwest's sugar plantations, many of them
quite vast, that were the distinctive feature of land husbandry in
these three provinces. These farms achieved enormous profits in
the years of Russia's rapid industrialization. Their practices and
organization require close attention, as the character of the peasant
movement in the southwest was fundamentally determined by conditions on these plantations.

Sugar Beets, Workers, and Refineries

Sugar beets were first raised in the right bank during the 1820s,
although few landlords planted beets until the 1850s. At that time,
many of the leading nobles of the region, including the Bobrinskii,
Pototskii, Brannitskii, Sangushko, Bezrobodko, and later the
Tereshchenko families began planting and refining this crop.[47]
They were following the example of their Prussian counterparts
who had also begun the conversion of portions of their estates to
sugar.[48] In fact, the first beet strains were German, and German
varieties continued to be predominant even after 1917.[49] These
first steps, however, were halting. Raising sugar beets required the
heavy use of labor at certain key moments in the life cycle of the
crop. Wage workers, rather than peasants, were more productive
at this sort of labor. Thus, the full-scale production of Russian
sugar had to await the emancipation.

Starting with the 1860s, output rose dramatically. As Russian
industrialization quickened and the cities grew, so did the demand
for sugar. The growth of production was extremely swift (see
Table 2). The expansion of land sown with sugar beets was equally
swift. In 1850, 21,000 *desiatiny* were planted with this crop; by
1900, over 300,000 *desiatiny* were under beets. Even during the
disturbances, between 1905 and 1907, 50,000 new *desiatiny* came

[47]G. I. Marakhov, *Pol'skoe vosstanie 1863 g. na pravoberezhnoi Ukraine* (Kiev, 1967), p. 26.
[48]Perkins, p. 20.
[49]*KS*, pp. 160–187.

Table 2. Sugar Production in the Right
Bank, 1865–1900

Years	Pudy*
1865–66	700,000
1881–82	803,298
1889–90	13,369,895
1899–1900	27,000,000 (est.)

Source: O. O. Nesterenko, *Rozvitok kapitalistichnoi promislovosti i formuvannia proletariaty na ukraini v kinsti XIX i na XX st.* (Kiev, 1952), p. 52
*one *pud* = 36.11 pounds

under cultivation. By 1912, a half million *desiatiny* would be devoted to sugar.[50]

Half the southwest's sugar came from Kiev, which was first among all provinces as a producer and refiner.[51] Podol'e ranked a close second. Much less sugar was raised in Volynia (9 percent of the region's total), and agriculture in this province more closely resembled practices in central Russia. As mentioned earlier, Volynia's northern half was largely forested, and sugar beets grew only in its southeastern districts, bordering on Kiev. The left-bank Ukraine and Kursk produced some sugar, but no region could challenge the right bank in the production of this cash crop.

Cash was, in fact, the primary attraction of sugar beet production for the landlords of the southwest. In Kiev during 1905, one *pud* of beets fetched five times the amount that could be earned from a similar amount of wheat, and six times the price of a *pud* of rye.[52] Costs were not that much greater than those entailed in the raising of other crops. As a result, profits were enormous.[53] Inevitably, larger numbers of landlords were attracted to raising sugar

[50]Leshchenko, 1955, p. 30.

[51]*Vestnik sakharnoi promyshlennosti* (hereafter VSP) 23 (1906), 986.

[52]Agronomicheskii otdel Kievskoi gubernskoi upravy po delam zemskogo khoziaistva, *Obzor sostoianiia sel'skogo khoziaistva Kievskoi gubernii v 1905 i 1906 gg.* (Kiev, 1906), p. 21.

[53]A. Iaroshevich, *Opis maetkiv po ekonomitsi pivdennozakhidnogo kraiu* (Kiev, 1909), p. 150.

beets, which had the added advantage of being a much more reliable crop than the most common grains.[54] Sharp variations in harvests, so common an element in the Russian countryside, were not typical for sugar beets.

Sugar raised and refined in the southwest was largely sold domestically. Russian landlords were not able to compete with their Prussian counterparts on the world market. The leading foreign customers for Russian sugar were Turkey and Persia, each of which purchased approximately half a million *pudy* per year. Austria-Hungary was the largest European buyer with annual purchases between 130,000 and 140,000 *pudy*.[55] In the years before the Revolution of 1905, international prices dropped and exports fell.[56] Domestic prices, however, rose slightly, and production did not fall off drastically. On the eve of the revolutionary turmoil, the Russian sugar industry, despite problems, was in a rather healthy state. Conditions were not quite as rosy as they had been in 1900, but sugar producers felt comfortable and economically unthreatened.[57]

The raising and refining of sugar beets was primarily a gentry enterprise. Those that did not participate in it directly profited from the sugar trade by renting their estates to joint-stock companies or directly to sugar refineries not owned by nobles. By contrast, peasants were less involved in raising this crop. Nevertheless, the fact that they had any interest in growing something that was not part of their normal diets is worth noting. Given the well-advertised peasant aversion to innovation, their willingness to plant any sugar beets at all may be considered surprising. Still, their efficiency and productivity were considerably lower than that of the large estates which remained the centers of Russian sugar production.[58] In 1905, 56 percent of the area sown with sugar beets was on large, noble-owned plantations. Firms renting estates accounted for 29 percent of the land under sugar, while peasants accounted for less than 15 percent.[59]

[54]Liubanskii, *Opisanie imenii Podol'skoi gubernii* (Vinnitsa, 1908), p. 28.
[55]*VSP* 40 (1907), 451.
[56]L. F. Volokhov, *Sakharnoi promyshlennosti Rossii v tsifrakh* (Kiev, 1913), p. 63. Oganovskii, p. 300.
[57]Volokhov, table 2.
[58]Ibid., table 7.
[59]Kievskoe Agronomicheskoe Obshchestvo, *Trudy*, vyp. III (Kiev, 1915), p. 13. Butsik, 1949, p. 89.

The conduct of operations on both landlord-run and privately rented estates was largely the same. Peasants, in particular, paid little attention to the distinction. There is no evidence to suggest that either kind of farm was a more desirable place for peasants to work. Although some few peasants raised a relatively small crop of sugar beets, their primary role in the southwest's sugar industry was the provision of manual labor on the larger estates.

None of the nobility's plantations were devoted entirely to raising sugar beet, but nearly all of them were organized along what for Russian agriculture would have been called modern lines. The largest holdings were primarily controlled by the gentry, but medium-sized and smaller estates were oriented to the market as well. The retention of primitive methods did not always preclude the production of sugar in the right bank, however. A significant number of farms had kept the three-field system, but instead of sowing rye as a summer crop, planted beets. A few of these apparently traditional operations even had refineries.[60] Nevertheless, sugar production in the right bank was centered in well-organized estates, practicing advanced farming methods and new, but not always benign, approaches to labor relations.

By any European standard all the estates of the right-bank nobility were immense. The typical holding of the East Prussian Junker was 200 hectares (one hectare = 2.2 acres).[61] These dimensions were small compared to even the mid-sized holding in Russia's southwest, where such estates ranged from 500 to 5,000 *desiatiny*. They were advanced, multifield operations producing a variety of corps of which sugar beet was the most profitable but not always the most widely sown. In the relatively simple five-field system of the Ustinov estate in Podol'e, sugar beets occupied 15 percent of the arable land; winter wheat 26 percent.[62] On the more complex eight-field rotation of the Zagrebel'nyi estate, also in Podol'e, sugar beet, winter wheat, and clover each covered 22 percent of arable.[63] Ten and twelve-field rotations were also quite common in the southwest. The estate of Elena Petrovna Demidova

---

[60]*KS,* pp. 155–58, 178–80.
[61]Perkins, p. 20.
[62]Iaroshevich, 1909, p. 148.
[63]Liubanskii, 1908, p. 10.

in Kiev (Lipovets district) employed a twelve-field system on its 2,535 *desiatiny* of arable (she owned 5,277 in all). Three of these fields were planted with sugar beets.[64] All of these holdings made extensive use of fertilizers, especially chemical ones; few estates, however, had made large investments in agricultural machinery.[65]

The famous Russian suprematist painter Kazimir Malevich grew up on a sugar estate in Podol'e during the 1890s. He later described work on one plantation:

> The sugar-beet plantations were large. A lot of manpower, provided by peasants, mostly, was needed to run these plantations. Peasants, young and old, worked on these plantations all summer and fall. As a future artist, I feasted my eyes upon the fields and the "colored" workers who weeded and dug up the beetroot. Platoons of girls in colorful clothes moved in rows across the whole field. It was a war. The troops in colorful dresses struggled with weeds, liberating the beetroot from unwanted overgrowths . . . The sugar plantations stretched as far as the eye could see, blending into the distant horizon, sloping down to the small cornfields, or running up the hills, engulfing towns and villages in their fields, covered with the monotonous texture of green plants.[66]

A small number of the operators of middle-sized estates had constructed refineries, but most landlords had to ship their beets to neighboring plantations for processing. Many of these holdings were of gargantuan proportions. In many parts of Russia, the owners of latifundia such as these had made no attempt to improve their lands, preferring simply to collect rents from peasants who were in no position to engage in significant agrarian advancement. The sugar plantations of the southwest did not follow this pattern. They were owned by the oldest and most respected noble families of the region. As already noted, the Bobrinskii, Pototskii, Brannitskii, Balashev, and other families had been the pioneers of the

[64]*KS*, p. 154.

[65]*VSP* 1 (1907), 7. *KS*, pp. 149, 152, 153, 158, 159, 163, 166, 167, 168, 169, 172, 180, 185, 186.

[66]Kazimir Malevich, "Chapters from an Artist's Autobiography," *October*, no. 34 (Fall 1985), 25 (translated by Alan Upchurch).

Russian sugar trade. They had proven extremely successful in adapting their lands for the production of commodities for the market. Many of their estates were models of modern commercial agriculture. They merit close attention for two reasons. They were the most distinctive feature of the right bank's agriculture, and, significantly, they were all centers of intense peasant agitation between 1905 and 1907.

The immensity of the southwest's sugar plantations cannot be overstressed. The four Kiev estates of Mar'ia Brannitskaia covered almost 97,000 *desiatiny*. Only one of those units *(ekonomii)* was a true farming center. More than 15,000 of its 31,158 *desiatiny* were planted in multifield systems which included many fruits, vegetables, and grasses, along with improved grains and sugar beets. Each of the four estates had a sugar refinery. Brannitskaia also operated two distilleries.[67] The Volynia estates of Roman Sangushko were nearly as large as Brannitskaia's holdings. Similarly, Moshnogorodishchenskoe, the Kiev estate of Ekaterina Andreevna Balasheva, covered 43,586 *desiatiny,* 11,000 of it arable. This immense, modern plantation was divided into several subunits, all of which were studded with new brick buildings, including stables, barns, distilleries, breweries, dormitories, and, or course, refineries. Balasheva and her staff of administrators used eight-field rotations, raising a broad variety of crops, fertilizing extensively, and processing the estate's produce in a number of different plants *(zavody)* on the plantation itself.[68] The Kiev estate of the Bobrinskii family was almost as large as Balasheva's and was similarly organized.[69] Various members of the Tereshchenko family owned and operated sugar plantations throughout the southwest. These ranged from 11,000 to 15,000 *desiatiny*. All were efficiently run and all had sugar refineries on their premises.[70]

Given the fact that estates of this size occupied so much land and controlled so many resources, it is only logical that they were not particularly numerous. Yet there were more of these latifundia in

[67]*KS*, p. 149.
[68]P. R. Slezkin, *Opisanie moshnogorodishchenskogo imeniia ee vysokoprevoskhoditel'stva Ekateriny Aleksandreevny Balashevy,* 2 vols. (Kiev, 1913), 1:36–65.
[69]*KS*, p. 160.
[70]TsGIAU, f. 318, o. 1, d. 364, l. 130. *KS*, pp. 175–77.

the right bank (forty-nine of more than 10,000 *desiatiny*) than in most other regions. Moreover, it would be wrong to see them as exceptional or unusual given their central role in the economy of the southwest. They generated tremendous wealth for their owners and provided work for vast numbers of peasants.

As was the case with most estates oriented toward farming, the southwest's sugar plantations employed small full-time staffs of administrators and managers, many of whom were foreign. These men were usually paid a sizable fixed sum, plus a percentage (5 or 6 percent) of profits. The administrators then hired a year-round staff of skilled workers who were paid a small amount (between twenty and thirty rubles) and provided with housing, grain, and fuel.[71] Stablehands, blacksmiths, house servants, and others made up this group which was supplemented by other workers, usually local peasants, who were taken on for a period of months. This segment of the work force *(srokovye rabochie)* was hired just before sowing and stayed on several weeks after harvest. Like the annual workers, this group too was relatively small.[72]

The great majority of those who worked the sugar plantations of the right bank were day laborers, recruited for the most part from the local peasantry. Although there are no precise figures on the number of such laborers, all sources do make clear that their use was widespread. Wage work made up a decisive portion of the income of those thousands of peasant households whose allotments were insufficient to sustain life. Very often the women and children went to work in the landlord's fields while the men stayed home. In fact, it was the general wisdom among landlords, following the Prussian example, that women and children were better workers.[73] Women, in particular, could work as long and hard as men but were paid a good deal less.

Wages varied from season to season, year to year, and estate to estate, but in no time or place could payment for work on the sugar plantations be described as anything but minimal. In fact, Bal-

---

[71]Kievskoe Agronomicheskoe Obshchestvo, *Trudy,* vyp. IV (Kiev, 1915), pp. 36–37. Slezkin, 1913, p. 84.

[72]Tsentral'nyi gosudarstvennyi istoricheskii arkhiv v Leningrade (hereafter TsGIAL), f. 1405, o. 107, d. 7932, l. 2.

[73]Perkins, pp. 19–21.

asheva's accountants estimated that paying a day laborer cost far less than keeping a horse (twenty-six as opposed to forty-one kopecks a day in 1905).[74] More precise wage levels will be treated in detail when the strike movement is examined. At this point it is sufficient to stress that while landlords employed very sizable numbers of day workers, they did not pay dearly for this labor. Wages represented a comparatively small and manageable portion (one fourth to one third) of the costs of those who operated all of the region's sugar estates, not simply the largest plantations.[75] The demand for labor on the sugar plantations was considerable, but the general poverty of the local peasantry was so acute that a large number of job seekers was guaranteed every year.

The central factor determining the sizable demand for wage workers was the labor-intensive character of sugar beet raising. The average person had to work almost twice as many days to raise a *desiatin* of sugar beets as opposed to a *desiatin* of most grains.[76] In addition, the cycle of the sugar beet created a number of crucial moments that demanded the immediate and careful attention of large numbers of working hands.[77] The fragility of the sugar beet at certain points in its development created opportunities for those engaged in its actual cultivation, giving peasants a limited and transitory power in their relationship with their employers. As a result, the contours of the peasant movement were very much influenced by the demands of sugar beet cultivation.

Great care had to be taken in deciding where and when to sow the beets. The readiness of each field had to be measured before proceeding. Temperatures had to reach sufficient levels (9 to 10 degrees centigrade), a point reached between late March and early May depending on the place and year. Plowing had to be deep given the sugar beets' long roots—metal plows were a necessity.[78]

[74]Slezkin, 1913, p. 88.

[75]Liubanskii, 1908, p. 10.

[76]Voblyi, 1925, p. 60.

[77]Tsentral'nyi gosudarstvennyi arkhiv oktiabrskoi revoliutsii (hereafter TsGAOR), f. 102, 1907, o. 236, d. 700, ch. 54, l. 145.

[78]S. L. Franfurt, *Chto nuzhno znat' zemledeltsu chtoby uspeshno vozdelyvat' sakharnuiu sveklovitsu* (Kiev, 1913), p. 66. P. R. Slezkin, *Sakharnaia svekla i ee kultura* (Kiev, 1908), p. 86.

Proletarian Peasants

The beets themselves had to be sown carefully, in neat rows, at sufficient distances from each other.

Sowing was a simple process compared to the next phase of the beets' development. The soil had to be constantly aerated and watered. When the first shoots appeared, it became necessary to begin an intense daily search for pests. Children usually performed this work. Weeding went on constantly in these early phases as did extensive fertilizing. This phase lasted through May and June.[79] Without this intense early attention, the crop would be ruined. After a rest of a week to ten days in late June, a new period of weeding, watering, and fertilizing began, lasting three weeks to a month. At this point, less attention was required until the harvest in late August or early September. Workers pulled the mature beets out of the ground with their hands, a literally back-breaking task. They then trimmed off the leaves and roots with a knife and carried the beets to waiting wagons or carts provided by the plantation owners. All of the work, from sowing to harvest, was strictly supervised by foremen. The crucial fact to keep in mind for present purposes is that the sowing and harvesting of the sugar beet were not the times of the year requiring the largest amount of labor. Instead, that moment came in May and June when the beets had to be watched over almost hourly.

Once the beets had been harvested, they had to be refined. By and large, this task was performed on the plantations in refineries that had been built either by landlords or their renters, some of which, later on, were joint-stock companies owned by Jewish merchants.[80] In 1830, there had been 6 sugar refineries in all of Russia. By 1900 there were 159 such establishments, 117 of which were in the southwest.[81] That year, these 117 refineries employed 68,435 workers, a figure that varied little in the years leading up to the

[79]Franfurt, p. 77. Telichuk, p. 108. Slezkin, 1908, p. 126.

[80]Arcadius Kahan, "Notes on Jewish Entrepreneurship in Tsarist Russia," in Gregory Guroff and Fred V. Carstensen, eds., *Entrepreneurship in Imperial Russia and the Soviet Union* (Princeton, 1983), p. 115.

[81]M. N. Leshchenko, *Selianski rukh na Ukraini v roki pershoi rosiis'koi revoliutsii* (Kiev, 1956), p. 22.

58

revolutionary turmoil.[82] In contrast to those who worked the fields, only 10 percent of refinery workers were women.[83] The total number of sugar refinery workers may not seem large when compared to the total peasant population of the region, yet they represented a significant proportion (29 percent) of industrial workers in the Ukraine.[84]

Sugar refinery workers were hired for six-month periods, beginning in mid-August. As no special skills were required, mill owners sent teams into neighboring villages to recruit peasants. Agents paid elders as much as a ruble a head for each worker hired.[85] Contracts were signed. Workers then appeared in groups from their villages and were placed under the authority of a foreman (*podviadchik*) who controlled their wages, along with their food and lodging, both of which were provided by the refinery. In the 1870s and 1880s, mills found it difficult to recruit peasants who were suspicious of industrial work. Once they began working in the refineries, many peasants simply ran out on their contracts rather than subject themselves to the new and difficult industrial conditions. As a result, foremen took to keeping their workers' passports (needed to travel between provinces). This practice also served to restrain acts of insubordination and labor unrest. Unions were clearly illegal, and the only protection afforded mill workers was provided by the government's factory inspectors, who, after the 1890s, succeeded in forcing considerable improvements on mill owners.[86]

Initially, conditions in the refineries had been quite harsh. Extremely hot boilers and distilling devices reached high temperatures and produced steamy, humid air. The heat inside would clash with cold outside air to produce a health hazard for the workers. Pneumonia and typhus were common, but medical care, provided by the landlords, was minimal. The accident rate among the largely

---

[82]Leshchenko, 1955, p. 23.

[83]K. Voblyi, *Narisi z isotrii rosiis'ko-ukrainskoi tsukro-buriakovoi prom-islovosti* (Kiev, 1931), p. 6.

[84]Ibid., p. 9.

[85]Ibid., p. 26.

[86]Ibid., p. 20.

unskilled workers was particularly high, as much as 25 percent in one plant. Clinics provided by owners were rarely if ever staffed by doctors. This would change under government pressure by 1900, but there were few changes in the danger and difficulty of the labor process itself. Unsanitary conditions in the factories were matched by the filth characteristic of the housing provided workers. Food, however, was plentiful if not always nourishing, as workers required the energy for two twelve-hour shifts. The factories worked around the clock during their busy season, and as one worker labored another was occupying his bed.

Malevich's father had worked in a sugar refinery which was described in the following way:

> The other part of the factory recalled some fortress in which people worked day and night, obeying the merciless summons of factory whistles. People stood in the factories, bound by time to some apparatus or machine: twelve hours in the steam, the stench of gas and filth. I remember my father standing in front of a large apparatus. It was beautiful with many pieces of glass of various sizes. . . . All the workers there carefully followed the movements of their machine, as though following the movements of a predatory animal. And in the same time, they had to keep a sharp eye on themselves and their own movements. A false move threatened either death or being crippled for life.[87]

Difficult conditions did produce some strikes and disturbances. Usually an accident provoked a disorder. But sugar workers were handicapped by the seasonal character of their work and by their general industrial inexperience. Given the fact that they were still, by definition, peasants, it often proved simpler for them to return home if unpleasantness occurred in the refinery. Later on when peasants would confront landlords in different and more massive ways, it became possible for refinery workers to join forces. Until 1905, however, they provided, for the most part, a source of cheap labor to the owners of sugar refineries. Landlords and renters had proven highly efficient in processing the output of the estates. The

[87]Malevich, p. 26.

ability of the right-bank gentry to survive and prosper was not typical of the landed nobility throughout Russia. Their success, however, made life all the more difficult for the peasantry of Kiev, Podol'e, and Volynia.

Peasant Landholding and Peasant Agriculture

In February 1906, N. Kleigels, the governor-general of the southwest, wrote to the Council of Ministers: "The mass of the people here is poor. In some places they have been reduced to begging. Despite the great wealth of the region, the vast mass of the population can provide for itself only at a comparatively low material level."[88] News of this sort could hardly have been deemed earth-shattering, even in St. Petersburg. Nevertheless, the poverty of the right bank's peasantry was especially acute. To make matters worse, their ability to improve their situations was very constrained. Landlord success was one obstacle. Another was the character of the commune in this part of the empire. Throughout most of Russia, peasants with small allotments could hope to improve their positions in forthcoming repartitions. In the Ukraine and parts of Bielorussia, villages practiced hereditary tenure (*podvornoe vladenie*). In the southwest, 97 percent of households were in hereditary communes.[89]

It is easy enough to imagine that the existence of hereditary rather than repartitional tenure might have created the potential for private peasant property and sharp divergences of wealth. So much had been made for so long of the special powers of central Russia's communal villages that it may be surprising to learn that the Ukrainian *gromada* (commune) did not differ very much in its daily operation from the more celebrated Russian *mir*. The secretary of the Kiev Agricultural Society, T. I. Osadchii, noted this fact in 1899: "The land, despite the hereditary form of its use, is exploited in common. It has not been divided up among the peasants once and for all. Rather, its location and situation changes from

88Butsik, 1949, p. 76.
89Anfimov, 1980, p. 88.

year to year."[90] In addition, Shanin has been able to demonstrate that the "substantive changes" that worked between repartitions in central Russia also operated in hereditary communes, blurring the distinction even further.[91]

Perhaps more significant, the practice of agriculture in the hereditary commune was not notably different from the central Russian experience. Both kinds of settlements demonstrated the primary characteristics of the historic open-field village seen throughout feudal Europe. Hereditary peasants had the same problems taking care of their own allotments as did repartitional peasants. Land was divided into the same complex and inefficient system of scattered strips seen in the Russian village.[92] Sowing, harvesting, and the entire panoply of agricultural tasks were performed together under the guidance of the assembly of heads of households (the *skhod*) which operated according to well-understood traditions. Common grazing, manuring, and building were practiced in the right bank as elsewhere.[93] The practices that brought peasants together were still vital in the southwest. The practices that divided them were still constrained. It was difficult to sell even a hereditary allotment. Enclosures were rare until the land reform of 1906 enacted by the prime minister, Peter Stolypin, who sought to eliminate the commune and institute individual private property for the peasants.

The communal traditions of the peasantry were not identical throughout all parts of the Ukraine. Villages in the left bank were more like those in central Russia. Private peasant landholding had made considerable strides in Kherson and Ekaterinoslav, while Kiev, Podol'e, and Volynia exhibited comparatively weak communal structures because they had only recently been part of Poland. Recent research on patterns of property inheritance in Kiev and Kharkov, however, did not reveal sharply divergent practices despite the wider dispersal of the hereditary commune in the right bank.[94] Novorossiia, the left bank, and the right bank, however,

[90]Ibid., p. 106.
[91]Shanin, 1972, p. 120.
[92]I. M. Reva, *Kievskii krestianin i ego khoziaistvo.* (Kiev, 1893), p. 30.
[93]Robinson, p. 71.
[94]Christine Worobec, "Patterns of Property Devolution among Ukrainian Peas-

were all Ukrainian. Peasants, with obvious regional variations, all spoke Ukrainian. Hereditary tenure, with some differences, was practiced throughout the entire Ukraine.

Culture played the same unifying role in the right-bank Ukraine as it did in other peasant societies. The traditional assembly of heads of households organized the agricultural and social life of the village. The *skhod* was, however, more oligarchical than it was democratic. Its members were nearly always male, and more powerful households were most often able to manipulate decisions for their own benefit.[95] All of the rules and rituals of peasant life were enforced informally by the *skhod* with the added power of highly conformist village social pressure. There can be no question that cultural forms of this sort played an enormous role in the daily life of all peasants, Ukrainians and Russians included. Any broader understanding of peasant life that would exclude these phenomena would surely be incomplete. Yet these considerations are not particularly helpful in answering the more specific questions raised by the peasant movement in the right-bank Ukraine during the Revolution of 1905. Events in the southwest were sharply different from those encountered in the other parts of the Ukraine, but similar cultural and communal forms could be found throughout the Ukraine. The peasant movement in 1905 displayed striking regional variations. The Ukraine was no exception. Distinctions of culture and ritual, though important in many ways, were not nearly so acute, nor was their dispersal so geographically precise. Important as they are to any understanding of peasant lives in this part of the world, these considerations do not provide answers to our more immediate questions.

Demographic pressures, themselves the product of changing village family norms, played a crucial role in the difficulties facing the right bank's peasants. Population growth had been swifter in the southwest than in any other region (90 percent between 1858, and 1897). The size of the average household (between five and six

---

ants in Kiev and Kharkiv Provinces, 1861–1900," paper for Conference on the Peasantry of European Russia, 1800–1917, University of Massachusetts, Boston, August 19–22, 1986.

[95]O. F. Kuven'ova, *Gromadskii pobut ukrainskogo selianstva* (Kiev, 1966), p. 20.

Table 3. Average Allotment per
Peasant Household, 1905

Province	*Desiatiny*
Kiev	5.5
Podol'e	3.8
Volynia	7.8
All Ukraine	6.9
All Russia	8.9

Sources: P. P. Telichuk, *Ekonomichni osnovi agrarnoi revoliutsii na
ukrainii* (Kiev, 1971), p. 43. D. P.
Poida, *Krestianskoe dvizhenie na pravoberezhnoi ukraine v poreformennoi
period (1866–1900)* (Dnepropetrovsk,
1960), p. 36.

members) changed little over time and hardly differed from the
households of central Russia.[96] The number of households, however, increased dramatically. This growth in population combined
with the gentry's ability to retain their lands, sharply reducing the
average peasant holding. In 1861 the amount of land per peasant
"soul" averaged 2.9 *desiatiny;* in 1880 it was 2.1; by 1906 it had
declined to 1.4.[97]

Population was especially dense in the southwest.[98] To compensate for the great increase in numbers, peasants had to supplement
their allotments with purchases of private land. In most regions
such lands were bought from nobles, but the landlords of the right
bank had made little land available to buy or rent. As a result,
peasant holdings in Kiev, Podol'e, and Volynia were among the
smallest in the Russian Empire (see Table 3).

Not only was the average allotment in the southwest comparatively small, but the great majority of peasants had holdings

[96]Chaianov, p. 55. V. I. Frolov, *Kharakteristika krestianskogo khoziaistva i
zemel'nogo fonda Podol'skoi gubernii* (Vinnitsa, 1917), p. 12.
[97]Anfimov, 1980, p. 151. For decline in peasant landholdings, see Leshchenko,
1955, p. 54.
[98]Butsik, 1949, p. 78.

considerably below the average. Large allotments were rather rare in the southwest. Even what might be called middle-sized holdings were less numerous in the right bank than in other parts of Russia and the Ukraine (see Table 4). The size divisions used in Table 4 should not necessarily be seen as corresponding to the standard Leninist class divisions of "poor," "middle," and "rich." Allotment size, by itself, did not include all the land a peasant household might control, and regional differences did not make 5 *desiatiny* in one part of the empire equivalent to 5 *desiatiny* in another. Nevertheless, these figures should make clear that land hunger, so central a peasant grievance throughout Russia, was especially acute in the southwest. Small and insufficient holdings were the norm in this region, and the ability of the peasantry to change this situation was severely limited.

Since the emancipation, peasants had been able to alleviate some portion of their land hunger through purchase and rental. The decline of the landowning nobility had made sizable tracts available, and the State Peasant Bank, founded in 1883, had aided some better-off peasants in making purchases. Fertility and climate, however, conspired against the southwest's peasantry. The success of landlords meant that a minimum of surplus land could be

Table 4. Percentage of Peasant Allotments by Size and Region, 1905

	Desiatiny		
Province or Region	Up to 5	5–10	Over 10
Volynia	27.2	50.6	22.2
Kiev	55.5	35.4	9.1
Podol'e	78.6	19.8	1.6
Entire right bank	57.5	32.9	9.5
Left-bank Ukraine	44.8	43.1	12.1
Novorossiia	28.1	41.3	30.6
Bielorussia	7.8	63.8	28.4
Central Black Earth region	23.7	56.1	30.2

Source: Tsental'nyi statisticheskii komitet Ministerstvo vnutrennykh del, *Statistiki zemlevladenia v Rossii 1905 g.* (St. Petersburg, 1907).

bought, and high prices made the little available land unattainable for most peasants. In 1905, land in the southwest sold for just over 200 rubles a *desiatin,* compared to the national average of 107 rubles.[99] Since 1889, land in the right bank had increased 108 percent in value. Variations from district to district made the pattern even more obvious. Where land was comparatively less fertile, peasants were able to make purchases. In the more desirable districts, they made little progress. In the sugar beet *uezd* of Vasilkovsk (Kiev), nobles owned 90 percent of private land. In less fertile Radomylsk (also in Kiev), they owned only 57 percent.[100] In fact, peasants bought less land in the right bank than in any other region, and the land that was purchased was bought by individuals rather than by communes as was common in the rest of the empire.[101]

Between the two universal surveys of 1877 and 1905, the right-bank peasantry added over 620,000 *desiatiny* of land to their holdings. In 1877, they had controlled almost 3 percent of private land. By 1905, they had 13 percent, but this amount was far less than peasants in the left bank and steppe had acquired. In these regions, peasants owned roughly one third of the available private, that is, nonallotment, land.[102] Merchants proved especially keen competitors for the private lands of the right bank, precisely because the sugar beet industry made speculative purchasing more viable than in other regions.[103] Quite simply, little land was put up for sale. Peasants begged landlords to sell them even small parcels, but large landowners, regardless of their nationalities or political feelings, were unresponsive to these pleas.[104]

Peasants in the southwest were even less successful in renting land. They were outbid by sugar companies who paid as high as twenty-six rubles a year per *desiatin.*[105] These firms also supplied

[99]Pershin, p. 85.
[100]Butsik, 1949, pp. 78–86.
[101]Telichuk, pp. 51–53.
[102]Butsik, *Seliani i sil'skii proletariat Kiivshchini v pershii rosiis'skii revoliutsii* (Kiev, 1957), p. 8. Teplytskii, p. 159.
[103]Skvortsov, pp. 133–35.
[104]*Russkie Vedemosti,* April 25, 1905.
[105]Butsik, 1957, p. 16. *Istoria selianstva,* 1:395.

their own seed, fertilizer, and tools, leaving the landlord to collect a handsome royalty without any significant investments. The success of capitalist agriculture in the region turned land into a full-fledged commodity.[106] Given the new economic assumptions, there was no reason to rent to peasants who could not possibly pay the going rate.[107] During 1905, 13 percent of the land sown by peasants in the left-bank Ukraine was rented. In Novorossiia, the figure was as high as 20 percent. By contrast, right-bank peasants rented little more than 5 percent of their land.[108]

Right-bank peasants had proven ill-equipped to combat their acute land hunger. Dire poverty, even starvation, could be escaped only through labor for others. In most cases, survival included work for landlords, as wealthy peasants were very few.[109] A pre-revolutionary study by the agronomist A. I. Iaroshevich found that the less land a household controlled, the more likely one of its members would be working for someone else.[110] No one would argue that Russian peasants in 1905 were either wealthy or comfortable, but it should be clear that peasants in the southwest were especially poor. Large numbers of households held extremely small allotments.[111] Western and Soviet scholars are in broad agreement that the largest segment of the peasantry in central Russia fit into the so-called middle peasant group. Soviet specialists, using familiar terminology and basing their judgments on size of allotment, have described the majority of the right bank's peasantry as "poor." Employing a variety of censuses and land surveys, P. P. Telichuk, a Ukrainian economic historian, divided the southwest's peasantry along the lines shown in Table 5. M. N. Leshchenko, the leading Soviet authority on the Ukrainian peasant movement, using similar sources, came up with a slightly less stark picture of the size of the poor peasantry in the right bank. Leshchenko, look-

[106]For useful definitions of agrarian capitalism see Kaplan, p. 39. See also Galeski, p. 39.

[107]Anfimov, 1980, p. 118.

[108]Teplytskii, p. 172.

[109]Telichuk, p. 149.

[110]A. Iaroshevich, *Ocherki ekonomicheskoi zhizni iugo-zapadnago kraia* (Kiev, 1911), vyp. 2, p. 2.

[111]Voblyi, 1925, p. 64. Butsik, 1957, p. 12. Frolov, p. 12.

Proletarian Peasants

Table 5. Right-Bank Peasant Stratification, 1905

Province	No. of households	Poor		Middle		Rich	
		number	%	number	%	number	%
Volynia	439,811	282,803	64.3	84,557	19.2	72,451	16.5
Kiev	539,141	372,724	69.1	115,310	21.4	51,107	9.5
Podol'e	524,669	399,187	76.1	88,746	16.9	36,736	7.0

Sources: P. P. Telichuk, Ekonomichni osnovi agrarnoi revoliutsii na ukrainii (Kiev, 1971), p. 138.

ing at the entire Ukraine, was able to demonstrate that a similar portion of the peasantry in the rest of the Ukraine also could be classified as "poor." So-called middle peasants were slightly more numerous in the left bank and Novorossiia, and wealthy peasants were considerably more common in Kherson and Kharkov.[112]

The picture in individual right-bank villages is virtually impossible to determine. Precise information is available only on one Volynia commune, Zemlitsy in Vladimirvolynsk district. Some 289 souls lived in Zemlitsy (130 men and 159 women). They made up forty-eight households, occupying 200 *desiatiny*. The poorest families were landless (eight households), while the wealthiest peasant had 10 *desiatiny*. Only six households had more than 6 *desiatiny*. The remaining thirty-four households had some land but could be said to fall into the "poor" category, if we use the admittedly crude criterion of allotment size. There was, however, a positive correlation between family size and landholding. The eight landless families averaged 4.25 members, while the four wealthiest households averaged 6.25. The picture given by the peasants of Zemlitsy corresponds to commonly accepted general patterns, but it should be clear that this single example proves little by itself.[113]

The standard Soviet categories, derived as they are from Lenin, have been correctly criticized in both the West and the Soviet Union. It has not always been possible to assume the political

[112]Leshchenko, 1970, p. 59.
[113]Zhitomirskii oblast'nyi gosudarstvennyi arkhiv (hereafter ZhOGA), f. 115, o. 2, d. 2521, l. 6.

behavior of the various subgroups no matter how acute or vulgar the criteria used in delineating them. If most right-bank peasants fell into the category of "poor," this can be seen first and foremost as proof of the overall poverty of the entire peasantry of the region. By itself, it does not signify the existence of a politically unified social class of poor peasants who acted in predictable ways. By itself, it does not mean that intravillage tensions were acutely perceived by the peasants themselves.

Nevertheless, if most peasants in central Russia could be included in the middle group, most rural cultivators in the southwest can properly be described as poor. The poverty of the right bank's peasants was even more desperate than that of their counterparts elsewhere in Russia and the Ukraine. These conditions, in turn, greatly constrained not only their political choices but their economic activities as well. Peasants in the southwest were not simply poor versions of central Russia's middle peasants. They confronted a specific set of circumstances, and their responses to those circumstances were equally specific.

The transformation of landlord agriculture in the right bank did not contribute to similar changes in peasant agriculture. Big, successful estates existed alongside small villages with tiny allotments. If anything, the existence of the capitalist farm made peasant progress even more difficult.[114] On the peasant allotments, little had changed. The three-field system was nearly universal.[115] Holdings consisted of garden plots *(usad'ba)* and small amounts of arable, usually devoted to grains, especially winter rye and wheat. Tools and livestock were minimal. A 1910 survey of Uman district would reveal that 35 percent of households lacked tools and 26 percent had no livestock. One half of the families surveyed lacked the means to be even minimally successful.[116] Right-bank peasants tilled the soil with a slightly more advanced type of plow called a *plug* as opposed to the more traditional *sokha* of central Russia. Metal plows were common but hardly widespread.[117] Technical

[114]Iaroshevich, 1911, p. 44.
[115]Telichuk, p. 152. Kolomiets, *Polozhenie krestian,* p. 95. TsGIAU, f. 442, o. 635, d. 20, l. 61.
[116]Iaroshevich, 1911, p. 5.
[117]Telichuk, p. 152. Anfimov, 1980, p. 158.

progress was minimal, and peasants planted and sowed according to the same traditional schedules that had been practiced for centuries. In fact, a team of *zemstvo* agronomists who toured Kiev in 1910 would describe peasant agriculture there as something out of the "middle ages."[118]

One element of feudalism the right-bank peasantry very much wanted to preserve was the *servitutnye prava,* preemancipation rights to the use of the landlord's forest and pasture. Throughout Russia, enterprising landlords had restricted peasants' ability to graze their livestock, often charging for what had once been a right. With agrarian progress came an abandonment of traditional obligations. *Servitutnye prava* were especially threatened in the right bank.[119] Disputes over the use of grazing lands were common throughout the decades before 1905, and many early disturbances were caused by arguments concerning these matters. Landlord unwillingness to allow peasant access eventually reduced the number of livestock that peasant households could maintain. The predictable result was greater poverty and dependency.

Peasant productivity was a great deal lower than that of landlords. In the left-bank Ukraine and the Central Black Earth region, landlords generally produced two thirds again the amount of grain raised by peasants. In the right bank, landlords raised 86 percent more than peasants did in 1904.[120] This figure is all the more striking given the gentry's considerable involvement in the cultivation of crops other than grain.

A few well-meaning agronomists and landlords sought to alleviate the problem by introducing peasants to the raising of sugar beets. Expanding rail networks had improved the transport of the beets to the refineries. It was now less necessary for the processing to take place right next to the fields.[121] This change created possibilities for peasants, but they were unable to adapt to the new conditions. As already noted, almost 15 percent of the region's land under sugar beets was planted by peasants. Their productivi-

[118]Telichuk, pp. 153–54.
[119] Pershin, p. 39. Telichuk, p. 20. Anfimov, 1980, p. 80.
[120]Tsentral'nyi statisticheskii komitet Ministerstva vnutrennykh del, *Urozhai na 1904 g.* (St. Petersburg, 1904), pp. 12–13, 30–31, 6–7, 64–67.
[121]Kievskoe Agronomicheskoe Obshchestvo, *Trudy,* vyp. III (Kiev, 1915), p. 5.

ty, however, was lower than that of landlord estates, and the quality of their beets was considerably poorer. Peasants were ill-equipped to provide the constant fertilizing, watering, and weeding required by this crop. They lacked proper storage facilities, making spoilage a problem. Often peasants who received advances from sugar companies simply spent the money and never delivered what was promised.[122] Most significantly, peasants were not always willing to plant sugar beets because doing so required an abandoning of the traditional three-field system. A few landlords had planted sugar beets and retained the three-field on their estates, but this proved impossible for peasants.

Despite the obstacles, a sizable number of peasants were willing to innovate along these lines, but the vast majority (over 90 percent) practiced primitive agriculture according to traditional methods. Landlord estates in the right bank were not like those elsewhere in Russia and the Ukraine. Peasant farms in the southwest, however, were much like those of central Russia. If capitalism had come to the fields of Kiev, Podol'e, Volynia, it was a gentry enterprise. Peasants in these provinces cultivated their own lands in much the same way as their central Russian counterparts. Rather, it was wage work that most sharply distinguished their lives from those of others in Russia and the Ukraine who worked the land.

Agricultural Workers—a True Rural Proletariat?

A rural proletariat was a sign of capitalist development and, appropriately, the commercial estates of the southwest employed large numbers of day laborers. One might then logically conclude that the right bank was home to a large body of landless wage earners. The poverty of the region's peasantry and the primitive character of its agriculture would seem even more likely to create conditions conducive to the emergence of this class. If a strictly defined rural proletariat were part of the rural scene anywhere in Russia, the right bank would seem to be a most likely place to find it.

[122]Ibid., p. 6.

Proletarian Peasants

The literature on the Russian and Ukrainian countrysides makes a consistent distinction between "peasants" who were members of village communities and "agricultural workers" *(agrarnye* or *sel'skokhoziaistvennye rabochie)* who were not members of the communities in which they worked. Agricultural workers sold their labor on large, agriculturally advanced estates, and wages, according to certain definitions, were their sole source of income.[123] In reality, this distinction between the peasant (the complete insider) and the agricultural worker (the complete outsider) often broke down. Many poor peasants throughout Russia, owners of little land, were forced to take wage work. As already noted, this was most common in the southwest. On the other hand, there were landless individual members of peasant households and communes. Often these were youths who had not yet succeeded to their allotments. These landless villagers have been described in the literature as *"batraks."* They did not move around from place to place, as did agricultural workers, and they did not always receive wages for the work they performed within the traditional context of the family.[124]

It is difficult to identify a rural proletariat of the sort defined by Sidney Mintz (landless and wage earning) because, like so many other social groups in prerevolutionary Russia, the rural proletariat was very much a transitional phenomenon. Logically, peasants rendered landless might be expected to go to industrially expanding cities. This was very much the case in Prussia in the second half of the nineteenth century. Junker landlords experienced a chronic labor shortage.[125] Seasonal oscillations between town and country were still quite common in Russia, however, and the cities began to absorb the surplus rural population only after 1905. Until the beginning of the revolutionary turmoil, a huge reserve army of labor could be found throughout the Russian countryside.[126] The mem-

---

[123]L. Kirillov, "Rabochie sel'skie," *Entsiklopedicheskii slovar'* (St. Petersburg, 1899), p. 7.

[124]P. Lokhtin, *Bezzemel'nyi proletariat v Rossii* (Moscow, 1905), p. 5. B. N. Knipovich, *K voprosu o differentsiatsii russkogo krestianstva* (St. Petersburg, 1912), p. 83. Kirillov, p. 8.

[125]Athar Hussain and Keith Tribe, *Marxism and the Agrarian Question,* 2 vols. (Atlantic Highlands, N. J., 1981), 1:52.

[126]Knipovich, p. 12.

bers of this army, the landless and the nearly landless, had to leave their native villages each spring in search of work to support themselves and their families. By 1906, industry revived from a depression and the laws concerning the commune were changed. Those who wished to leave the land and migrate to the cities could now do so more easily. Soon thereafter the number of those wandering the Russian and Ukrainian countryside each spring and summer began to decrease.[127]

Not all those who labored for wages were landless, nor were all those without land necessarily wage workers. As a result, this potential rural proletariat was not as large a social group as might be expected. Its numbers were limited, especially when compared to the rest of the peasant population. Despite these caveats, this phenomenon of migrant labor (known as *otkhod*) was a significant element of rural life throughout the Russian Empire. Each spring a massive movement of agricultural workers began throughout the countryside. If they had no land or not enough land, if there were too many working hands in the household, or if the previous harvest had been poor, peasants had to abandon their native villages to find employment on large, commercially organized estates.[128] Most of these workers moved from the infertile central provinces to the booming borderlands, but migration within provinces and even within districts was also common. Strangely enough, estates in a particular region might recruit from outside, despite the existence of a local labor surplus. This irrational situation existed in the southwest, where a considerable number of migrants *(otkhodniki)* were hired to work on the sugar estates. Local agricultural conditions and individual landlord attitudes usually accounted for these anomalies. At the same time, so sizable was the surplus agricultural population of the right bank that many had to leave the region to find work.[129]

Conditions faced by *otkhodniki* throughout the empire had many similarities. To leave their homes and go to another prov-

[127]Ia. Ia. Polferov, *Sel'skokhoziaistvennye rabochie ruki* (St. Petersburg, 1913), p. 39. Dubrovskii, 1975, p. 333.

[128]P. Maslov, *Agrarnyi vopros v Rossii*, 2 vols. (St. Petersburg, 1908), 1:345. Polferov, p. 2. S. M. Dubrovskii, *Sel'skoe khoziaistvo i krestianstvo Rossii v period imperializma* (Moscow, 1975), p. 344.

[129]*Volyn'*, July 26, 1905.

ince, peasants had to obtain a passport from the local authorities. This process was the full extent to which peasant migration was in any way registered or counted. Many peasants left without gaining permission, and no one seriously checked them thereafter.[130] Those who migrated in search of employment had no guarantee of finding it. Previously arranged contracts were extremely rare for migrating peasants. There were no formal labor exchanges, no advertisements. Migrants, most of whom were male, would go where they had found work in the past or where a friend or relative had experienced success in another year. The growth of railroads sped this process, and each spring the Ministry of Communications was forced to lay on extra trains. The majority of *otkhodniki*, however, still made the journey on foot, usually in groups of ten or fifteen from the same village.[131] Trips in search of work could last as long as a month but the typical peasant journeyed for one or two weeks. Travel in the spring meant wading through rivers of mud as the winter snows melted.

The journey was completed when the group arrived at an informal labor market, usually a fair, bazaar, or railway station. There were twenty such points in Kiev and Podol'e, all in close proximity to large sugar plantations.[132] Workers then negotiated contracts in groups for the entire growing season which varied from region to region. Although they had little choice, workers preferred not to sign such contracts. The terms of one such document from the estates of the Pototskii family make this reluctance fully understandable:

> I, a peasant of the village of——enter into an agreement of my own free will to do wage work on the estate of Count Pototskii in whatever way I am instructed. In all I will work 144 days and receive 34 rubles of which 10 rubles will be given in advance and the remainder to be given as I work.
>
> 1. I will go out to work with the rising of the sun and work until it sets.

[130]E. I. Lugova, *Sel'skokhoziaistvennyi proletariat iuga Ukrainy v poslednei chetverti xix veka*, avtoreferat dissertatsii (Kiev, 1961), p. 13. Maslov, 1:425. Dubrovskii, 1975, p. 345. Polferov, p. 2.

[131]Maslov, 1908, 1:420. Dubrovskii, 1975, p. 344.

[132]Leshchenko, 1977, p. 90.

2. If I quit work without a legal reason, I shall return two times the advance and receive no wages for any other work.

3. I must appear for work as soon as I am called.

4. If the estate calls me to work on a holiday or Sunday, I do not have the right to refuse.

5. If I go on a holiday without permission, I must make up double the work missed.

6. If I fall sick or die, a member of my family must fulfill this contract.

7. Under no circumstances may I quit work before the agreed upon period.[133]

Contracts of this sort were often broken, and disputes were common. Workers would depart if they learned of better wages elsewhere. On the other hand, groups of laborers were often summarily dismissed. In such instances they received nothing, not even for the work they had already performed.[134] Labor discipline was severe, and corporal punishment was common.[135] Employers really had no choice but to beat workers, given working conditions on the estates. Arrest meant nothing to agricultural workers. So wretched was the housing provided by the landlords (when it was provided at all) that a night in prison guaranteed a roof over one's head and better rations. Workers often had to sleep in the open.[136] Sometimes they dug trenches and slept in them. Others were allowed to live in barns; a few were housed in dormitories that were, by most descriptions, worse than the barns.[137] These problems were less acute in the right bank where much of the labor force came from neighboring villages, lived in their own homes, and ate their food. Landlords did provide meals to those workers living on

[133]G. I. Moiseevich, *Sel'skokhoziaistvennye rabochie vo vremia pervoi revoliutsii 1905–1907 gg.* (Moscow, 1925), pp. 18–19.

[134]Polferov, p. 24.

[135]Maslov, 1908, 1:425.

[136]A. B. Shestakov, *Sel'skie rabochie, ikh zhizn' i borba* (St. Petersburg, 1907), p. 17. Timothy Mixter, "Migrant Agricultural Workers in the Hiring Markets of the European Russian Steppe, 1894–1914," paper presented to the Seminar on the History of Russian Society in the Twentieth Century, Philadelphia, January 30–31, 1982.

[137]Maslov, 1908, 1:424. Dubrovskii, 1975, p. 334.

the plantations. Breakfasts were usually bread, hot water, and potato broth. Lunches were the largest meals, consisting most often of *borshch* and a bit of meat or dried fish. Dinners were small versions of lunch, with soup, bread, and potatoes the usual fare.[138]

Agricultural workers throughout Russia labored from dawn until dusk. Between two and three hours were taken out by meals. During harvests, it was common for workers to continue into the night under torches or electric lights. Machines, when employed, were as much a hazard as a help, and landlords complained about the low "mental and moral level" of the workers who "resisted" efforts to modernize the estates.[139] Where machines were introduced, long workdays and unfamiliar equipment led to a high accident rate, but landlords, who had no legal responsibility for the medical care of their employees, argued that these men and women simply did not know "how to walk near machines."[140]

It is not easy to exaggerate the difficulty of agricultural wage work. Not all these conditions prevailed in the southwest: Novorossiia and the Baltic provinces were larger importers of migrant labor. Yet the long days, hard work, harsh discipline, and low wages were the same in the right bank as elsewhere. In some ways the situation of the wage worker was worse in the southwest than in other parts of the empire. Rural cultivators in the region received a good deal less for a day's work than their counterparts elsewhere. Because households supported their wage-earning members through the normal slack periods of the agrarian cycle, it was possible for landlords to pay less than subsistence wages. The prerevolutionary Marxist scholar G. Drozdov found significant differences between the right bank and other regions (see Table 6).

Sixty years later, the Soviet specialist on the rural economy I. D. Kovalchenko came up with roughly similar findings.[141] Somewhat surprisingly, official government figures, based on reports from landlords, were actually lower than these more sympathetic re-

---

[138]*Istoria selianstva*, 1:400. Telichuk, p. 110, Shestakov, 1907, pp. 17–18.

[139]*Zemledelie*, April 28, 1905. This was the official organ of the Kiev Agronomic Society, a group dominated by landlords.

[140]Polferov, p. 96.

[141]I. D. Kovalchenko and L. V. Milov, *Vserossiiskii agrarnyi rynok* (Moscow, 1974), p. 330.

Table 6. Average Daily Wage in Agriculture, 1902–1904

Region	Kopecks
Right bank	48.3
Left bank	65.0
Novorossiia	78.6
Central Black Earth region	61.3
All Russia	64.0

Source: G. Drozdov, *Zarabotnaia plata zemledelcheskikh rabochikh v Rossii v sviazi s agrarnym dvizheniem 1905–1906gg.* (St. Petersburg, 1914), pp. 14–18.

searches. In 1904, according to the Ministry of Interior, men in the right bank earned from twenty-five kopecks a day in the spring to forty-five kopecks a day in the fall. Women's wages ranged from twenty kopecks in the spring to thirty kopecks in the fall.[142] Although the demand for wage work on the sugar plantations was considerable, the supply of willing hands was tremendous. The excess working population of the right bank has been counted as high as 3 million.[143] Landlessness was one possible explanation for the abundant supply of those seeking work in Kiev, Podol'e, and, to a lesser extent, Volynia. Lack of land was one of the characteristics of a rural proletariat, and the number of households without allotments was higher in the right bank than in other regions (see Table 7).

Migrant workers were not the majority of laborers on the estates of Kiev, Podol'e, and Volynia. Instead, local peasants, including large numbers of women and children, composed the sugar plantation labor force. Female laborers tended to be the younger members of local households.[144] As noted, most landlords thought women were as productive as men but paid them considerably less. Nevertheless, right-bank women received a higher percentage of

[142]Ministerstvo zemledeliia i gosudarstvennykh imushchestv, *1904 god v sel'skokhoziaistvennykh otnoshenii* (St. Petersburg, 1904), pp. 78–79.

[143]Kolomiets, *Polozhenie krestian,* p. 10. Leshchenko, 1970, p. 83.

[144]Slezkin, 1913, p. 21. Telichuk, p. 114.

Proletarian Peasants

Table 7. Landless Households in 1893

Region	Number	Percentage
Kiev	44,995	16.6
Podol'e	25,367	10.1
Volynia	14,035	8.2
All Ukraine	196,862	11.1
All Russia	726,338	8.7

Source: P. Lokhtin, *Bezzemel'nyi proletariat v Rossii* (Moscow, 1905), p. 176.

the wage paid to men (69 percent) than in any other region.[145] Most of these women were members of local households and, unlike agricultural workers in other parts of Russia, they were not entirely dependent on their wage for survival. As a result, they were able to play a highly militant role during the revolutionary period. The activism of right-bank women contrasted with the moderating, even conservative, role played by women everywhere else in Russia during 1905. The combativeness of right-bank women also conflicts with common assumptions about the political and social passivity of peasant women in general.

Agricultural laborers (landless, wage-earning rural proletarians) only constituted a small portion of the workers on the estates of the right bank; no one could claim that these men and women made up a large percentage of the rural population throughout Russia. Precision about the size of this strictly defined rural proletariat is difficult to obtain. Similarly, the numbers of those engaged in wage work on the southwest's plantations can only be estimated. Using the 1897 census, Lenin, in the 1908 edition of *The Development of Capitalism in Russia,* came up with a figure of approximately 3 million agricultural workers out of a peasant population of nearly 80 million.[146] At about the same time, Drozdov and the leading Menshevik authority on agriculture, Peter Maslov,

[145]Lenin, *The Development of Capitalism in Russia,* p. 241.
[146]G. Drozdov, *Zarabotnaia plata zemledel'cheskikh rabochikh v Rossii v sviazi s agrarnym dvizheniem 1905–1906gg.* (St. Petersburg, 1914), p. 10.

78

arrived at roughly similar numbers.[147] S. M. Dubrovskii repeated this figure in his 1975 book.[148] The more thorough researches of Kovalchenko and his colleagues (published in 1974) revealed the number of those who fit the strict definition of the rural proletarian to be something less than 2 million.[149] Maslov, Kovalchenko, and Leshchenko all estimated the number of agricultural workers in the right bank, subsisting entirely on their wages, to be around 150,000.[150] Looked at either nationally or regionally, it is apparent that men and women who could properly be called rural proletarians were simply too few in number to dominate either agrarian labor in general or a peasant movement in particular.

Constructing an estimate of the size of the wage-labor force in the right bank is an even more slippery proposition. No universal data of any sort exist. Given the oft-noted importance of women workers on the sugar estates, information on the gender of the southwest's rural cultivators would be of decisive significance. Yet no statistical materials answer this question. Estimates vary wildly. Telichuk claimed more than a million workers were required to work the sugar plantations of the entire Ukraine.[151] Given the preponderance of the right bank in the sugar trade it would not be an exaggeration to guess there were as many as 900,000 such workers in the southwest. Leshchenko, ever alert for even the slightest sign of a rural proletariat, has placed the number of sugar workers as low as 300,000.[152] We do know that as many as 1,000 day workers were employed on each of the several estates belonging to the Tereshchenko family.[153] A 1913 study of eight estates in Kiev found that these estates provided 393,150 workdays to day laborers. If we take the Pototskii contract as typical of a season (144 days)—and other sources make this likely—then these eight Kiev estates (of varying sizes) employed 2,730 people in 1913.[154]

[147]Maslov, 1908, 2:98. Drozdov, p. 5.
[148]Dubrovskii, 1975, p. 312.
[149]Kovalchenko and Milov, 1974, p. 320.
[150]Maslov, 1908, 2:98. Leshchenko, 1970, p. 69. Kovalchenko and Milov, 1974, p. 47.
[151]Telichuk, p. 105.
[152]Leshchenko, 1977, p. 68.
[153]Telichuk, p. 106.
[154]AD, 2:106.

Whatever the precise figures, it is obvious that there were not enough rural proletarians, strictly defined, for this group to dominate the peasant movement in the right bank. Nevertheless, it was still possible that this most distressed of elements could have played a classical Leninist vanguard role. At the same time, it was altogether possible that peasant wage workers, whose households held some land, might behave in ways that could be characterized as classically proletarian.

One can only guess how many of these cultivators were women. Landlords' descriptions of their estates give considerable attention to the role of the female labor. Government reports paint a similar picture, as does the scientific literature on agriculture in the region. Given the fact that women left household work in order to supply day labor on the sugar estates, it is reasonable to assume they were a sizable share, even a majority, of the wage labor force. One report from Podol'e stated that women from both poor and prosperous families predominated in the labor force on local sugar plantations.[155] This set of circumstances made the southwest highly exceptional in the context of Russian agriculture. In other regions where agrarian workers received wages, most notably Novorossiia and the Baltic, men performed these tasks.[156] The impact of such extensive female wage work on the patriarchal structure of right bank households has not been studied, but it is safe to assume that traditional patterns were undermined, and the exceptionally prominent role of right-bank women in the strikes and disturbances of 1905 would seem to attest to a disequilibrium of the old structures.

Agriculture in the southwest had followed many contours of the Prussian path toward capitalist development. The right bank was clearly an advanced region with extensive production for expanding markets. Many landlords, along with numerous entrepreneurs, had been able to benefit from these swift changes. Peasants, on the other hand, paid the price for this transition. Their allotments were reduced, and their opportunities for agrarian innovation remained

[155]Kievskoe Agronomicheskoe Obshchestvo, *Trudy,* vyp. IV (Kiev, 1915), pp. 34–35.
[156]Lugova, p. 11. Maslov, 2:98.

limited. Even the most energetic and ambitious peasants had been unable to rent or buy large amounts of land. They farmed the southwest's fertile soil, using methods that differed little from those encountered in the most backward areas outside of the black earth zones. To survive, members of their families had been forced to accept poorly paid, arduous work on estates that produced commodities rarely found in peasant homes. These conditions differed greatly from those found in central Russia, but they contained much the same potential for unrest that would soon sweep the rest of the empire.

3

A Strike Movement—
Demands and Tactics

The First Russian Revolution throughout Rural Russia

The Revolution of 1905 did not fall like a bolt of lightning from a cloudless sky. These events were the culmination of tensions that had been building for half a century, if not longer. The peasant emancipation of 1861 changed many personal and economic relationships on the land, but it did not usher in an era of progress and prosperity in rural Russia. In return for their personal freedom and control of their allotments, peasants had to give up a part of their land and compensate the nobility above and beyond the market value of what were already inadequate holdings. Peasants also lost the free use of the landlords' woods and pastures. The forest had been a vital source of fuel and food, and the meadows had been grazed by peasant livestock. The loss of these customary rights (*servitutnye prava*) represented a severe blow to peasants who reacted to the disappointing emancipation settlement with violence and rage. Disturbances and disorders were numerous throughout the early 1860s. The emancipation decree had been intended to quell peasant discontent. Instead, it sparked even more instability.

In the last decades of the nineteenth century, rural Russia experienced a profoundly disorienting transition that dimmed hopes of progress not only for the peasantry but for the nobility as well.[1] Much of rural Russia proved ill-equipped to transform agricultural practices in ways that would allow the production of massive surpluses. Yet, the empire now required these changes in order to develop the kind of industrial base that could support a modern army. To finance industrial growth and encourage exports, the state severely taxed the entire agricultural sector in a variety of ways. The autocracy took these steps at a particularly difficult moment. Worldwide economic depression began in the mid-1870s and lasted for twenty years. The massive influx of American grain into Europe lowered prices precipitously. Long-standing anti-entrepreneurial attitudes and lack of capital did not make Russian nobles especially good candidates for the new role of gentleman farmer. Low prices for grain made the rewards minimal and, accordingly, the chances of success slight. As a result, nobles relinquished massive amounts of land in the last decades of the nineteenth century. By 1905, they had sold some 40 percent of their holdings; most of these lands went to peasants.

But the acquisition of so much land did not improve peasant lives. Although peasants now controlled more land, there were now many more peasants. Between 1858 and 1897, the peasant estate grew by nearly 60 percent. The reasons for this massive population growth are uncertain, but its results were clear enough. The gains achieved by the peasantry as a whole were nulified by demographic pressures. Land hunger (*malozeml'e*) became the

---

[1] The existence of a prerevolutionary agrarian crisis has recently been called into question. For the familiar view, see Robinson, pp. 94–116; Bensidoun, pp. 81–150; Manning, pp. 3–24. Challenges have come from James Simms, Jr., "The Crisis in Russian Agriculture at the End of the 19th Century: A Different View," *Slavic Review* 36 (September 1977), 377–98. See also Paul Gregory, *Russian National Income, 1885–1913* (Cambridge, 1980), pp. 222–31. Gary Hamburg, *Politics of the Russian Nobility, 1881–1905* (New Brunswick, N.J., 1984), pp. 71–190, has sought to reestablish the existence of the crisis, especially as it pertains to the gentry. See also S. G. Wheatcroft, "The Agrarian Crisis and Peasant Living Standards in Late Imperial Russia: A Reconsideration of Trends and Regional Differentiation," paper presented to Conference on the Peasantry of European Russia, 1800–1917, University of Massachusetts, Boston, August 19–22, 1986.

dominant fact of life for most peasants. If most nobles could not make the switch to modern methods, peasants, with their supposed devotion to custom and their primitive practices, were thought to be even less likely to achieve success although peasant innovation was not unknown. By the end of the nineteenth century the traditional peasant goal of subsistence was no longer simply an implicit cultural norm of the village. While overall productivity rose during this period and yields increased, the gains were not evenly distributed among lords and peasants.[2]

By the 1890s, the problems caused by the transformation of rural Russia were evident to most outside observers. Even so, overt peasant responses to these difficulties were episodic and isolated. Although still sporadic, disputes over the use of forests and meadows became ever more common, and the level of illegal wood cutting, livestock grazing, and crop stealing increased with each passing year. In the spring of 1902, however, the left-bank Ukrainian provinces of Kharkov and Poltava witnessed thousands of peasants involved in massive destruction of property and widespread arson. What had been a series of random and separated incidents now showed signs of becoming a movement. These disorders were met with severe government repression, and peasants had a new series of grievances against the authorities, who now joined the landlords as their hated enemies. In the next two years, the number of disorders continued to grow.

Instability in the countryside was matched by disaffection in the cities. Strikes by workers and students became more numerous and militant, and members of Russia's rapidly growing free professions also came to join a national chorus demanding a wide variety of reforms. In order to take the nation's mind off its many problems, the autocracy, in 1904, offered Russia a "short, victorious war" with what it thought would be a weak Japanese adversary. The result was quick, ignominious defeat.

On January 9, 1905, soldiers fired, without provocation, on a mass demonstration of workers who had come to the Palace Square in St. Petersburg to petition the tsar for a redress of their

[2]Richard Robbins, *Famine in Russia 1891–1892: The Imperial Government Responds to a Crisis* (New York, 1975).

grievances. The subsequent massacre became known as "Bloody Sunday." This event touched off a wave of strikes and protests that did not escape the attention of those in the countryside. With a large part of the army at the front, peasants realized that the moment had come to settle old scores. The army, itself composed of peasants, was rife with mutiny.[3] Peasant frustration became all the more intense with a series of crop failures that made both the winter and summer harvests among the poorest of the last decade. The immediate difficulty of surviving on their allotments intensified the peasants' long-standing belief that their central problem was severe land hunger.

According to the research conducted in central archives in the 1950s by the Soviet specialist S. M. Dubrovskii, there were 7,165 manifestations of what was called the "peasant movement" in Russia during 1905, 1906, and 1907.[4] Nearly 30 percent of these incidents occurred in the six provinces of the Central Black Earth region (Kursk, Orel, Riazan, Tula, Tambov, and Voronezh). Of all the other regions of the empire, the three provinces that made up the southwest ranked second with 985 disturbances. These numbers cannot be seen as scientifically accurate. In the decades since Dubrovskii and his assistants combed the repositories of Moscow and Leningrad, scores of other Soviet historians have worked in local archives. It is now claimed that more than 18,000 disorders of various kinds occurred in this period.[5] Despite this new research, the contours of the movement described by Dubrovskii remain the same, and the Central Black Earth region and the right-bank Ukraine are still seen, along with the Mid-Volga, as the leading centers of peasant activity.

Disorders in the countryside during these years assumed a wide variety of forms, and the ways in which rural cultivators chose to express their discontent tell us much about peasant society and peasant politics. Disturbances could entail isolated crop stealing by a single peasant or massive strikes involving hundreds of wage workers. The most common forms of the movement involved vio-

[3]John Bushnell, *Mutiny amid Rebellion: Russian Soldiers in the Revolution of 1905–1906* (Bloomington, Ind., 1985), pp. 44–49.

[4]Dubrovikii, 1956, p. 60.

[5]Simonova, p. 1.

lence against property. Arson accounted for 18.1 percent of the disorders uncovered by Dubrovskii. Another 15.7 percent of the disturbances involved destruction of estates; illegal woodcutting occurred 15 percent of the time.[6] Most of the manifestations of the movement were spontaneous, primitively organized, and directed almost entirely against landlords.[7] When peasants articulated demands, during 1905, they expressed vague hopes for the long-awaited "total repartition" that would rid them of the gentry and give them all of Russia's land. If their goals were specific, they usually harked back to some mythical golden age when the land was theirs and the nobility was absent. Millenarian but backward-looking goals of this sort were typical of traditional peasant disorders in a wide variety of precapitalist societies and were in no way limited to Russia.[8]

Confrontations with police and soldiers were common and most often bloody. More than ever before, the state became an object of peasant hatred along with the landlords. At such moments, villages acted cohesively. According to Soviet and Western scholars, class tensions within the commune, during 1905, were less important than common hatred for the aristocracy, state, and merchants. If any specific group within the peasantry could be said to have played a leading role, it was the so-called middle peasantry, which was in truth the traditional peasantry. Younger men, many of them literate, everywhere demonstrated considerable militance. As was common in most peasant societies, women and old people throughout the empire played small roles and some even sought to retard the movement out of fear.

It was also common for villages to act apart from neighboring settlements, directing their wrath only against their own landlords. When peasants articulated their grievances, they invariably cited *malozeml'e*, land hunger. When they specified demands at all, it was clear their ultimate goal was the confiscation of all gentry, state, and church lands to be divided by the peasantry, acting on their own. All these forms of behavior were far more reminiscent of the rural disorders that had taken place not only in Russia but in

[6]Maureen Perrie, *The Agrarian Policy of the Russian Socialist-Revolutionary Party* (Cambridge, 1976), p. 120.
[7]Dubrovskii, 1955, p. 65.
[8]Hobsbawm, 1959, pp. 13–107.

premodern Europe as well. They bore little resemblance to the more organized strikes and politically conscious demonstrations then sweeping Russia's cities. Rather, they repeated patterns that had been seen throughout the premodern world for centuries.

The peasant movement first became visible in February 1905, but it was not until June that the number of disorders became massive. By fall a general strike gripped the cities. To quell the discontent tsar Nicholas II issued a manifesto on October 17, proclaiming civil liberties, but failing to address the land question in the same way. In response, peasants engaged in even more numerous and destructive disorders. By February 1906, the countryside had quieted down in the face of heavy repression by police and soldiers. That summer, however, the disturbances resumed at much the same level as the previous fall.[9] The movement then continued at a diminished pace, flaring up again the next summer and dying down by the end of 1907. Most historians, Soviet and Western, ascribe the eventual return of peace in the countryside to peasant exhaustion and government repression.

Agitators from a variety of political groups were active in the countryside before and after 1905. Yet no single group led or controlled peasant actions. Proclamations and pamphlets were found throughout rural Russia.[10] Activists from the Socialist Revolutionary party, as well as many Social Democrats, had been organizing among the peasantry for years, but when the moment came, the peasants mobilized themselves. Their actions were spontaneous, and their militance was largely self-generated.[11] Peasants articulated but did not emphasize such political goals as constituent assemblies, universal suffrage, and freedom to organize politically. Their first concern was the land question, and when the Duma finally began operating as part of Russia's new semi-parliamentary system, they saw it primarily as one more institution to which they could address their demands on what was for them the central issue.

The movement throughout the empire spread through its own momentum. Rumor played a more powerful role than any single

[9]Manning, p. 141.
[10]Owen, p. 12.
[11]Peter Maslov, *Krestianskoe dvizhenie v Rossii v epokhu pervoi russkoi revoliutsii* (Moscow, 1924), p. 3. Shestakov, 1926, p. 4.

agitator. Bazaars and fairs were crucial points for transmitting what was often garbled information. Newspapers, carrying dispatches from the front, circulated widely in the countryside, and peasants then read other news of widespread disorder and discontent. Peasant illiteracy was no impediment to the influence of the press—literate peasants simply read aloud to their neighbors. The village was hardly isolated from the outside world. In fact, it was well aware of the turmoil throughout Russia. Workers from the cities and veterans returning from the front brought news of larger struggles, which fortified peasant militance. Railwaymen, who played a decisive role in the October general strike of 1905, also were instrumental in spreading the movement in the countryside through which they journeyed. The example of fellow peasants was the main force contributing to the growth of unrest, however. One peasant action usually convinced neighboring villages to move against their landlords as well. Accordingly, it was common for the movement to appear in pockets of intense unrest rather than to be spread evenly throughout all of Russia.

Ultimately, it became clear to most observers of events in central Russia that the cohesion and the solidarity of the peasantry were fortified by the continuing vitality of the commune. The traditional assembly of heads of households provided a ready-made forum for the discussion of tactics and demands. It reinforced the tension between insiders and outsiders and mitigated class tensions within the village. Because they were not members of communes in the places they worked, strictly defined rural proletarians also played the role of outsiders. They did little to influence peasant decisions, and they were often the victims of peasant violence. Yet this tension between traditional peasants and landless laborers paled before the hatred all rural cultivators felt for their common enemy, the landlords. So profound were peasant grievances in 1905 that these antagonisms lost much meaning once the fires were lit and the manor houses burning.

The Southwest before 1905

While peasant unrest was extensive throughout rural Russia in the last decades of the nineteenth century, the level of discontent was especially high in the right bank. Peasants in Kiev, Podol'e, and Volynia had received larger allotments than their central Russian counterparts at the time of the emancipation. It had been the government's intention to aid what it chose to call Russian peasants at the expense of the Polish landlords who dominated agriculture in the southwest. But the autocracy's comparative largesse did little to assuage peasant disappointment. M. N. Leshchenko, with lavish statistical generosity, claimed that 2,185 disorders occurred in the right bank during the 1860s. This was roughly two thirds of all the incidents in the entire Ukraine.[12]

By the second half of the decade, peasant activity, as elsewhere, dropped off sharply. Thereafter, it increased steadily, accelerating during the 1890s, as the agrarian crisis intensified. D. P. Poida's research on the right bank revealed a more modest level of discontent than that found by Leshchenko, although Poida did show a continuous rise in the number of disturbances of all sorts. In 1866–70, there were 48 disturbances; in 1871–75, 96; in 1876–80, 98; in 1881–85, 142; 1886–90, 159; 1891–95, 191; and in 1896–1900, 212. In the last two decades of the century, unrest in the Ukraine was even more concentrated in the right bank than earlier. Of the 1,192 disorders counted by the indefatigable Leshchenko, 912 took place in the southwest.[13] O. M. Kolomiets, who, like Poida, is more circumspect than Leshchenko about calling any incident a full-fledged disturbance, studied the period 1900–1904 and found evidence of 425 serious disorders in the right bank.[14]

The differences in these numbers reflect deeper arguments among Soviet scholars concerning the nature of the peasant movement, the comparability of different forms of struggle, and the seriousness of what can truly be called a disturbance. Nevertheless, there is broad agreement concerning both the special volatility of the right bank and the character of the movement there before 1905. Only in 1902, when massive arson and destruction swept Kharkov and Poltava, did the southwest assume a secondary position as a center of discontent.

[12]Leshchenko, 1959, p. 20.

[13]Poida, 1960, p. 422. Leshchenko, 1970, pp. 223, 265, 288.

[14]O. M. Kolomiets, "Stanovishchne selian i selianskii rukh na pravoberezhnii ukraini," *Ukrainskii istorichni zhurnal* 3 (1969), 96.

The forms assumed by the movement in the right bank before 1905 differed little from those found elsewhere in Russia. Over half the incidents in the region between 1861 and 1905 involved crop stealing and forest offenses.[15] In the wake of the events of 1902 in the left bank, arson (*podzhog*) flared up in the right bank.[16] Peasants were also constantly in dispute with nobles over the use of forests and pastures. As landlords sought to convert their estates to more profitable crops and to increase arable land, peasants were forced to protest to a wide variety of authorities and courts. They sought to prevent innovations by the landlord, and, in so doing, they fell back, given the absence of any other alternative, on the defense of traditional practices.

In 1901, on the huge Volynia estate of F. I. Tereshchenko, peasants resisted the conversion of the landlord's crop rotation from the traditional three-field system to a multifield approach.[17] During 1903, peasants on the immense Kiev sugar plantation of Count Alexander Bobrinskii contested in court the landlord's attempt to move them off a section of the estate on which they had always been allowed to graze their livestock. Local justices upheld their claim to part of the pasture, but the peasants wanted the entire plot and soon began grazing their livestock there. Soldiers then intervened and drove the peasants off.[18] In 1904, when another member of the Tereshchenko family sought to build a fence around 400 *desiatiny* on his Kiev estate, he was met by a crowd of 400 women who prevented any construction from beginning. On the next day police came to protect those building the fence. They were met by a similar-sized crowd of men, armed with pitchforks, axes, sticks, and rocks. When one peasant cried, "The authorities came to defend the lords, not us. Come on, let's smash them," the battle was joined. A bloody confrontation ensued with injuries on both sides.[19]

Given the prevalence of wage work, one might think that strikes

[15]Leshchenko, 1970, pp. 241 and 258. Kolomiets, 1969, p. 14.
[16]Leshchenko, 1970, p. 63.
[17]F. E. Los' et al., eds., *Revoliutsiia 1905–1907 gg. na Ukraine* (hereafter UD), 3 vols. (Kiev, 1955), 1:124
[18]Ibid., p. 488.
[19]TsGIAL, f. 1405, o. 107, d. 9621, l. 1.

on the large estates would be common. Such was not the case. Several villages in Balt district of Podol'e experienced strikes for higher wages as early as 1881. Sugar factories also experienced periodic work stoppages, but there was no full-fledged strike on a sugar plantation until 1897.[20] Even in the years immediately preceding the revolution (1900–1904), strike activity comprised a minute percentage (2 percent) of the recorded disturbances.[21] Nevertheless, some peasants did withhold their labor, and patterns were set that would be followed in the ensuing years. On July 17, 1902, in the Kiev village of Shandry, 400 peasants asked the renter of a large estate for a higher portion (one tenth) of the winter grain harvest. He refused and invited peasants from a neighboring settlement to work on the estate. The local peasants attacked the strikebreakers and drove them off. The peasants then elected what was called a committee of elders to present their demands to the renter, but they could not put the demands in written form because the village scribe felt the strike was illegal and refused to assist. Again their request for one tenth of the harvest was rejected. This time the peasants of Shandry went around to the neighboring villages and warned them not to accept work at the estate. Again the renter sought to bring in strikebreakers who were again met with violence. Police then intervened and arrested eighteen peasants, called "leaders" by the authorities. Fearing further disorder and needing peasant labor at the crucial point in the harvest, the renter eventually gave in to peasant demands.[22]

At this point, however, strike activity was exceptional. Even though landlord agriculture had evolved swiftly in a capitalist direction, peasants still responded to this trend with what could be called traditional tactics. They showed clear signs that they felt the innovations of the southwest's landlords had upset the moral economy of the region. In this sense their actions differed little from those of their counterparts in central Russia. The forms assumed by the movement in the right bank were much the same as those seen elsewhere in Russia. In 1905, that situation would change drastically.

[20]*Istoria selianstva*, 1:418–23.
[21]Kolomiets, "Stanovishchne selian," p. 96.
[22]*UD*, 1:186.

The Statistical Extent of Agitation in
the Southwest, 1905–1907

In the midst of the Revolution of 1905, the peasant movement in the right-bank Ukraine expanded dramatically in its extent and changed sharply in its character. As already noted, Dubrovskii, writing in 1956 and using the archives of Moscow and Leningrad, counted 985 manifestations of the peasant movement in the southwest between 1905 and 1907.[23] Leshchenko, in 1955, combed the repositories of the Ukraine and claimed to have found 2,635 incidents in the right bank.[24] By 1977, Leshchenko had unearthed evidence for what he said were 3,924 disturbances of all sorts in Kiev, Podol'e, and Volynia.[25]

Leshchenko also found that these events touched 2,371 populated points in the southwest and that these settlements had a combined population of 3,725,817, comprising 43.1 percent of the total population of the right bank.[26] This level of participation was higher than either of the other two regions of the Ukraine and was considerably higher than the average for the empire. In 1926, A. Shestakov used the cruder device of the number of districts in a region effected by the movement. He too found the southwest to be a highly volatile place. Seventy-eight percent of Russia's districts had been touched by disorders during the revolution. All but one of the right-bank's thirty-six districts (97.2 percent) witnessed disturbances.[27] Compared with the rest of Russia, the Ukraine in general and the right bank in particular were clearly at the forefront of the peasant movement.[28]

These figures cannot in any way be seen as precise. The differences in the numbers reflect the methodological disagreements among Soviet students of the peasantry. In particular, Leshchenko has been criticized by his colleagues for his willingness to count modest signs of peasant unhappiness as full-fledged disturbances. Many Soviet historians also feel his emphasis on the various forms assumed by the struggle is similarly misplaced. Other criteria have

[23]Dubrovskii, 1955, p. 65.
[24]Leshchenko, 1955, pp. 84–87.
[25]Leshchenko, 1977, p. 349.
[26]Ibid., p. 208.
[27]Shestakov, 1926, p. 52.
[28]*Istoria selianstva,* 1:471.

been suggested, and new categories have been advanced.[29] At this, point, however, it would be hard to argue that the dispute has been resolved.

Regardless of the specific approach taken and regardless of the precise numbers, broad consensus exists on the general contours of the peasant movement. When the same methods are used to study different regions or periods, the relationships generally remain the same. Given the fact that Western scholars have neither the time nor manpower to examine the archival evidence thoroughly and systematically, there is little reason to expect a more precise picture to emerge. Nor is there any special reason to believe that more refined Western statistical practices would seriously revise our picture of the movement.

Industrial strike activity expanded immediately in the wake of the events of Bloody Sunday. Yet disorders did not become widespread in the right bank until May. The movement reached its peak during June and July. Things quieted down in the fall. The outburst of peasant indignation that came in the wake of the October Manifesto was not repeated in the southwest. The next spring, the agitation reached a level almost as high as that of 1905. The fall witnessed a similar slowing of peasant turmoil. By 1907, the movement had spent much of its force. A slight revival occurred that summer, but by the end of the year, quiet had returned to the countryside.[30]

---

[29]Poida has suggested comparing the total population of points touched by the movement with the total population in a district or province to gain an idea of the intensity of the movement. He has dismissed Leshchenko's concern with forms. B. G. Litvak, while defending Leshchenko, has noted the possible confusion when one disturbance might combine several forms of struggle. Significantly, this has been an open, scholarly debate fought on the pages of Soviet scholarly journals. It shows the broad range of disagreement among Soviet historians. It also demonstrates their willingness, with little fear, to challenge each other's views. See D. P. Poida, "Po metodiku vivchennia selians'kogo rukhu periodu domonopolistichnogo kapitalizmu," *Ukrainskii istorichni zhurnal* 5 (1966), 25–31. M. N. Leshchenko, "Udoskonalivati metodiku doslidzhennia selians'kikh rukhiv," *Ukrainskii istorichni zhurnal* 5 (1966), 32–38. B. G. Litvak, "Koordinatsiia metodiki vivchennia selians'kogo rukhu zavdannia printsipovoi vazhlivosti," *Ukrainskii istorichni zhurnal* 1 (1967), 100–114. B. G. Litvak, *Opyt statisticheskogo izuchenia krestianskogo dvizhenia v Rossii XIX veka* (Moscow, 1967), pp. 23–54.

[30]Maslov, 1924, p. 162.

Proletarian Peasants

Table 8. Disturbances in the Southwest, 1905–1907

Year	Kiev	Podol'e	Volynia	Total
1905	551	278	238	1,067
1906	383	493	161	1,037
1907	235	213	83	531
Totals	1,169	984	482	2,635

Source: M. N. Leshchenko, *Selianskii rukh na pravoberezhnii ukrainii v period revoliutsii 1905–1907 rr.* (Kiev, 1955), pp. 84–87.

The Russian sugar industry was concentrated in Kiev and Podol'e, and these two provinces were the centers of peasant activity. Volynia was considerably less volatile; conditions there more closely resembled those found in central Russia.[31] Leshchenko's earlier figures (1955) give a good picture of the geographical and chronological distribution of the movement in the right bank in 1905–7; see Table 8. In all three years, well over half the disorders occurred in May, June, and July, suggesting that the cycles of agrarian life played the decisive role in the timing of the movement. Political crises in the cities caused a ripple effect at certain moments, but events in the right bank had their own rhythm. The incidence of the disturbances, in terms of both time and place, showed a close relationship to the character of agriculture in the southwest. In particular, it is important to determine both the forms of the movement and the times of the year the disorders occurred. Once these facts are established, it is possible to pinpoint the causes of unrest in the right bank.

The Forms of the Movement

Before 1905, the actions of right-bank peasants fit traditional patterns. They were, to use Henry Landsberger's typology, "expressive" of elemental rage rather than "instrumental," that is,

[31]E. Vinogradov and P. Denisovets, *Revoliutsiina borot'ba trudiashchikh volini v pershoi rosiis'kii revoliutsii* (Lvov, 1955), p. 34.

planned and organized with realizable aims and appropriate tactics. This latter approach was commonly imputed to urban labor movements. Once the revolution began, this old pattern changed sharply. The forms assumed by the movement in the southwest differed fundamentally from those encountered elsewhere in rural Russia both before and during 1905. Throughout the empire no single form predominated. Arson, forest offenses, and destruction of estates were the most common ways peasants chose to express their dissatisfaction and to convince landlords to leave the estates in the hands of those who worked with their own labor. During the years of the revolutionary upsurge, the peasants of Kiev, Podol'e, and Volynia made different choices.

In the first few months of 1905, peasant activity was limited to crop stealing and forest offenses, but in the spring that situation changed dramatically. Beginning in May, and continuing through the spring, the southwest was swept by a wave of organized and highly conscious agrarian strikes that affected most of the major estates of the region. Once this pattern was established, it became the norm for the peasant movement in the right bank. Depending on the compiler, between 55 and 60 percent of the disturbances recorded in the right bank between 1905 and 1907 were strikes against large landowners and renters. The victims were the wealthy of all nationalities, social origins, and political persuasions. It therefore should be stressed that the central focus of any study of peasant activity in the southwest must be this movement of planned, organized, and conscious strikes.

Leshchenko's most recent figures (1977) seem high (see Table 9). Nevertheless, the patterns he revealed have been corroborated by all other observers, both contemporary and scholarly. Leshchenko also advanced a distinction between what he called "active" and "passive" strikes. In a passive strike, peasants merely stated their demands and refused to work. Some form of negotiation ensued, and the peasants would return to work. "Active" strikes involved confrontations, usually violent, between peasants and either strikebreakers, police, or soldiers. Nearly 80 percent of the strikes fell into the so-called active category.[32] Peasants in the southwest were

---

[32]Leshchenko, 1955, p. 128.

Table 9. Forms of the Peasant Movement in the Right Bank, 1905–1907

Forms	Podol'e	Kiev	Volynia	Total
Strikes	1,109	846	374	2,329
Struggles over disputed land	185	162	164	511
Destruction of estates	20	17	10	47
Arson	244	100	57	401
Confrontations with authorities	26	62	28	116
Illegal meetings	92	168	24	284
Other	11	26	9	46
Mixed	70	83	37	190
Totals	1,757	1,464	703	3,924

Source: M. N. Leshchenko, *Ukrainsk'e selo v revoliutsii, 1905–1907 rr.* (Kiev, 1977), p. 346.

hardly shrinking violets, and they did not hesitate to use force when necessary. Yet, actions that involved violence were comparatively limited. In comparison to other regions, very few estates were destroyed. Arson was quite limited initially, but as frustration grew and repression became more severe, right-bank peasants found little choice but to resort to the methods employed by their counterparts elsewhere. Only 19 fires were set in 1905, but in the next two years, there were 319 cases of arson (Leshchenko's 1955 figures).[33] When peasants in the southwest did not strike, they were most commonly involved in struggles over disputed land. Sporadic outbursts of discontent, such as crop stealing, illegal pasturing, and forest offenses, were far more common in central Russia and in the other parts of the Ukraine.

This last fact is especially important. The peasant movement in the right-bank Ukraine differed significantly from that in the left bank and in Novorossiia. In the other regions of the Ukraine, there were far fewer disturbances, and the incidence of violence was considerably higher than in the right bank.[34] In all three areas, the hereditary commune predominated, and in all three places, peasant language, culture, custom, and nationality were, despite variations,

[33]Ibid., p. 127.
[34]I. M. Reva, *Selianskii rukh na livoberezhnii ukraini 1905–1907 rr.* (Kiev, 1964).

Table 10. Forms of the Peasant Movement in the Ukraine, 1905–1907

Forms	Right Bank	Left Bank	Novorossiia	Total
Strikes	2,329	223	195	2,748
Struggles over disputed land	511	295	134	940
Destruction of estates	47	358	278	683
Arson	401	230	96	727
Confrontations with authorities	116	78	54	248
Illegal meetings	284	381	221	886
Other	46	30	29	105
Mixed	190	173	102	465
Totals	3,924	1,688	1,190	6,802

Source: Compiled from data in M. N. Leshchenko, *Ukrainsk'e selo v revoliutsii 1905–1907 rr.* (Kiev, 1977), p. 346.

Ukrainian. (Table 10 compares the forms of the peasant movement in the Ukraine.) Accordingly, an explanation of the specific character of the peasant movement in the right bank cannot be found solely in terms of the region's cultural peculiarities. If the culture and traditional institutions of the peasantry were roughly similar throughout the Ukraine and the peasant movement differed sharply from region to region, then the reasons for these differences must be sought elsewhere.

This is not to belittle the significance of these concerns for a wide range of other aspects of peasant life. But it must be stressed that the patterns of noble and peasant landholding in the right bank were not repeated in the other regions of the Ukraine. Although commercial agriculture was extensive throughout the Ukraine, a high level of specialization in cash crops was found primarily in the southwest with its emphasis on sugar beets. It is therefore significant that peasant activity in Volynia, where sugar production was not well developed, followed patterns found most often in central Russia and the left-bank Ukraine.

The Timing of the Disorders

Strikes comprised the vast majority of disorders in the southwest. They occurred in the spring, most often in late May and early

June. Of the 3,924 disturbances counted by Leshchenko, 1,895 occurred in these months. He did not specifiy which forms fell in which months, but all other accounts make clear that the late spring was the strike season.[35] Elsewhere, most disorders occurred in June and July (2,572 of the 7,165 counted by Dubrovskii nationwide (including the right bank).[36] A great surge of discontent swept central Russia in November and December of 1905 once peasants came to realize that the October Manifesto would not deal with the land question, but peasants in the southwest did not repeat this pattern. The disturbances carried on by all Russian peasants were influenced by the rhythms of rural life, but this tendency appears to have been even more marked in the right bank.[37]

Late May and early June was the decisive period in the early gestation of the sugar beet. This crop was usually sown in late March or early April, but the crucial moment in its life cycle came in May as workers on the estates were required to pay minute attention to the progress of the beets, weeding, fertilizing, watering, aerating, and looking for pests. Without this care, the crop would be ruined. May, therefore, was clearly the moment of the peasants' greatest bargaining power. Landlords desperately needed their labor and were not prepared to withstand lengthy strikes. Less attention was required later in the summer, and, accordingly, strikes were fewer.[38] Few disorders of any kind took place at harvest time, as all peasants comprehended the overarching importance of this moment on the agricultural calendar. If strikes took place at this time, they were generally peaceful and weakly supported.[39]

Because of the agricultural calendar, strikes by wage-earning field hands were rarely coordinated with stoppages by sugar refin-

[35]Leshchenko, 1977, pp. 206 and 224.

[36]Dubrovskii, 1955, p. 42.

[37]Recently John Bushnell has suggested a fairly close correspondence between urban and rural disorders throughout the empire. See Bushnell, p. 46. Shanin's most recent work, however, uses much the same sources and reaches the opposite conclusion. See Shanin, 1985, pp. 174–83.

[38]TsGAOR f. 102, 4-oe dp., 1907, d. 108 ch. 38, ll. 1–32.

[39]TsGIAU f. 442, o. 856, d. 526, l. 11.

ery workers. The refineries began their seasonal operations in September, once the harvest was in. They continued to work until January. In rare cases, a peasant might find work in the fields during spring and summer and in a refinery in fall and winter. Strikes in the sugar factories were far less frequent given the simple fact that far fewer people (less than 70,000) worked in them.

As elsewhere, forest offenses in the southwest occurred during winter, as peasants searched for fuel. Crop stealing usually took place at harvest time. By 1907, strikes had become less successful. Landlord resistance stiffened as the police and army regained their cohesion and confidence. The withholding of labor had been a successful tactic in 1905 and 1906. By 1907, this approach was no longer producing results, and peasants in the right bank turned to the weapon used so often by their counterparts in central Russia. Arson, which had been little in evidence in 1905 and 1906, became common in the southwest as peasant frustration mounted.[40]

Causes of the Peasant Movement in the Southwest

Land hunger was the universal long-term cause of the peasant movement of 1905. In this, the right bank was no exception. If anything, the situation of *malozeml'e* in the southwest, Kiev and Podol'e in particular, was more acute than elsewhere. In no part of the empire were peasants satisfied with the size of their allotments, but in the right bank, peasant poverty was so severe that the movement took on special characteristics.[41] Strangely enough, the smallness of peasant holdings forced peasants to emphasize a variety of other concerns during the revolution. Low wages and dreadful working conditions were mentioned frequently by peasants as the reason for their actions, but those problems too had their roots in the acute land hunger felt by the region's cultivators.

Observers of all sorts shared the peasants' conviction that lack of land was the most fundamental peasant grievance. Both the governor of Kiev and the Kiev prosecutor stressed this fact in reporting to

[40]Shestakov, 1926, p. 51.
[41]Dubrovskii, 1955, p. 74. *AD*, 2:310.

superiors on the disorders in the spring of 1905.[42] Duma deputies received numerous petitions from peasants who mentioned a wide variety of other reasons for their discontent. Nevertheless, peasants in the right bank never failed to place land hunger at the center of their concerns.[43] The peasants of Malaia Bobrika (Podol'e) wrote to their representatives that the achievement of political freedom was not enough, especially in the light of their swiftly deteriorating position vis-à-vis the modernizing landlords: "It has gotten harder for us to live these last years. We need land as well as freedom, as we are completely dependent on the [large] landowners."[44] Peter Maslov, the leading Menshevik spokesman on agricultural matters, took pains to stress that the weakness of peasant participation in the rental market and the low wages were both the ultimate results of lack of land.[45] This impression was confirmed by the correspondents of the Free Economic Society who were unanimous in assigning paramount importance to land hunger as the root cause of the disorders in all three provinces.[46]

Peasants in the right bank, like those throughout Russia, ascribed their land hunger to the vastness of landlord holdings. In the southwest this conclusion was inescapable. Everything else flowed from this fact. Large landholders became the primary victims of peasant discontent. The immensity of many of the sugar plantations made these estates especially obvious targets, and the use of wage labor on them made the strike the most appropriate tactic for confronting what peasants thought was the cause of their misery.[47]

Peasants made no distinction in choosing those whom they attacked—they struck not only owners but also large-scale renters (usually sugar companies). Neither the nationality, political persuasion, nor personal characteristics of landlords or renters mattered to the peasants. Ukrainian peasants were as quick to strike a supposedly Ukrainian Tereshchenko as they were a Russian Bobrinskii or a Polish Dovgiello. Jews, such as the Brodskii family

[42]TsGIAU f. 442, o. 855, d. 115 ch. 2, l. 12. TsGAOR f. 102, o. 233 (1905), d. 2550 ch. 4, ll. 5–8.

[43]UD, 2:214. TsGIAL f. 1278, o. 1, d. 288, ll. 44–45.

[44]TsGIAL f. 1278, o. 1, 291, l. 298.

[45]Maslov, 1924, p. 22.

[46]AD, 2:74, 120, 140.

[47]Mirza-Avakiants, pp. 6–8.

who rented large blocs of land for sugar beet farming, were also not exempt.[48] Some landlords, like K. K. Sangushko, had a reputation for personal cruelty. As a result, the several strikes on his estates were especially bitter. On the other hand, personal kindness was no guarantee that one's peasants would remain quiescent.[49]

Extremely low pay was the primary cause of the strikes, and wages in the right bank were particularly low because the supply of labor was especially abundant. The reason so many sought wage work was simple enough. They could not survive on their allotments. As elsewhere, lack of land was the root cause of the peasant movement, but in the southwest, land hunger was so acute that it pushed peasant actions, tactics, and choices in special, distinctive directions.

The poor winter and summer harvests of 1905 were important immediate causes of the peasant movement in central Russia.[50] The violence and panic of the disorders in the Central Black Earth and Mid-Volga regions were more typical of short-term subsistence crises. In the right bank, on the other hand, the last four harvests had been good and the winter harvest of 1905 was no exception.[51] According to the government's statistics, winter grain production rose 1 percent between 1904 and 1905, and peasant production actually rose 6 percent. In contrast, the winter grain harvest in the left bank fell 3 percent, while production in three (of six) Central Black Earth provinces (Tula, Tambov, and Kursk) fell a disastrous 38 percent (see Table 11). Newspapers reported that the winter harvest in the right bank went well, despite the serious labor difficulties of the spring.[52] Nature offered few obstacles: during the first revolutionary years, weather conditions in the southwest were conducive to good harvests. Rainfall was more than adequate, and the average temperature during the growing season was slightly above normal.[53] By 1907, rainfall fell and temperatures dropped. The growing season shrank to 197 days (it

[48]*AD*, 2:169.
[49]Ibid., pp. 31, 113, 146.
[50]Robinson, p. 153. Pershin, p. 55.
[51]*AD*, 2:38.
[52]*Kievskaia Gazeta*, July 3, 1905. *Kievlianin*, June 13 and 16 and July 6, 1905. *Volyn'*, May 4, 1905.
[53]Slezkin, 1913, 1:15.

Table 11. Winter Grain Harvest, 1904–1905

	1904 (in 1,000 pudy)	1905 (in 1,000 pudy)	Percent Change
Landlord Harvest			
Right Bank	88,221	83,806	−5
Podol'e	30,234	30,868	2
Kiev	31,151	31,397	1
Volynia	26,836	21,541	−20
Left Bank	44,678	43,640	−2
Kharkov	11,932	10,808	−9
Poltava	20,829	23,534	13
Chernigov	11,917	9,298	−22
Central Black Earth	65,313	47,594	−27
Tambov	35,024	20,801	−41
Tula	13,997	8,474	−39
Kursk	16,287	18,319	12
Peasant Harvest			
Right Bank	101,041	107,601	6
Podol'e	31,189	37,282	20
Kiev	37,502	39,879	6
Volynia	32,350	30,440	−6
Left Bank	62,515	59,963	−4
Kharkov	18,464	16,644	−10
Poltava	21,285	24,574	15
Chernigov	22,766	18,745	−18
Central Black Earth	109,141	61,297	−44
Tambov	55,467	24,660	−56
Tula	17,451	8,386	−52
Kursk	36,223	28,251	−22
Total Harvest			
Right Bank	189,260	191,405	1
Podol'e	61,424	68,150	11
Kiev	68,652	71,275	4
Volynia	59,184	51,980	−12
Left Bank	107,193	103,603	−3
Kharkov	30,396	27,452	−10
Poltava	42,114	48,109	14
Chernigov	34,683	28,042	−19
Central Black Earth	174,449	108,892	−38
Tambov	90,491	45,462	−50
Tula	31,448	16,860	−46
Kursk	52,510	46,570	−11

Source: Tsentral'nyi statisticheskii komitet Ministerstva vnutrennykh del *Uro-zhai na 1904 god* (St. Petersburg, 1904) and *Urozhai na 1905 god* (St. Petersburg, 1905). Prepared with the assistance of Penny Waterstone.

had lasted 256 days in 1906).[54] In the southwest, the appearance of unfavorable meteorological conditions appeared at the time of the decline, rather than the emergence, of the peasant movement.

Bad harvests provided a partial explanation for the emergence of the peasant disorders in 1905, yet they clearly had little to do with the sudden and massive growth of the strike movement in the southwest. Events in the cities had some demonstration effect, but one can also find causes in the predominant agricultural practices of the region. The position of the sugar industry was decisive. Wages played a crucial role in the budgets of peasant families in the right bank, and those who labored on the plantations of the region received less for their work than did agrarian workers anywhere else in the empire.[55] The contemporary Bolshevik agrarian specialist Shestakov sought to extend the contrast. He claimed agricultural laborers in the right bank received eight times less than field workers in the United States and four times less than those who performed similar work in England.[56]

Under the impact of the strike movement, wages rose dramatically in 1905, in some cases by as much as 50 percent for both men and women (see Table 12). These kinds of increases occurred nowhere else in the empire.[57] Wages became the central demand of right-bank peasants, first, because pay was so low, and second, because outside earnings played so decisive a role in the survival of the peasant family. These facts were so brutally obvious even the government's representatives could not ignore them. In April 1905, the Podol'e Administration for Peasant Affairs reported to the governor that "Landlords and renters must recognize that wages, particularly day wages, are so low that they are insufficient to feed a worker's family."[58] Similarly, police reports on strikes in Volynia cited "extremely low wages" as the primary cause of the disorders.[59]

The ease with which peasants subsequently extracted wage in-

[54]Ibid., p. 19.
[55]Maslov, 1924, p. 80.
[56]Shestakov, 1907, p. 15.
[57]Drozdov, p. 20.
[58]TsGIAL f. 1405, o. 107, d. 7618, l. 82.
[59]TsGIAU f. 442, o. 855, d. 109, l. 111.

Table 12. Agricultural Wages in the Southwest, 1904–1907

Women's average wages (in kopecks)

	1904	1905	% change 1904–5	1906	% change 1905–6	1907	% change 1906–7
Spring							
Podol'e	20	25	25	25	0	**	**
Kiev	20	25	25	30	20	**	**
Volynia	**	15	**	20	33	**	**
Summer							
Podol'e	20	30	50	40	33	35	−13
Kiev	25	35	40	40	14	35	−13
Volynia	20	25	25	30	20	25	−17
Fall							
Podol'e	30	35	17	50	43	35	−30
Kiev	30	40	33	50	25	35	−30
Volynia	25	25	0	**	**	30	**

Men's average wages (in kopecks)

	1904	1905	% change 1904–5	1906	% change 1905–6	1907	% change 1906–7
Spring							
Podol'e	25	30	20	35	17	**	**
Kiev	25	35	40	40	14	**	**
Volynia	30	30	0	30	0	**	**
Summer							
Podol'e	30	40	33	60	50	45	−25
Kiev	35	55	57	70	27	50	−29
Volynia	40	40	0	50	25	45	−10
Fall							
Podol'e	40	45	13	60	33	50	−17
Kiev	45	60	33	70	17	55	−21
Volynia	40	40	0	**	**	45	**

Source: Ministervo zemledeliia i gosudarstvennykh imushchestv, *1904* (and) *1905 god v sel''skokhoziaistvennykh otnosheniakh* (St. Petersburg, 1904 and 1905). Prepared with the assistance of Penny Waterstone.
**Data not available.

creases was largely the result of the extremely low pay they received in the first place. Quite simply, landlords could afford to give peasants more and still make substantial profits. Landlords and renters reported increased wage levels to the government in 1905 and again in 1906. Yet it does not appear that peasants believed they had made much progress. During the spring sowing of 1906, the Kiev Agronomic Society, a group dominated by landlords and professors of agronomy, interviewed 959 peasants throughout the province. The peasants were asked whether they felt wages had risen, fallen, or stayed the same. Fully 726 respondents replied that they felt wages had fallen. Only 139 peasants thought wages were higher.[60] There is no way of knowing the methods used by the society in choosing this sample, but the contrast between the official statistics and peasant perceptions is striking. The contradiction could, perhaps, be resolved if the peasants' real wages failed to rise. Limited evidence suggests that this may have been the case.[61]

According to official figures, prices for meat, butter, and cloth rose sharply between 1904 and 1905 in the right bank. The increases were especially severe in Kiev and Podol'e, the centers of strike activity. Prices in the left bank also rose, but less dramatically than in the southwest. In the Central Black Earth region (Tula, Tambov, and Kursk in particular) meat prices actually fell, cloth rose moderately, and only butter increased at a rate comparable to the rises in the right bank (see Table 13). A variety of government observers in the countryside also stressed the significance of steep increases in the cost of fuel and fodder in the right bank.[62] Police accused a number of landlords of raising prices in "company stores" on their estates.[63] Throughout the right bank, these price rises were first felt early in the spring of 1905. In May 1905, A. A. Eiler, the governor of Podol'e, reported to the Ministry of Interior that wages in his province had fallen slightly just at the time of rises in the cost of fuel and fodder.[64]

The combination of low wages and high prices was obviously volatile. These trends suggest a specific, immediate cause for the emergence of the strike movement in the right bank during 1905. Wages, after all, had been scandalously low for some time, but

[60]*Obzor kievskogo agronomicheskogo obshchestva* (Kiev, 1906), p. 13.
[61]Drozdov, p. 26.
[62]TsGIAU f. 442, o. 855, d. 525, l. 7. TsGAOR f. 102, 1905, o. 233, d. 2550 ch. 5, ll. 5–8.
[63]TsGIAU f. 442, o. 855, d. 109, l. 109.
[64]Ibid., d. 113 ch. 1, l. 56.

Table 13. Prices of Beef, Butter, and Cloth, 1904–1905

	Beef (in rubles)			Butter (in rubles)			Cloth (in rubles)		
	1904	1905	% change	1904	1905	% change	1904	1905	% change
Right Bank									
Podol'e	3.10	3.28	6	14.90	16.60	11	4.95	6.15	24
Kiev	3.00	3.58	19	15.65	16.80	7	5.30	6.65	25
Volynia	2.90	3.22	11	15.15	14.60	-4	8.15	8.00	-2
Left Bank									
Kharkov	3.35	3.25	-3	14.50	14.90	3	5.45	5.75	6
Poltava	2.58	3.19	24	12.45	12.55	1	4.15	5.25	27
Chernigov	2.77	3.15	14	11.95	11.95	0	6.80	7.65	12
Central Black Earth									
Tambov	3.17	2.95	-7	13.40	15.00	12	8.95	9.15	2
Tula	3.25	3.10	-5	15.00	17.25	15	9.00	10.80	20
Kursk	3.17	3.16	0	13.60	14.55	7	8.20	8.50	4

Source: Ministerstvo zemledeliia i gosudarstvennykh imushchestv, *1904* (and) *1905 god v sel'skokhoziaistvennykh otnosheniakh* (St. Petersburg, 1904 and 1905). Prepared with the assistance of Penny Waterstone.

inflation, in part the result of war, was a new element. Again, events outside the village played a role in sparking the manifestation of discontent in the countryside. Poor harvests did not touch off the many strikes in the right bank. Disorders in these provinces did not have the characteristics of short-term subsistence crises. Instead, the interaction of the labor and commodity markets produced the peasants' difficulties. Their response was not the traditional, violent, and disorganized bread riot. Instead, conditions led them to choose a more modern tactic, the strike.

Scenes of revolution in the cities also led peasants to challenge the structures of power, property, and authority in the countryside. This was true throughout the empire, and the southwest was no exception. Put most broadly, the general mood of the moment, the vague example of urban events, led peasants to confront landlords and renters. Strikes in the cities suggested, however imprecisely, similar tactics in the countryside.

Disputes over contested land became increasingly common and bitter. Struggles of this sort occurred in many regions, but they were especially acute in the right bank where landlords were active in modernizing their estates. Illegal pasturing was one of the most direct ways of protesting landlord-directed changes. On the Volynia estate of Anna Dovgiallo, peasants had been able to use the meadows until 1904. In 1905, the entire estate was turned over to a large-scale renter who planted the disputed land with wheat. No sooner had the meadow been sown than the peasants moved their livestock onto it.[65] In the spring of 1905, Kiev peasants actually took to sowing unused land belonging to landlords.[66] Peasant societies later brought similar disputes to the attention of their Duma deputies. In all these cases, lands that they had used for many years had been taken away from them, in some instances despite the existence of written documents guaranteeing their rights.[67]

Whether they were appealing to the Duma or to local authorities, peasants presented clearly written, well-reasoned petitions that exhibited neither obsequiousness nor stridency. In nearly

[65]Ibid., d. 109, l. 138.
[66]TsGAOR f. 102, 1905, o. 233, d. 2550 ch. 4, l. 12.
[67]TsGIAL f. 1278, o. 1, d. 288, l. 12. TsGIAL f. 1278, o. 1, d. 785, ll. 34–39.

every case, they were protesting changes in their rights, unilaterally instituted by landlords. The complaints of the village of Novomylska to the Volynia Administration for Peasant Affairs were typical of hundreds of similar petitions. The situation had been tolerable until the estate had been sold a few years ago (the date was not specified) to S. S. Galiatinskii. For years the peasants had driven their livestock onto their allotments through a forest belonging to the lord. Peasants had enjoyed this right since 1868. Now Galiatinskii was demanding two rubles from each household to allow the animals through the forest. Beyond this, a well on Galiatinskii's property had been used by peasants for what they claimed was "centuries." Not only could they no longer use the well, but now Galiatinskii had taken to herding his livestock through the peasants' allotments. Unable to feed their animals, peasants were forced to sell livestock. The villagers of Novomylska noted that they had protested this situation in several courts and to a number of authorities, all to no avail.[68]

Disputes of this type had been going on for some time. Unlike the strike movement, they did not represent anything particularly new. Now, under the general impact of the revolutionary situation, struggles over land use became more frequent and intense. Peasant resistance was extensive and strong precisely because the landlord attack on customary rights was especially severe in the right bank with its high level of noble-inspired agrarian capitalism. This trend could properly be seen as a disruption of the traditional moral economy of the region. Peasants in the right bank, like those elsewhere, did not believe that the changes would benefit them. Nevertheless, attempts to restore older agricultural practices played a secondary role in the peasant movement in Kiev, Podol'e, and Volynia. Instead, rural cultivators sought to find more effective ways of adjusting to the new situation.

The Spread of Peasant Agitation

Disturbances and strikes were largely episodic and localized, although peasants were by no means unaware of struggles outside their villages. By the spring of 1905, disorders were no longer

[68]ZhOGA, f. 115, o. 2, d. 2786, l. 1.

isolated incidents. Provincial governors received a daily flood of telegrams from distressed landlords as the movement spread rapidly. Peasants learned of events in other places through a variety of means. The most obvious source of information was the newspaper. Illiteracy was no barrier for peasants who wanted to gather information—if only one member of a community could read, that was enough. Dailies, weeklies, and monthlies from a wide spectrum of political tendencies appeared in the countryside. Peasants, many of whom sought news of their sons on the Far Eastern front, read them avidly and in doing so, learned of the urban struggle. It could not be said that news of disorders in the cities touched off the strike wave in the southwest; however, there can be no doubt that the press played a crucial role in broadening and deepening the movement.[69]

A variety of government observers in the countryside stressed the significance of the reading of newspapers. It could be said that bureaucrats and policemen would, perhaps, be too attentive to possible sources of outside influence. Yet it is significant that they all noted the fact that any newspaper, regardless of its political coloration, could sow unrest in a village. In one village in Podol'e, the peasant society actually had a subscription to *Birzhevie Vedemosti,* the daily organ of Petersburg's commercial and financial bourgeoisie.[70] In most cases, newspapers appeared in rural areas with less regularity. Nevertheless, the stream of information, however haphazard, was constant. Not only revolutionary agitation, but any information from the outside world, could upset the equilibrium of the village. Peasants certainly were not ignorant of events beyond the limits of their communities. In the spring of 1905, A. Rafal'skii, an assistant of the Podol'e governor, prepared a detailed survey of reports from the lowest government officials in the localities (*mirovye posredniki*). Rafal'skii was struck by the "enormous" dispersal of all kinds of periodicals throughout the province and, on the matter of rural awareness of urban struggles, he noted, "In all the villages, the peasants are fully informed about the strikes of factory workers."[71]

[69]AD, 2:95.
[70]TsGIAU f. 442, o. 855, d. 526, l. 9.
[71]Ibid., l. 3.

As mentioned earlier, literate peasants read aloud to their fellow villagers or someone outside the commune, a teacher or sympathetic priest, would oblige. In other cases, peasant reading was more organized. Rafal'skii reported that in the Podol'e settlement of Solobkovtsy a group of ten men had actually formed an ongoing circle in which they read newspapers aloud to each other.[72] Literate peasants in Uniev (Volynia) made a habit of using the public reading room in the neighboring town.[73]

In some instances, the reading of a newspaper might be the actual spark that provoked a strike or disorder. This occurred several times in the Gaisin district of Podol'e.[74] Elsewhere, the Volynia vicegovernor blamed newspapers for strikes on the Sangushko and Pototskii estates during the spring of 1905.[75] In 1907, the governor of Volynia complained that press accounts of speeches by left-wing Duma deputies had set off a series of illegal pasturings in Novogradovolynsk district.[76] This was no hallucination. Peasants did read radical and socialist newspapers.[77] At the same time, the right kind of information in a conservative or liberal paper had similarly explosive effects.[78] Some governors were urging the police to ban all newspapers. On December 1, 1905, Savich, the governor of Kiev, wrote to Stolypin, "the peasants have greater belief in the printed word than in the living word of a government figure."[79] One could only ask what else he expected.

Rural disorders have usually spread in more amorphous ways than by newspaper. Rumors, perhaps leading to panic, could move quickly through the countryside, as frightened travelers and refugees gave garbled versions of events in other places. In *The Great Fear*, Georges Lefebvre noted that distorted accounts spread rapidly throughout the French countryside of 1789, inducing a

---

[72]Ibid., l. 1.

[73]TsGIAL f. 796, o. 187, d. 6725, l. 2.

[74]TsGAOR f. 102, 1905, d. 2550 ch. 41, l. 84.

[75]TsGIAU f. 442, o. 855, d. 109, l. 4.

[76]Ibid., o. 857, d. 195, l. 1.

[77]TsGAOR f. 102, 1906, o. 236, d. 700 ch. 54, l. 106. TsGIAL f. 1405, o. 108, d. 6895, l. 3.

[78]*Volyn'*, May 28, 1905. TsGAOR f. 102, 1907, d. 53 ch. 1, l. 15.

[79]TsGAOR 102, 1905, o. 233, d. 2550 ch. 4, l. 95.

wide variety of thoroughly irrational forms of behavior.[80] In Russia, rumors of this sort usually centered around promises peasants might claim had been made by the tsar. Naive monarchism had been a highly visible element of peasant politics throughout Russian history. By 1905, especially after the disappointing October Manifesto, peasant faith in the autocrat began to erode.[81] In the right bank, very few peasants justified their actions by citing imaginary decrees of the tsar.[82] One of the few instances in which peasants claimed to be following the tsar's will happened in the village of Studentsy (Volynia). Instead of hearing of the tsar's "edict" from some itinerant traveler, peasants said they had learned of the autocrat's wishes in a newspaper. It is difficult to imagine any periodical that might carry such news, but it is especially interesting to hear peasants claiming they learned of this development in the press.[83]

When word of strikes and disorders spread through the southwest, news was transmitted in far more concrete ways then mere rumor. This information was not usually distorted, and accounts were rarely garbled. Instead, contacts among villages were most often direct and usually occurred during or immediately after a strike. Confrontations with one landlord would then be followed by disorders on neighboring estates. In many cases, landlords themselves were the unwitting messengers. When a strike began, word was passed immediately to nearby villages, as landlords searched for strikebreakers. Instead of helping to acquire substitute labor, the news only provided an example for peasants elsewhere. Patterns of this sort arose often in Kiev and Podol'e during the spring of 1905.[84] In May 1905, strikes took place on the enormous sugar plantations of the Sangushko and Pototskii families. According to the vice-governor of Volynia, the entire *guberniia* knew of these events within days.[85] Very quickly the leaders of one strike would become agitators in other villages, carrying news of their

[80]Georges Lefebvre, *The Great Fear of 1789* (Princeton, 1973), pp. 148–51.
[81]Daniel Field, *Rebels in the Name of the Tsar* (Boston, 1976), p. 20.
[82]TsGIAU f. 442, o. 855, d. 115 ch. 2, ll. 95–96.
[83]Ibid., d. 109, ll. 96–97.
[84]*UD*, 2:33 and 353.
[85]TsGIAU f. 442, o. 855, d. 109, ll. 105–113.

struggles and triumphs to neighbors. In Tarashchansk district of Kiev, peasants who had successfully struck a sugar plantation journeyed to nine nearby villages, urging other peasants to take similar actions.[86] In May 1905, nine villages soon followed the example of the peasants of Ol'shevskii (Podol'e), striking for the same demands and acting in unison to prevent the hiring of strikebreakers.[87]

Direct village-to-village contact was not always possible. Instead, bazaars and fairs became common vehicles for sharing experiences and spreading the movement.[88] In March 1905, peasants in the settlement of Solobkivtsy (Podol'e) asked their landlord for a ruble a day to work the fields. The next day at a fair, they spread word of their action.[89] Itinerant salesmen passed through local bazaars and with their wares brought news of events in other places. Later on, political agitators found it convenient to pose as traders, selling pictures and trinkets while passing out leaflets.[90] In June 1906, peasants from Pilipy-Aleksandrovi (Podol'e) traveled to the town of Novo-Ushits to learn the various prices being offered for day labor throughout the district. This group returned to the village and informed the assembly of heads of households (the *skhod*) of prevailing wage levels. The peasants then voted to strike unless they were paid the going rate.[91]

Less concrete information could also be communicated at local fairs, and more than a few rumors were hatched at bazaars. In May 1905, peasants on the Podol'e estate of Prince Abamelek-Lazarev were in the midst of disputes with the manager of the domain. A group of them attended the local market. There they were told the tsar had "ordered" the nobility to sell land to the peasants at the price of two rubles a *desiatin*. This "news" served only to enflame peasant expectations which, in this case, quite clearly were not going to be met. The resulting confrontation was the most violent of all the disturbances that took place in the right bank during the

[86]TsGAOR f. 102, 1905, o. 233, d. 2550 ch. 4, l. 56.
[87]Ibid., ch. 41, l. 2.
[88]*AD*, 2:58.
[89]Leshchenko, 1955, p. 129. *UD*, 2:143.
[90]TsGIAU f. 442, o. 856, d. 526, l. 5. TsGIAL f. 1405, o. 107, d. 7618, l. 82.
[91]TsGAOR f. 102, 1906, o. 236, d. 700 ch. 54, ll. 104–5.

revolutionary period.[92] Much of the manor was destroyed, and the prince's managers had to flee for their lives.

Returning veterans were thought to have played an important role in spreading and deepening the movement throughout Russia. In the right bank, however, the influence of demobilized soliders was largely limited to Volynia, the least distinctive of the three southwestern provinces.[93] In the fall of 1905, the governor of Volynia blamed the problems of the previous spring on sailors, returning home from Odessa and Sevastopol'.[94] Early in 1906, he informed the police that soldiers had been spreading rumors that peasants would be relieved of redemption payments.[95] That winter, veterans in several places in Volynia were involved in a series of forest offenses.[96]

A few former soldiers actually turned to more active forms of agitation. Fillip Shevchuk and Nestor Fillipovich were arrested in December of 1905 in the Volynia village of Bogdanovka. Shevchuk was twenty-three years old. He was Ukrainian, literate, and unmarried. He had been demobilized on November 4, 1905, and returned to Bogdanovka, his native village. Shevchuk took a job working for a railroad where he met Fillipovich who had left the army in September when he refused to arrest a peasant engaged in a forest offense. Fillipovich was a twenty-five-year-old illiterate Bielorussian who had been born near Minsk. Together, he and Shevchuk had become itinerant traders, selling pictures of the Russo-Japanese War, while distributing revolutionary pamphlets at fairs and bazaars. Quite quickly, they were able to organize a gathering of 500 peasants in Bogdanovka. According to their indictment, this activity lasted little more than a month, when they were seized in the house of Shevchuk's uncle.[97]

Soviet historians have continued to stress the importance of contacts between peasants and militant urban workers. Given the capitalist character of agrarian labor in the southwest, proletarians and

[92]UD, 2:362.
[93]AD, 2:61.
[94]UD, 1:759.
[95]TsGAOR f. 102, 1906, d. 700 ch. 37, l. 1.
[96]TsGIAU f. 442, o. 855, d. 109, l. 123.
[97]TsGIAU f. 318, o. 1, d. 732, l. 37.

peasants in the region could very well be expected to find a common language. Scholars of the 1920s, for example Shestakov, repeatedly claimed a role for city workers in the right bank.[98] In 1955, F. E. Los' argued along similar lines, and Leshchenko never stopped asserting the importance of urban proletarians in the rural struggle.[99]

Soviet historians are able to offer evidence of some contact, but their claims are, by and large, not corroborated by the contemporary correspondents of the Free Economic Society. These observers found limited evidence of worker involvement in the peasant movement of the right bank. Only in Kiev was there any significant contact, and nowhere did workers take the lead in agrarian strikes or other struggles.[100] In June 1906, police did report the presence of urban proletarians in the course of a strike on the Kiev estate of Count A. A. Bobrinskii.[101] Still, incidents of this sort were exceptional.

Sugar factory workers also did little to spread the peasant movement. At best, they played roles in local struggles. Their work was seasonal, and the refineries were located in the countryside. Most workers had been recruited right out of neighboring villages and could hardly be considered carriers of any sort of advanced, urban proletarian consciousness. In the spring of 1905, workers in the Skomoroshskii factory in Kiev province and in the Balashev estate refinery in Podol'e went on strike.[102] There were several other moments of coordination between peasants and those working in the few Volynia refineries.[103] But the work in the fields did not overlap with the peak season in the refineries, so chances for powerful coordination were rare. Beyond this, refinery workers were simply not sufficiently numerous (about 70,000) to have had a major impact. In fact, it proved possible to find only one recorded case of sugar factory workers leading a strike of peasants.[104]

[98]Shestakov, 1930, p. 25.
[99]F. E. Los', *Revoliutsia 1905–1907 rokiv na Ukraini* (Kiev, 1955), p. 180.
[100]AD, 2:25, 61, and 108.
[101]UD, 3:216.
[102]AD, 2:171 and 183.
[103]Vinogradov and Denisovets, p. 22. Butsik, 1957, p. 42.
[104]*Russkie Vedemosti,* June 3, 1905.

As has already been mentioned, the railroad network in the right bank was especially well developed. The system that had been built to carry grain and sugar to the cities now helped spread the peasant movement. Agitators moved swiftly from place to place by train, and peasants often came to local stations to learn of developments outside their villages.[105] Shevchuk and Fillipovich, in particular, had used the railroads to cover the region quickly.[106] During December 1905, railwaymen at the Podol'e station of Strunkovka gave out newspapers and pamphlets to local peasants. Although peasants had doubts about the leaflets, they were, according to the police, tremendously impressed by the newspapers, which included the short-lived populist daily *Syn Otechestva* and *Russkaia Gazeta*.[107] In November 1905, 150 peasants from the Kiev village of Ol'shanitsa gathered at a nearby station to hear a railway worker read them the October Manifesto. The peasants then decided to send two delegates, both decorated veterans, to attend the liberal-inspired Peasant Union which would soon gather in Moscow.[108]

The railroads also allowed villages to maintain contact with each other. Savich noted a pattern, during the spring of 1905. Most of the points touched by the first manifestations of the strike wave were, he claimed, near railroad stations.[109] In fact, on May 22, 1905, a crowd of fifty women appeared at the Pogrobishche station (Kiev). They had come from the village of Adamovka where peasants were on strike against the Dziunkovskii sugar plantation. They urged the railwaymen to quit work. The women then stopped several workmen who were delivering beer to the estate. They drank some of the beer and destroyed the rest, after which they proceeded to prevent the delivery of sugar from the estate to the station. At this point, police were summoned, and the women returned to the village peacefully.[110]

Political activists from many parties and organizations were present in the southwest throughout the revolutionary period. Yet

[105]*AD*, 2:118.
[106]TsGIAU f. 318, o. 1, d. 732, l. 37.
[107]*UD*, 1:751.
[108]Butsik, 1957, p. 39.
[109]*UD*, 2:355.
[110]TsGIAU f. 442, o. 855, d. 115 ch. 2, ll. 2–3.

there is little evidence to suggest that outsiders either started or controlled the peasant movement. Representatives of many political groups flooded the countryside in 1905, but they became a significant presence only in 1906. Agitators had little or nothing to do with the first outbreaks of the movement in the right bank.[111] When villages acted, they did so on their own.[112] Even contemporary orthodox Soviet historians have accepted the disorganized and spontaneous character of the peasant movement. Both Dubrovskii and Leshchenko have readily acknowledged this fact.[113] The more flexible Soviet authors of the 1920s also believed that the influence of political parties was not decisive.[114]

No particular party or group could claim to control the movement. Peasants were often willing to cooperate with agitators, but such moments were episodic. No group, not the Socialist Revolutionaries, not the Social Democrats, not the Peasant Union, could claim to have a powerful, functioning network in any part of the countryside, including the right bank. Most important, peasants did not make precise distinctions among the various parties. Instead, they gave temporary audiences to anyone who made sense to them. In some cases, police found agitators carrying the literature of all three groups.

It should come as no surprise that landlords, bureaucrats, and police officials were quick to blame the disturbances on political agitators. The forces of order had a massive psychological and political investment in the peasantry's loyalty and conservatism. It was, after all, nothing new for targets of discontent to accuse outsiders of inspiring popular protests against those conditions created by the very propertied groups threatened by disorder. Claims of this sort were made throughout the empire. Here, the right bank was no exception.

In the summer of 1906, Eiler, the governor of Podol'e, sent a circular to all police personnel in the province. He warned them to be on the lookout for "agitators and other suspicious personalities." It was necessary to treat such figures harshly, because,

[111]AD, 2:109.
[112]AD, 2:216.
[113]Dubrovskii, 1955, p. 66. Leshchenko, 1955, p. 146.
[114]Mirza-Avakiants, p. 36. Maslov, 1924, p. 53. Shestakov, 1926, p. 79.

according to Eiler (a relatively moderate figure for a high-level bureaucrat), agitators were the main cause of the disorders.[115] A year earlier, Rafal'skii, who was particularly sympathetic to the peasants' situation, had stressed the influence of socialist literature.[116] At the same time, the head of the Podol'e gendarmerie informed his superiors of the influence of "socialist agitators."[117] At a spring 1905 meeting of Podol'e sugar producers, blame for the strikes was similarly fixed on the now familiar "outside agitators." The Kiev governor, Savich, also saw the first strike wave as the "result of political propaganda."[118] None of these reports, however, mentioned specific names or places.

The claim of a countryside overrun by revolutionaries was clearly exaggerated, if the discussion is limited to 1905. Nevertheless, by 1906, political activists of all sorts had entered the villages. Peasants paid little attention to the affiliations of these agitators, but they were extremely interested in their messages.[119] Soviet writers have always highlighted the presence of activists, especially Social Democrats. Leshchenko has cited a report by Savich that mentioned 140 cases in which Social Democratic literature was found in Kiev during 1905 and 1906.[120] Even Menshevik authors of the 1920s, Maslov in particular, have admitted a specifically Bolshevik influence in the right bank.[121] Yet the evidence usually cited, though considerable, can hardly be considered massive given the universal character of the peasant movement itself. Even 140 cases of illegal pamphleting, while significant, seem miniscule when compared to the thousands of strikes and disorders that occurred in Kiev during the revolutionary years. In addition, it must be considered that Kiev province, given the decisive presence of the city of Kiev, would be the most likely place to find successful political activity.

If the level of agitation was not as high as landlords feared and

[115]TsGIAU f. 442, o. 856, d. 526, l. 5.
[116]Ibid., o. 855, d. 526, l. 8.
[117]TsGAOR f. 102, 1905, d. 2550 ch. 4, l. 19.
[118]TsGIAU f. 442, o. 855, d. 115 ch. 2, l. 12.
[119]AD, 2:64.
[120]Leshchenko, 1955, p. 177.
[121]Maslov, 1924, p. 199.

political activists hoped, there can be no doubt that much pro-
pagandizing and organizing did go on. A surprisingly wide variety
of people were arrested for all sorts of troublemaking. Some fit the
stereotype of the student or the agitator from the city. Others were
members of the so-called rural intelligentsia of teachers and doctors. One could even find the occasional priest.

According to the Kiev prosecutor, an "unknown agitator" addressed a "large meeting" of "local peasants" in the village of
Lebedin, site of the Brodskii sugar refinery, on Sunday, June 18,
1906. The "agitator," a young outsider, called the gathering by
ringing the local church bell. He urged the peasants not to trust the
authorities and claimed that many soliders were now on the side of
"the socialists." The next day, he organized a similar large meeting. As a result of his influence, strikes soon occurred both in
Lebedin and on the neighboring Rkazynaogovskii estate.[122] Events
of this sort fit perfectly both landlord nightmares and orthodox
Soviet stereotypes. Other cases of agitation revealed a broader
variety of carriers of the revolutionary message.

Most priests supported the landlords and authorities during the
disorders. Some tried to act as mediators; a small number actually
were arrested for fomenting discontent among the peasantry. The
reasons for clergy activism were usually more personal than political. Father Tyniavskii of Sorokomiazhinets (Podol'e) had disputed
the attempts of the local landlord to redraw land boundaries at the
expense of the church's holdings. When local peasants struck the
estate in July 1905, Tyniavskii offered them his support.[123] In 1907,
a Father Pavel' Vikul' was arrested in Bashtanovka (Podol'e). He
had been agitating for two years among the local peasants after his
sixteen-year-old son had been jailed for subversion.[124] A few teachers at church schools were also arrested. Their activities were usually
more explicitly political and often involved the distribution of literature produced by various political parties.[125]

The old populist tradition of agitation by rural doctors did not

[122]UD, 2:pt. 2, p. 220.
[123]TsGIAU f. 442, o. 855, d. 113 ch. 2, l. 1.
[124]TsGIAL f. 796, o. 188, d. 7007, l. 1.
[125]TsGIAU f. 442, o. 855, d. 115 ch. 2, l. 176. TsGAOR f. 102, 1906, d. 700 ch.
37, ll. 34–36.

entirely disappear in the southwest. In Vinnitsa district (Podol'e), police reported on the activities of a Doctor Donskoi who roamed the countryside with his son, organizing secret meetings and convincing the peasants of their right to the land (as if the peasants needed convincing). He had achieved a considerable following, and local landlords urged the police to remove him from the province.[126]

Small merchants, members of the social estate called the *meshchanstvo*, also played a role in fomenting and spreading disorder. The motives of these figures were also mixed. Like the priests, these members of the petty bourgeoisie in the structural rather than polemical sense criticized the authorities for reasons that were decidedly mixed.[127] Nevertheless, their involvement could be explicitly political. Such was the case of Samuel Gel'man, a Jewish merchant of modest means. Starting with the summer of 1905, Gel'man and his sons traveled to many villages near their home in Ol'shanitsa (Kiev). Gel'man was especially active in November 1905 when he helped organize a number of public and private meetings for peasants, including the aforementioned gathering at the Ol'shanitsa station. In addressing peasants, Gel'man took a very general approach and focused on the land question above all. When he was arrested in February 1906, it was claimed that he had distributed literature from the Social Democrats, Socialist Revolutionaries, and the Peasant Union. Gel'man, like the many other agitators who were Jewish, had no difficulty in finding an audience amont the Ukrainian peasantry of the right bank.[128] Peasants in the southwest had not suddenly been overcome with the spirit of brotherhood and cosmopolitanism, however. Rather, their concern for their own aims and interests was stronger than their perhaps too-well-advertised anti-Semitism. As shall be seen later, right-bank peasants also could express less positive feelings for their Jewish neighbors. Yet this did not prevent peasants from welcoming Jewish agitators into their midst when the views of the two groups coincided.

[126]TsGIAU f. 442, o. 855, d. 113 ch. 2, l. 1.
[127]Ibid., o. 856, d. 442, l. 1.
[128]TsGIAU f. 318, o. 1, d. 302, ll. 3 and 223.

It was also possible for peasants themselves to play a role in fomenting disorders. Early in 1905, a peasant named Badiuk was arrested in Liubanki (Podol'e) for holding a series of meetings in his house at which he gave out literature from several parties.[129] Later that year in Krasnoiosk (Kiev), a Leonid Kovan was taken in for distributing a pamphlet published by the Social Democrats entitled "How to Take the Land from the Landlords." Despite his leafleting, Kovan, who was forty and married with four children, was himself illiterate.[130] When Timofei Kruk was arrested in Turichany (Volynia) on May 3, 1907, nine illegal brochures from a variety of groups were found. Born in the neighboring settlement of Novosel', Kruk, no hot-headed youth at forty-nine, had been touring the region for a year. He was already known to the peasants of Turichany who invited him into their homes to hold meetings at which he read aloud from the literature he was carrying. Kruk was given three years. The two peasants whose house he used were also arrested. They received light sentences.[131]

Duma members provided a final mechanism for the spread of the peasant movement. They had broad parliamentary immunity and were allowed to travel the countryside freely to address meetings of peasants. This practice became an especially acute problem for the authorities once the second Duma, with its more radical membership, was elected early in 1907. In two cases in Kiev, strikes followed immediately in the wake of appearances by deputies in the countryside.[132] Often the mere promise of a speech by a Duma member was enough to spark an incident.[133] Peasants also came together to draw up instructions (*nakazy*) for their deputies, and in doing so, they were led to take more direct forms of action.[134]

Peasants in the southwest, like those elsewhere, directed their actions primarily against their own landlords, but this did not mean that they lived in hermetic worlds. Their awareness of events

[129]Kolomiets, *Polozhenie krestian*, p. 16.
[130]TsGIAU f. 318, o. 1, d. 409, l. 39.
[131]Ibid., o. 1, 1847, ll. 2–100.
[132]TsGIAU f. 442, o. 857, o. 193, l. 1. TsGIAL f. 1405, o. 193, d. 1674, l. 3.
[133]*AD*, 2:202.
[134]Maslov, 1924, p. 199.

outside the villages may have been imprecise, but there can be no doubt that even the most remote and primitive settlements knew about struggles other than their own—strikes in the cities and confrontations throughout the region. Right-bank peasants also learned of the outside world in direct and modern ways. As mentioned, the press played a decisive role, and low literacy rates were no impediment. Political agitators may not have always gotten their points across, but their very presence in the countryside was sufficient to awaken peasants to the significance of the revolutionary moment. Finally, the landlords themselves spread word of strikes through their calls to neighboring villages for working hands. If the estates of the southwest had not been capitalistically organized, steps of this sort would not have been required. In short, right-bank peasants were not ignorant prisoners of their customs and traditions. They knew of events external to their world, and outside forces influenced their actions.

Demands

Throughout central Russia, the demands of peasants were largely implicit in their actions. It was not necessary for peasants to state their aims openly in the course of crop stealing, arson, or illegal woodcutting. Upon their arrest, some individuals admitted their goals to the authorities, but those engaged in these kinds of activities felt no particular need to specify their aspirations. In central Russia, vague hopes of removing the landlords and acquiring the land were the norm. During the strike movement in the right bank, however, this was not the case. The logic of a strike required that the demands of those working on an estate be fully spelled out. Rural cultivators in the southwest had to formulate (sometimes with outside help) clear and specific demands. In many cases, it proved necessary for peasants to write out what it was they wanted.[135] This process forced them to clarify and think through their aspirations with far greater specificity than was required of their central Russian counterparts.

[135]TsGIAU f. 442, o. 855, d. 113 ch. 1, p. 266.

The conditions under which rural cultivators worked in the southwest very directly determined the character of their demands. Agriculture in the region was dominated by landlord-owned capitalist farms, employing large numbers of day laborers. Nobles, and those who worked with them, thoroughly controlled the lands of Kiev, Podol'e, and Volynia. They showed few signs of giving up their estates. Accordingly, wages, rather than land, became the most direct and visible concern of the region's rural cultivators. This expressed preference did not mean that right-bank peasants did not share the universal desire that all the state, gentry, and church lands be given them without compensation to the previous owners, only that it was not their most explicit demand.

Right-bank peasants also raised questions about a variety of working conditions; they even made specifically political demands from time to time. As the strike movement developed with each passing month, peasants and agricultural workers downplayed other demands and came to concentrate on wages. The reasons for this trend are not obscure. Wages were the only issue on which the strikers enjoyed much success. Peasants of the southwest rarely expressed traditional and millenarian goals (total repartition in particular). Instead, they came to concentrate on the more immediately realizable. In doing this, they chose methods (the strike) that were effective instruments for the attainment of their goals. Rural cultivators in the southwest rarely engaged in elemental, destructive outbursts that sought a return to a mythical golden, precapitalist way of life. In the right bank that era was long gone. Given the impossibility of moving backward, right-bank peasants sought the best possible deal for themselves under the conditions then existing in the region.

Wages in the right bank were extremely low, and early in the spring of 1905, peasants sought dramatic increases in their pay. In the spring of 1904, men had received twenty-five kopecks a day in Kiev and Podol'e. Women in both provinces got twenty kopecks.[136] In April 1905, peasants in Ushits and Kamenets districts in Podol'e asked for fifty for men and thirty for women.[137] Elsewhere, peas-

[136]TsGAOR f. 102, o. 233, d. 2550 ch. 4, l. 16.
[137]AD, 2:168. TsGAOR f. 102, 1905, d. 2550 ch. 41, ll. 85–86.

ants sought a doubling of wages up to fifty or sixty kopecks.[138]
After initial refusals, peasants very often got all or a large part of
what they had demanded. Most landlords were doing well financial-
ly. The price of sugar was steady on the world market, and external
and internal sales were solid. Given the initial low wage levels, it was
possible for them to grant sizable increases and still make substantial profits. According to official statistics, wages for men went up
20 percent in Podol'e and 40 percent in Kiev. Women in both
provinces raised their pay by 25 percent. It was rare that peasants
asked for equal wages for all, despite the fact that women played a
highly visible and important role in all aspects of the movement, not
to mention the economy, in the right bank. There were, however, a
few cases of explicit demands for the same wages for all adults. This
occurred in May, 1905, on the Kashperovsky Company sugar plantation in Kiev.[139] At roughly the same time, the correspondents of
the Free Economic Society reported six instances of villages asking
for equal wages for women and men.[140] Yet the peasant communities of the southwest, despite their special circumstances, were still
substantially patriarchal, and cases of this sort were rare.

During the next two springs, peasants demanded similar wage
increases. The specific amount varied from place to place. During
1906, it still was possible to find demands for such modest levels as
forty-five kopecks in Podol'e.[141] As late as 1907, peasants in the
Kiev village of Nadtochievka sought forty-five kopecks a day.[142]
At the same time, the villagers of Kashperovka (Kiev) asked for and
got fifty kopecks.[143] Requests of this type represented the lower
levels of peasant wage demands, however.

Very quickly, peasants came to fasten on the clear, simple, and
militant demand of one ruble for one day's labor. To ask for a
ruble a day did not require a precise calculation of realizable goals
to be gained in the course of negotiation. Instead, it was a clear and

[138]TsGIAU f. 318, o. 1, d. 336, l. 57. *UD*, 2:334.
[139]*Kievlianin*, May 27, 1905.
[140]*AD*, 2:53.
[141]TsGAOR f. 102, 1907, o. 236, d. 700 ch. 54, l. 64.
[142]TsGIAU f. 442, o. 857, d. 193, l. 30.
[143]Ibid., l. 17.

readily understandable peasant aim that signified a decisive victory over the landlords. Nowhere was this goal achieved, but in asking for what could be a tripling or quadrupling of their pay, peasants were able to win large wage increases. Some of the real value of these gains was eroded by inflation. In addition, wage levels in the southwest were still comparatively low, despite the increases. Nevertheless, pay proved to be one area in which peasants did gain much of what they wanted, and the demand of a ruble a day became an effective rallying point.

Peasants began asking for a ruble a day (for men) as soon as the strike movement began in the spring of 1905. In itself, this was nothing new. As early as 1896, peasants in Podol'e had asked for a ruble a day in the wake of Nicholas II's inauguration.[144] On March 30, 1905, the assembly of heads of households in Solobkivtsy met and decided to ask for a ruble a day for men and fifty kopecks for women.[145] The next month in Zavadovka (Kiev) peasants asked for a ruble (seventy-five kopecks for women).[146] Almost instantaneously, the call for a ruble a day became widespread throughout the southwest. Peasants, for the most part, raised this demand on the sugar plantations of Kiev and Podol'e.[147] The grain-producing estates in Volynia were by no means immune to the call.[148]

The campaign for a ruble a day became the single most common demand throughout the region during the revolutionary period.[149] Nevertheless, documented instances of this demand diminish in 1906 and 1907.[150] When it became clear that landlords could not give them the full, symbolically significant amount, peasants moderated their demands. To get a ruble a day, even if only for men, would have been a significant and unmistakable victory over the landlords. Peasants were unable to win this demand, but they did gain sizable increases in their wages. By striking at the moment of

[144]AD, 2:7.
[145]Leshchenko, 1955, p. 129.
[146]TsGIAU f. 318, o. 1, d. 351, l. 1.
[147]AD, 2:169.
[148]UD, 1:760.
[149]Russkie Vedemosti, May 28, 1905. Kiev, June 24, 1905. Butsik, 1957, p. 28.
[150]TsGIAU f. 442, o. 636, d. 401, l. 2. TsGIAU f. 442, o. 857, d. 195, l. 1.

peak labor demand, they found landlords unwilling to endure long work stoppages. In addition, those who owned the sugar plantations were in a sufficiently advantageous economic position to grant large pay raises and still make healthy profits.[151]

The diminution of demands for a ruble a day is significant. This trend demonstrates that right-bank peasants were able to moderate their demands and focus on more pragmatic goals. Asking for a ruble a day was seen by some in the countryside as unrealistic. It was thought that the true motive of those working on the plantations was to force the landlords to abandon their estates. Industrialists, faced with the demands of striking workers, could protest that large wage increases would drive them out of business, rendering the workers jobless. By contrast, peasants knew what to do with any estate a landlord might abandon. According to this reasoning, peasants in the southwest appeared to have aims similar to their counterparts in central Russia. They too wanted the land immediately. Enormous wage demands were seen as a useful tactic for achieving this traditional peasant goal.

Yet peasants in Kiev, Podol'e, and Volynia did not cling stubbornly to the call for a ruble a day. Instead, they modified their demands as conditions changed, showing an ability to make precise and rational decisions in the course of the struggle. Had they maintained the goal of a ruble a day, one could confidently say that this demand was a ploy, masking traditional claims. But this willingness to show moderation undermines contentions that wage demands, by themselves, had no meaning.

Having said this, it would also be impossible to dismiss the land aspirations of peasants in the southwest. Even though the long-term goal of total repartition was not in the foreground of right-bank peasants' demands, one cannot deny that it constituted a significant element in their thinking. Petitions of southwest peasants to their Duma deputies reveal strong concern with the land question.[152] On this count, the peasants shared the obsession of their counterparts in central Russia, Novorossiia, and the left bank. Drozdov, Maslov, and Dubrovskii have stressed the dis-

[151]Ibid., o. 855, d. 113 ch. 1, ll. 55–59. TsGIAL 1405, o. 107, d. 7578, l. 11.
[152]Terence Emmons, *The First Russian Elections* (Stanford, 1984), p. 244.

tinctiveness of peasant demands in the right bank. On the other hand, such diverse scholars as Geroid Robinson and Leshchenko, citing the "land" basis of huge wage claims, have argued that the peasants of the southwest, much like peasants throughout Russia, sought simply to drive the landlords from the countryside.[153] In this sense, the wage demands could be seen as less than serious. Robinson drew his conclusion from the survey of the Free Economic Society in which those correspondents reporting this phenomenon were, for the most part, landlords and estate managers.[154] Leshchenko, relying primarily on bureaucratic and police documents, found a similar preoccupation among the guardians of order and property.[155] Invariably, those government reports claiming to have unearthed the true nature of peasant demands came from the pens of provincial governors.[156] Given the social origins of those characterizing peasant aims in the right bank, it could be argued that both Robinson and Leshchenko were too prepared to accept the worst fears of the gentry.

Fundamentally, however, there is little real contradiction between those who take right-bank wage demands seriously and those who dismiss them. Peasants in Kiev, Podol'e and Volynia were allotment holders and were well aware of the smallness of their holdings. It would have been unrealistic to expect them not to be concerned with the land question. Land hunger was, after all, the fundamental cause of the movement in this region, just as it was everywhere else. The special acuteness of the problem in the southwest forced peasants to take wage work; this labor contributed a significant portion of the household budget. For this reason, they could not ignore short-term concerns, even if long-term goals were never absent from their thoughts.

Nevertheless, open calls from right-bank peasants for total repartition were exceedingly rare.[157] Not surprisingly, the few peas-

[153]Drozdov, p. 20. Maslov, 1924, p. 40. Dubrovskii, 1955, p. 72. Robinson, p. 206. Leshchenko, 1955, p. 141.

[154]AD, 2:170.

[155]UD, 2:337.

[156]TsGIAU f. 442, o. 855, d. 113 ch. 1, l. 266. TsGAOR f. 102, 1906, d. 700 ch. 54, l. 106. TsGAOR f. 102, 1905, d. 2550 ch. 41, l. 19.

[157]AD, 2:100.

ant demands for the immediate departure of the landlord were nearly all from Volynia, the least agriculturally advanced of the three right-bank provinces.[158] Instead, peasants concentrated on two other types of demands. They asked that parcels of disputed land be given entirely to the village, and they called for landlords to make more land available to rent at reasonable rates.

In 1906, the peasants of Popovaia-Grebnia (Podol'e) wrote to the Duma, asking that hay fields they had used before the emancipation be returned to them. They had tried all legal avenues. They had struck, and now they were turning to the Duma.[159] On Countess Brannitskaia's estate in Kiev, peasants demanded that 50 *desiatiny* they claimed were taken from them in 1861 be restored.[160] The violent disorders on the Podol'e estate of Prince Abamelek-Lazarev were touched off by peasant calls for the use of land that had been in dispute since the 1880s.[161] The governor of Volynia, reporting in November 1905, remarked that one common demand of peasants was for the use of idle land belonging to nobles.[162] On June 19, 1906, peasants in Rubki (Volynia) demanded 27 *desiatiny* for hay raising. The landlord refused, and a strike ensued.[163]

In the right bank, peasants had been unable to compete for land on the open market. Landlords rented their estates to large firms at much higher rates than peasants could possibly afford.[164] Accordingly, peasants often asked that land be made available to them at what they called reasonable rental rates. Demands of this sort were a great deal more common than calls for immediate land siezure.[165] In July 1905, the peasants of Kuzmin, on the Podol'e estate of Alexander Poltovich, asked him to rent 300 *desiatiny* that were not part of his arable land. He refused, and they struck.[166]

[158]Los', p. 245. *AD*, 2:193. TsGIAU f. 442, o. 855, d. 113 ch. 13, l. 17. ZhOGA f. 115, o. 2, d. 2593, l. 10. TsGAOR f. 102, 1906, d. 700 ch. 37, ll. 34–36.
[159]TsGIAL f. 1278, o. 1, d. 291, l. 256.
[160]Ibid., d. 785, l. 253.
[161]*UD*, 2:362.
[162]TsGIAU f. 442, o. 855, d. 391 ch. 4, l. 83.
[163]TsGAOR f. 102, 1906, d. 700, l. 19.
[164]Maslov, 1924, p. 25.
[165]Leshchenko, 1955, p. 101.
[166]TsGIAU f. 442, o. 855, d. 113 ch. 2, l. 36.

During a 1906 strike in Tolmach (Kiev), peasants simply asked for more land to rent at what were called reasonable rates.[167] For strikers in Podol'e, reasonable rates were six rubles per *desiatin*.[168] On the Sakhnovskii estate in Kiev, they were willing to pay five rubles a *desiatin*.[169] As the going market rate varied between twenty-five and thirty rubles a year, it becomes clear that peasants had to resort to extra-economic means to improve their position. As in the case of wages, they were willing to make compromises and accept less than they wanted, but on the matter of renting land they achieved few successes.

Demands for a part of the land were not central to the movement in the southwest. Wages were the most common concern. Almost as widespread was the call for limiting employment on the estates to "local people." In twentieth-century terms, this demand could be termed a "closed shop." On the other hand, it is possible to interpret it as a traditionalist attempt to affirm the cohesion of the village against the outside world. Whatever the case, such demands made sound tactical sense. Faced with strikes, landlords almost always sought to break peasant resistance by hiring workers from nearby villages. Unless they could prevent the use of strikebreakers, the peasants' efforts were doomed to failure. In addition, if they succeeded in limiting the pool from which landlords could draw, they could reasonably hope for higher wages. Thus, peasants always sought limitations on the hiring of "outsiders."[170]

Attempts to limit hiring to local people occurred throughout all three revolutionary years in all three provinces on all kinds of estates. Peasants even voiced this demand in the course of the few strikes that took place in the fall or winter.[171] At other moments, they asked for an interesting variation on limitations against outsiders. In June 1905, in Sumovka (Podol'e), peasants demanded work for all who wanted it. They demanded that the landlord hire

[167]*AD*, 2:196.
[168]Ibid.
[169]TsGIAU f. 318, o. 1, d. 347, ll. 2–51.
[170]*AD*, 2:53, 172, and 198.
[171]TsGIAL f. 1405, 1907, o. 193, d. 2460, l. 5.

all seeking employment or no one would work.[172] On May 7, 1907, peasants in Okninaia (Kiev) opposed a landlord who sought to hire only women. The next day a crowd of 300 men and women appeared on the plantation to demand work for all.[173] By the time the revolutionary period came to an end, the demand for restrictions on the employment of outsiders had become almost as common as calls for higher pay.

Rural cultivators in the right bank also sought to impove their working conditions. They made these demands less often than calls for better pay and restricted hiring. Most often, peasants asked for a shorter working day, usually an eight-hour day. Peasants demanded better conditions throughout the southwest, but most commonly in Kiev and Podol'e, the main sites of sugar production. Peasants had little luck on this issue.[174] Owners of sugar plantations were especially opposed to any concessions on working hours.[175] Even more moderate demands for a nine-hour day or simply shorter hours were rarely met.[176] Part of the landlords' resistance may have been based on what had become the well-known symbolic meaning of the eight-hour day in the urban struggle. This demand had acquired a highly charged political significance in the wake of the crushing of the Moscow uprising during December 1905. That movement had made the eight-hour day its central aim, and it had been on this issue that the unity of the antitsarist movement had split in the wake of the October Manifesto. For peasants to have asked for an eight-hour day demonstrated an awareness, however dim and imprecise, of events in the cities.

Those who worked the estates of the southwest also sought "respectful and humane treatment" from their employers. This demand bears special attention. It appeared nowhere else in rural Russia during the revolutionary period. More important, it suggests a consciously proletarian, political, perhaps even revolution-

---

[172]TsGAOR f. 102, 1905, d. 2550 ch. 41, l. 133.
[173]TsGIAU f. 442, o. 857, d. 193, l. 19.
[174]Shestakov, 1907, p. 27.
[175]VSP 15 (1905), 1.
[176]Butsik, 1957, p. 11. Leshchenko, 1955, p. 134.

ary awareness on the part of peasants and agricultural workers in
the right bank. It would be an exaggeration to describe this demand as universal. Nevertheless, it did appear with some frequency.[177]

Correspondents of the Free Economic Society reported that
peasants made requests for respectful treatment but reporters did
not always specify what the peasants meant by the term.[178] A
police report from Podol'e stressed the strikers' strong protest
against the "inhuman treatment" by a large-scale renter who did
not allow them to drink water during the working day.[179] Peasants
in Didovshchina (Kiev) refused to agree to return to work, despite
some concessions, because of the "lack of respect" shown them by
the landlord.[180] In Novyi Chartori (Volynia), striking peasants
made this an explicit demand along with calls for higher wages and
the eight-hour day.[181] Strikers on Count Bobrinskii's Kiev estate,
where urban workers actually were involved, asked for the same
things.[182]

Labor relations on K. K. Sangushko's Volynia estate were particularly poor. He had experienced several strikes, and peasants complained to local authorities that they especially resented his "lack
of respect" for them.[183] They were incensed with the behavior of
Sangushko's estate manager who forced peasants to bow down
before him.[184] In Pikova (Podol'e), villagers protested the "inhuman treatment" carried on by the large-scale renter of the Ol'shevskii estate.[185] During a strike in Koshevati (Kiev) peasants demanded that the plantation administrator explain why he beat
their children.[186] Strikers at Zhidovets (Kiev) presented a list of
twenty demands including respectful treatment and the right to
elect their own foremen.[187]

---

[177]Shestakov, 1930, p. 33.
[178]AD, 2:15, 100, and 408.
[179]UD, 2:353.
[180]AD, 2:203.
[181]Ibid., p. 188.
[182]Ibid., p. 177.
[183]TsGIAU f. 442. o. 855, d. 109, l. 105.
[184]TsGIAU f. 442, o. 855, d. 109, l. 111.
[185]TsGAOR f. 102, 1905, d. 2550 ch. 4, l. 32.
[186]Butsik, 1957, p. 27.
[187]Ibid., p. 11.

The insistence on personal dignity is striking for two reasons. First, the southwest was the only rural region where this demand appeared during the Revolution of 1905. Second, these kinds of concerns were extremely significant in the highly militant and political strike movement in Petersburg on the eve of the First World War and in the army during 1917. In both cases, the consequences of these demands were explosive. That peasants and other laborers in the right bank should have such aims is not surprising, given the character of agriculture in the region. The lord-peasant relationship had been eroded but not destroyed in central Russia. Despite its obvious exploitative character, it was still a human relationship in which the lord had certain obligations to the peasant. Landlords in the southwest were seeking to abandon that traditional relationship as they modified agricultural practices. In making this shift, landowners abandoned paternalism. They now viewed the peasants simply as employees.

The demand for respectful treatment usually appeared along with calls for a constituent assembly and universal suffrage. This coupling suggests the influence of outside political agitators.[188] Yet political activists in the countryside offered a number of demands and programs to peasants and other rural cultivators. Not all these ideas elicited a positive response. Those who worked the plantations of Kiev, Podol'e, and Volynia came to adopt a demand that would later become a central aspect of a highly politicized, urban movement. The entire structure of peasant demands in the right bank underscores this fact. The concerns of rural cultivators were largely dictated by the conditions that confronted them. They behaved differently than peasants elsewhere in Russia and the Ukraine, because the conditions they faced were different.

A familiar dialectic appeared to be at work. The appearance of capitalist agriculture had induced peasants to copy the tactics and demands of city workers. The conversion to sugar beet production on landlord estates had caused rural cultivators in the right bank to become partly proletarianized. In confronting the estate owners, the women and men who worked the plantations did not act in the supposedly irrational ways associated with traditional peasants. Lenin had ascribed a measure of proletarian consciousness to rural

[188]Maslov, 1924, pp. 124–26. TsGIAL f. 1405, o. 108, d. 6824, ll. 2, 6, and 7.

workers whose lives had been affected by agricultural progress. The actions of right-bank peasants appear to support his contention.

Yet capitalism had come to Kiev, Podol'e, and Volynia by the "Prussian path." Commercial agriculture was a landlord, not a peasant, venture. This fact meant that capitalist relations of production influenced the lives of right-bank peasants primarily in their contacts with estate owners. Peasant agriculture was still primitive. Within the villages, many traditional structures and practices persisted. For this reason, those in the southwest who worked the land could emulate only some of the practices of urban proletarians. They chose the strike weapon, but they did not always use it in the same manner as their counterparts in the cities.

The economic situations of right-bank peasants mirrored the experience of the urban worker only in limited ways. By some standards (primarily wage work) the peasants had become proletarianized. By others, they still retained the characteristics of peasants. They were, in fact, semi-proletarian, and their political actions were similarly mixed.

4

A Peasant Movement—
Patterns and Participants

Because agrarian capitalism in the southwest was organized by landlords, peasant agriculture had advanced little. The availability of wage work on the estates allowed peasants to stay in the countryside, rather than move to the cities. They continued to live in communes that retained many traditional practices. Peasant capitalism would have undermined the old structures, but peasant capitalism was scarcely in evidence in the right bank. The persistence of traditional institutions meant that the peasants of Kiev, Podol'e, and Volynia organized their strikes in specifically rural ways. Social cohesion proved to be the norm. The assembly of heads of households played a crucial if diminished role, and landless laborers found themselves on the outside at most crucial moments.

Strike Scenarios

Between the spring of 1905 and the summer of 1907, more than 2,000 strikes took place in the right bank. Nearly all of these manifestations appeared to follow a well-understood script from which there were few variations. The logic of wage labor on the southwest's large estates dictated actions undertaken by the peasants. There was little need to improvise. Both the Social Democrat, Shestakov, and the governor of Kiev, Savich, were struck by this fact. The strikes, they each noted separately, were "all of one type."[1] Indeed, a reading of the available police reports on the strikes leaves one with the impression that the peasants had received instructions from some central source. So uniform were their actions that it is possible to construct a scenario of the typical strike. The only significant variation concerned violence between local peasants and strikebreakers. These kinds of confrontations occurred 80 percent of the time.[2] The peasants of the southwest quickly learned the methods, logic, and order of the agrarian strike. They used this weapon until it was no longer effective.

In their homes or in the fields, peasant men and women discussed their grievances and refused to work. Often this step came in response to a specific provocation from the landlord. In other cases, peasants learned of higher wages in other villages and sought the same for themselves. At this point, they called a meeting of the assembly of heads of households. Demands were formulated, and the *skhod* informally assumed the role of a strike committee. No one hesitated to use this traditional institution in this manner. It was, after all, the place peasants met to discuss most matters of importance. Even in the hereditary communes of the west and south, the assembly contributed to peasant cohesion.[3] Ad hoc meetings in the woods and independent strike committees took

[1]TsGAOR f. 102, 1905, o. 233, d. 2550 ch. 4, l. 23. Shestakov, 1930, p. 23. *Kievlianin,* June 2, 1905.

[2]Leshchenko, 1955, p. 128. Soviet archival authorities made available detailed police or bureaucratic reports on 244 strikes. If we are to believe Leshchenko's probably inflated figures, this material would comprise 10 percent of the total of strikes. Unfortunately one can do little to quantify the information in the documents I was allowed to see. Roughly the same number of reports was made available from all three provinces. Yet, 90 percent of the strikes occurred in Kiev and Podol'e. Although the archival accounts correspond in their details to the descriptions in published materials, one can make no easy assumptions about their typicality. The overrepresentation of Volynia in the sample of documents is, in part, the result of my access to the Zhitomir regional archive. Zhitomir was the capital of Volynia. Similar materials were not available for Kiev and Podol'e.

[3]TsGIAU f. 442, o. 857, d. 221, l. 2. TsGAOR f. 102, 1907, o. 236, d. 700 ch. 54, l. 60.

place far less frequently, especially in the initial stages of the movement.

After the village assemblies met, peasants organized deputations to present demands to manor houses or company offices. In nearly every case, the initial requests were refused. Strikes then began in earnest. In response, landlords hired strikebreakers. These outsiders were either landless laborers or, more often, peasants from other villages.[4] Local villagers understood full well the disastrous implications of allowing strikebreakers to work on the estates. Peasants consistently demanded limiting employment to "local people." Accordingly, peasants bent all efforts to preventing strikebreakers from working the large estates. If force was required, then force was used. Clashes between outsiders and local peasants were the rule, not the exception. On the roads leading to estates, peasants, armed with the usual arsenal of pitchforks, axes, sticks, and rocks, confronted strikebreakers. Later on, peasants from other villages, whether from fear or solidarity, would refuse to accept work as strikebreakers.[5] Initially, however, bloody clashes were common.

The hiring and subsequent repelling of outsiders always proved a crucial moment in any strike. These clashes provided the excuse for landlords to summon the authorities to repress the strikers.[6] In general, the government, especially after the appointment of Stolypin as Minister of Interior in 1906, sought to defend the gentry. In the localities, however, soldiers and policemen from time to time expressed reluctance to come to the aid of the more odious landlords. Yet, by and large, the guardians of order engaged in a wide range of summary arrests, executions, beatings, and burnings of peasant dwellings in order to defend landlord property.[7]

Soldiers or gendarmes would appear at a striking village. Strike leaders would be arrested, but the work would not resume.[8] Often

[4]UD, 2:337. TsGIAL f. 1405, o. 108, d. 6861, l. 3. TsGAOR f. 102, 1905, d. 2550 ch. 4, l. 1. TsGIAU f. 442, o. 855, d. 526, l. 26.
[5]AD, 2:125, 229, and 231.
[6]Ibid., p. 36.
[7]UD, 2:203.
[8]AD, 2:198. Maslov, 1924, p. 26. Leshchenko, 1955, p. 81.

peasants demanded the release of their arrested comrades, leading to clashes with the police. Soldiers might be stationed in a village, but the strike would continue. Peasants would not return to work until at least some of their demands had been met. Women day laborers, in particular, were able to rely on the food and money generated by the allotments worked by their families. Usually, strikers won victories on wage matters: sugar beet prices were rising, and landlords had the funds to pay increases to workers. By 1907, however, repression was so universal and severe that not even the right-bank peasants could resist it. By then the countryside was peaceful once again.

Events in Popovaia (Podol'e) during May 1905 closely followed the well-understood script. Some 160 men and women stopped work on the local sugar plantation and asked the manager for a raise from thirty to sixty kopecks a day. When they were refused, they went on strike and succeeded in getting day workers from a neighboring village to join them. On May 23 (the next day), a crowd of 500 men and women marched onto the plantation's fields and removed 60 landless wage laborers who left without a struggle. The next morning 1,000 peasants appeared on the estate and met 800 strikebreakers who had been brought in from neighboring villages. With some limited force, these outsiders were driven off. The local peasants then surrounded the lord's livestock to prevent it from grazing and convinced his household servants to join the strike. In a few days, the estate owner gave in to their demands.[9]

Other strikes followed slightly different patterns. Also during May in Germanovskaia Slobodka (Kiev), during the second day of a strike on the sugar plantation of Mikhail Savchenko, a crowd of 600 men and women marched on the lord's manor house. Very shortly, 50 peasants were chasing Savchenko's wife around her house, shouting, "The devil take you. Give us work. We want to eat." Quickly and wisely, Savchenko yielded to their demand of fifty kopecks a day. The peasants, however, insisted on a written agreement witnessed by local authorities.[10] Earlier in May, much

[9]TsGAOR f. 102, 1905, d. 2550 ch. 4, ll. 85–86.
[10]UD, 2:349.

the same pattern prevailed on the Podol'e estate of Peter Balashev, one of the province's wealthiest lords. Strikebreakers were also brought in, but local peasants convinced them to leave, after which Balashev acceded to their wage demands.[11]

Nonstrike Scenarios

Not all the disorders in the right bank were strikes. Disturbances like those in central Russia were far from uncommon. On May 24, 1905, an accidental fire began in a building on the Podol'e estate of Stanislav Kholonevskii. To extinguish the blaze, Kholonevskii set off with water taken from a well he had forbidden the peasants to use. Learning of this, 100 men and women surrounded him. Yelling and screaming, they threatened him with the usual peasant arsenal. He promised to let them use the well in the future, but the peasants simply encircled him and allowed the building to burn to the ground.[12]

Peasants in Volynia were equally threatening and direct. Several of them were arrested near Zhitomir for stealing mushrooms in the course of a forest offense. When asked why he had taken the mushrooms, one peasant replied with characteristic directness, "I don't like *borshch* without mushrooms."[13]

Other nonstrike activity involved resistance to the plans of modernizing landlords. Peasants did not welcome the conversion of an estate to sugar production. This step may have created jobs, but, more important, it took away land. In April 1907, peasants in Kachanovka (Podol'e) continued a confrontation with a landlord who was converting from a three-field to an eight-field rotation. In doing this, he diminished the amount of fallow land peasants could use to graze their livestock. On April 24, they let their animals loose on the disputed land. They repeated this act over several days despite an increasing police presence. Eventually arrests took place.

[11]TsGIAU f. 442, o. 855, d. 526, l. 24. TsGAOR f. 102, 1905, d. 2550 ch. 41, l. 36.

[12]TsGIAL f. 1405, o. 108, d. 6823, ll. 14–15.

[13]*Volyn'*, June 12, 1905.

In response, 1,000 peasants massed and marched to the estate's office in order to free their fellow villagers. In the face of such a crowd, the police had no choice but to let the arrested go. Illegal pasturing then resumed. When police appeared to halt this new round of activity, the village church bell was rung, and a crowd of 1,000 quickly appeared in the fields to confront the police. The peasants had pitchforks, axes, sticks, rocks, shovels, and rakes. The police had guns. Vastly outnumbered, the police used their weapons to disperse the peasants, wounding two in the process.[14] Incidents of this sort were common in central Russia between 1905 and 1907. They also happened in Kiev, Podol'e, and Volynia, but strikes proved the most common form of the movement.

Peasant Violence, Official Force

Peasants in the southwest set few fires and destroyed few estates, but this did not signify any special restraint in the use of force. Peasant violence in the right bank was primarily defensive, initiated either to prevent arrests of fellow villagers or stop work by strikebreakers. Yet violence was common, and it gave landlords suitable reasons for summoning the army and gendarmerie. Of course, members of these repressive forces could not, by themselves, till the fields of the southwest's plantations, but they were able to exact a heavy toll on the peasantry. Most detailed accounts of peasant confrontations with the authorities came from local police. These reports usually describe the actions of a group of guardians of order who were summoned to protect the property or person of a local landlord. The soldiers or police would order peasants to cease whatever illegal acts they were committing. They also might enter a village with the intention of arresting so-called instigators. When peasants resisted these demands, police and soldiers felt they had no choice but to use force. They always claimed to have fired warning shots. When peasants continued to resist, the next step was a volley into the crowd. Inevitably, deaths and injuries resulted, and these were always reported.

[14]TsGIAL f. 1405, o. 194, d. 117, l. 3.

One of Savich's reports to the governor-general of the southwest, N. Kleigels, described this pattern of police action. Savich depicted the events of May 24, 1905, on the estate of Baroness Wrangel' in Kozatskii (Kiev). Some 200 peasants refused to work for thirty kopecks a day. They then marched to the estate's distillery where they got the staff to join them. Soon, this crowd was confronted by 10 soldiers who had orders to arrest Kornei Sych, a peasant they claimed was the leader of the strike. It was, after all, a crime, in the police's words, "to disturb economic relations between workers and landowners."[15] Sych, however, refused to go along. The crowd was then supposed to have said, "If you take Sych, you'll have to take all of us." At this point, according to Savich, the 200 peasants attacked the 10 soldiers, seeking to take away their rifles. After a warning shot, a peasant named Luka Kudym told his fellows, "Don't be afraid, brothers. The soldiers are shooting with blanks." The soldiers fired again, this time into the crowd, killing 2 peasants. The crowd quickly dispersed.[16]

The account of July 1906, in Korzheva (Kiev) was also typical of official views of peasant violence. According to the indictment of the Kiev court (*Kievskaia sudebnaia palata*), peasants on the estate of Vladislav Podgarskii demanded more money for the harvest of winter grain. They stopped working and, using force, got day laborers and household servants to join them. On July 19, 1906, 50 cossacks, the most feared guardians of order, were sent to the village to arrest leaders. The cossacks entered a meeting of the *skhod* and informed the peasants of the illegality of their acts. The peasants refused to turn over anyone to the cossacks. In fact, the peasants claimed they had no idea who the leaders were. In response to this resistance, the cossacks went door to door, taking grain and chickens. Soon a crowd of 200 massed in front of the village church to protest the expropriations. The cossacks then claimed they heard three revolver shots. In response, they fired the usual warning shot which went unheeded, whereupon they fired on the crowd, killing 2 women.[17]

[15]TsGIAU f. 318, o. 1, d. 349. l. 59.
[16]Ibid., f. 442, o. 855, d. 115 ch. 2, ll. 26–27.
[17]*UD*, 2:227.

Correspondents of the Free Economic Society gave an even more graphic picture of repression in the right bank. They described soldiers pulling peasants out of their huts and destroying their homes in several Kiev villages. They claimed cossacks were "unrestrained" in whipping, beating, and shooting peasants.[18] In Ol'shanitsa, during the spring of 1905, dragoons occupied the village for six weeks, forcing peasants to feed and supply them.[19] In 1906, police in a number of Kiev villages broke up meetings of several assemblies of heads of households.[20] Peasants complained to their Duma deputies. For example, villagers from Zherdenevka (Podol'e) said that soldiers had been lodged there for ten days. They had broken into their cupboards, demanded money, taken grain and poultry, and attacked fourteen-year-old girls.[21]

Some bureaucrats, soldiers, and police often had mixed feelings about their duties. Within the administration, there was a range of views, concerning the propriety and limits of government action on behalf of the landlords who, of course, expected immediate assistance in moments of peril.[22] Governor-General Kleigels, in particular, advocated swift and ruthless action.[23] Many troops were away at the Far Eastern front and the movement was so massive that provincial governors often had to choose whom to defend. Police were not fond of intervening on behalf of landlords with especially bad reputations; for example K. K. Sangushko, who had a particularly difficult relationship with the Volynia gendarmerie.[24] Soldiers also did not like the constant patrol that was required in the first months of the movement, during the spring of 1905.[25] On the other hand, landlords were unhappy with the work of the lowest level of government bureaucrat in the countryside, the *mirovye posredniki*. These figures worked closely with the peasantry. Landlords thought they had advance knowledge of disturbances and strikes, knowledge

[18]*AD*, 2:198.
[19]Ibid., p. 175.
[20]Ibid., p. 260.
[21]TsGIAL f. 1278, o. 1, d. 695, l. 8.
[22]*AD*, 2:36.
[23]TsGIAU f. 442, o. 855, d. 109, l. 23.
[24]Ibid., l. 111.
[25]TsGAOR f. 102, 1905, o. 233, d. 2550 ch. 4, l. 12.

that was not shared with the landlords. At times, *mirovye posredniki* even called assemblies of heads of households to warn peasants of the illegality of their impending actions. This, however, did not satisfy many landlords.[26]

In contrast to Kleigels and Savich, A. A. Eiler, the governor of Podol'e, sought to have those below him play a mediating role.[27] He warned landlords that they could not count on protection unless they made concessions on wages.[28] In particular, Eiler became embroiled in a heated controversy with one landlord, Prince Gudim-Levkovich, who used convict labor on his estate in order to avoid paying the local peasantry. Eiler pointed out the potential dangers of this course, not the least of which involved allowing prisoners out of jail. Gudim-Levkovich was, predictably, incensed and wrote to both Eiler and Kleigels, claiming that Eiler was merely seeking a way to avoid his responsibility to repress the peasantry.[29]

In the light of the autocracy's need to favor industrialization, the interests and views of the government and the landed nobility had long ceased to be identical. Differences of this sort were inevitable, but generally exceptional. In the end, the guardians of order came to the defense of the landlords and exacted a severe price from the peasantry. This repression led to the loss of thousands of peasant lives in the southwest, as well as in the rest of the empire. More than any other single factor, it was the state's use of force that brought the peasant movement to an end.

Patterns of Participation

The steps taken by striking peasants shed light on one of our central questions. Which of the village strata took part in the movement? Long before 1905, revolutionaries had searched for those elements of the peasantry most likely to exhibit militant opposition to the landlords and the state. After 1905, policymakers

[26]TsGIAU f. 442, o. 855, d. 526, l. 11.
[27]Ibid., d. 113 ch. 1, l. 12.
[28]Ibid., l. 34.
[29]Ibid., ll. 187, 198, and 213.

and scholars continued to debate this most central of political questions, much as they do today. Historians have generally stressed the cohesiveness of the entire rural population during what is called the first Russian revolution. Soviet writers have not sought to challenge this conclusion. Instead, they have argued that the experience represented only a first phase of the struggle in which the entire peasantry opposed the gentry and the autocracy. With the central Russian experience in mind, S. M. Dubrovskii was reluctant to assign a paramount role to poor peasants and landless laborers even in the right bank.[30] On the other hand, Leshchenko and Los', the leading Soviet specialists on the Ukraine, continually stressed the role of what they called "day laborers and *batraks*." Leshchenko went so far as to argue that "agricultural proletarians and semi-proletarians were in the vanguard of the movement."[31] On the surface, there would appear to be some basis for such a claim, especially given the importance of wage labor and the overall poverty of the peasantry.

Moshe Lewin and Teodor Shanin have made abundantly clear that the standard categories for dividing the peasantry are quite imprecise. Criteria that may seem meaningful in a general sense often become useless when analyzing specific situations. The terms "poor," "middle," and "rich" are best used relatively, for what was rich in the right bank might have been poor by the standards of central Russia. The uncertain definition of the term *kulak* would later have the most deadly consequences after the revolution at the time of collectivization. Nor is it possible to be entirely sure that the *batrak* (landless peasant) was the pure rural proletarian on which the Bolsheviks would place so much hope, both in 1905 and later.

The imprecision of the meaning of *batrak* has special significance in the analysis of the strike movement in the southwest. The sources, published and unpublished, make repeated references to "*batraks*," "agricultural workers," "day laborers," "monthly workers," and "period workers." Yet the same sources emphasize the role of "peasants" and the organizing function of the assembly

[30]Dubrovskii, 1955, p. 15.
[31]Los', p. 183; Leshchenko, 1955, p. 5.

of heads of households during the disturbances. These facts made it clear that *pure* rural proletarians, agricultural workers, were not at the center of the strike movement. The large number of female wage workers, members of allotment-holding households, suggests that landless male laborers were far from a majority of those who worked the estates in this region. Despite the extent of wage labor in the right bank, landless laborers dominated neither village life nor the strike movement.

Instead, poor peasants, Lenin's semi-proletarians, led the disturbances in the southwest. They did not do this, however, by consistently opposing rich or middle peasants. Because landlords had retained so much land and because they rented little of it to peasants, the total amount of land available to peasants in the southwest was extremely small. If one uses, as do most Soviet scholars, the admittedly crude criterion of sown area, the majority of peasants in the right bank fell into the so-called poor category. Middle peasants were a minority, and rich, landowning peasants were rare.[32] The movement, therefore, was led by peasants who were truly poor. The majority of the region's rural cultivators were poor peasants, just as middle peasants were thought to be the largest of the village strata in central Russia. This meant that the special theoretical significance of the role of the right bank's poor was necessarily limited.

In the words of a correspondent of the Free Economic Society in Zvenigorod district (Kiev), "Here all the peasants are the same—poor. . . . In the villages a rich peasant is a rarity."[33] In short, if poor peasants led the movement in the southwest, this occurred because most peasants there were poor. As in central Russia, the movement appears to have been carried out by most of the region's peasantry. In central Russia, the majority of peasants fell into the middle category. In the right bank, most of them were poor. This fact led to the appearance of the same kind of political cohesion in the southwest that Shanin and others claim existed elsewhere in Russia. Although the forms of the movement in the right bank were sharply different from those elsewhere in Russia, the absence

[32]AD, 2:103.
[33]Ibid., p. 105.

of intrapeasant class tension was much the same as the general experience.

Surprisingly, the correspondents of the Free Economic Society were the only firsthand observers who were concerned with the class character of the participants in the movement. They generally noted that all social and economic levels of the southwest's villages participated not only in strikes but in the more spontaneous and disorganized disturbances as well.[34] The general need of all was so great that differences within the peasantry appeared minimal in the face of the struggle with the landlords.[35]

Although Free Economic Society correspondents stressed cohesion, they did note that the movement was met with indifference or even hostility by what were called "prosperous" (*zazhitochnyi*) peasants.[36] This term was broadly used to describe anyone from a stable middle peasant up to a *kulak*. Landowning peasants did not take part in the strike movement. They did participate in forest offenses, and at exceptional moments were, themselves, the victims of peasant violence.[37] Peasant attacks on *kulaks* and other wealthy villagers were rare, however.

At the Voitsovtsy strike, all levels of wealth and age took part.[38] Poor peasants controlled the strike at the F. I. Tereshchenko estate, but middle peasants also participated there.[39] On the Podol'e estate of Admiral Chikhachev, the Free Economic Society's correspondent reported that "the solidarity, order, and lack of opposition were staggering."[40] In Iampolsk and Gaisin districts (Podol'e), middle peasants led strikes while the poor and rich stayed on the sidelines.[41] The same phenomenon took place in Bratslav (Podol'e) and Chigirin districts (Kiev).[42] Elsewhere in Chigirin and in nearby

[34]Ibid., p. 58. TsGAOR f. 102, 1906, o. 236, d. 700 ch. 54, l. 93.

[35]*AD*, 2:139. TsGIAU f. 442, o. 855, d. 526. l. 3.

[36]*AD*, 2:21.

[37]TsGIAU f. 318, o. 1, d. 817, l. 2. TsGAOR f. 102, 1907, o. 236, d. 700 ch. 54, l. 75.

[38]*AD*, 2:142.

[39]Ibid., p. 174.

[40]Ibid., p. 170.

[41]Ibid., pp. 58 and 193.

[42]Ibid., pp. 27 and 60. Correspondents did not always name specific villages in their reports. Instead, they merely mentioned the district (*uezd*) in which disorders occurred.

Radomylsk district (Kiev) poor peasants led strikes that were opposed not only by the wealthy but by the middle strata as well.[43]
Only in the villages of Lebedin (Chigirin district, Kiev) and Prus
(Cherkass district, Podol'e) did the pattern of participation resemble the expected Bolshevik scenario, with poor and middle peasants opposing *kulaks* and landlords. According to the Free Economic Society's correspondent in Lebedin,

> The strike was carried on in a friendly manner. There was class
> emnity for the landlord. Nevertheless, the leading elements were the
> youth and the poor peasants. The middle groups were not especially
> interested in the strike as they did not work on the estate. . . . The
> rich simply chuckled.[44]

In Prus, "all were divided into two camps. The poor and middle
peasants participated in strikes, while the rich acted as one with the
landlord."[45]

This highly mixed picture given by the Free Economic Society's
correspondents is not contradicted by any of the available archival
evidence. Policemen, judges, and bureaucrats produced this material, and they were uninterested in this particular issue. They did
not care to know the precise level of the village from which striking
peasants came. Quite simply, the local authorities thought all those
involved were dangerous. They were not seeking allies, only criminals. Although it is true poor peasants led the strike movement, it
appears they did not do so with consistent opposition from any
other element among the peasantry. Only those who had purchased land were antagonistic to the strikers, but such peasants
were so few that they could not be said to have played a significant
role in the right-bank.

Agricultural workers have so far been omitted from this discussion. Their situation proved highly precarious, and they found it
difficult to play the role assigned them by Lenin and most Soviet
scholars. Though landless laborers most often took part, in no way
could they be described as "the vanguard of the movement." Rural

[43]Ibid., p. 106.
[44]Ibid.
[45]Ibid., p. 22.

proletarians confronted situations that were fundamentally different from those facing their supposed urban counterparts. They
were not members of the village communes where they worked.
They could not participate in the functions of the central social
institution in the Russian and Ukrainian countryside. This body
(the *skhod*) was responsible for much of the cohesion that the
peasantry was able to demonstrate. Rural proletarians had no similar mechanism to bring them together.

The social relations that supported political cohesion were not
created by the labor process itself, as was the case in the city. The
plantation field was not a factory. The processes of interaction that
took place on the factory floor and in the working-class neighborhood did not occur in the fields with quite the same ease.
Laborers were often physically separated from each other. There
were few regularly frequented meeting points, and dispersed living
conditions made constant contact and exchange difficult. Mobiliz-
ing rural proletarians was far more difficult than organizing urban
workers. This has been true in modern commercial agriculture as
well: as has been seen since the 1960s in California, the task of
organizing farm workers on the vast factory farms of the Central
and Imperial valleys has been a difficult and trying process.

Peasant mistrust of outsiders was a central element of their political behavior. Of course landless laborers were not the same sort of
enemy as landlords or soldiers, but they were also outsiders and
therefore mistrusted. Landlords continually used these workers as
strikebreakers. This practice created an obvious tension between
rural proletarians (strictly defined) and poor peasants with some
land, the so-called semi-proletariat. Agricultural workers were social and cultural outsiders. Their work situations created few significant social and political relationships. Accordingly, those within the community viewed agricultural workers with suspicion. The
situation of the rural proletariat was by no means identical with
that of the poor peasantry. As a result, these two groups behaved
quite differently in the course of the strike movement.

The record of landless laborers in the southwest was not one of
unremitting militance and leadership. Rather, those who fit the
strict definition of rural proletarian played a hesitant and fearful
role. Their reluctance had its roots in the processes described by

Eric Wolf.[46] The precariousness of their situation was more a source of fear than of revolutionary fervor. Instead of behaving like employed city workers, they acted much like Marx's urban *lumpenproletariat* of drifters, beggars, and petty criminals who composed an amorphous pool of support for political conservatives and proto-fascists. Their fear made landless laborers well suited for strikebreaking. In time, it became possible to overcome that fear. Meanwhile, assuring the participation of the propertyless required the best efforts of the peasantry, the poor peasants in particular.

The landless depended on a daily wage for survival. As a result, they lacked what Wolf called "tactical mobility." They could not retreat to their allotments to ride out a strike.[47] When work was halted, they always demonstrated an initial reluctance. According to Savich's report on events in Kiev, "*batraks* and day laborers" joined strikes only after they had been forced to do so by regular peasants.[48] They had been reluctant to take part, in Savich's opinion, precisely because of their complete dependence.

Initially, peasants had to use physical force to coerce the landless into participating. Soon, however, more benign forms of solidarity emerged. Peasants began to subsidize the landless with food collections.[49] Often, the village assembly would designate a portion of the harvest to aid the landless.[50] In Mogilev (Podol'e), striking peasants simply took up a collection to aid agricultural workers who had at first expressed fear.[51] The hesitancy of the landless was not the result of any conscious political antipathy toward peasant goals. Rather, the absence of militance was caused by the lack of tactical options in a strike situation. Despite many cases of rural proletarians exhibiting full solidarity with peasant strikers, there is no case in the available sources of the landless actually leading a strike, playing a "vanguard" role.

Some observers went so far as to say that this initial reluctance was simply a self-protective tactic to avoid reprisals from land-

[46]Wolf, 1969, p. 52.
[47]*AD*, 2:211.
[48]*UD*, 2:334.
[49]*AD*, 2:23.
[50]Ibid., p. 212.
[51]Ibid., pp. 60, 170, and 232.

lords; therefore, it was incorrect to assume a lack of militance on the part of the landless. Maslov claimed such an approach was common throughout Podol'e.[52] Correspondents of the Free Economic Society confirmed this view.[53] But opinions of this sort were decidedly in the minority.

The experience of rural proletarians in the right bank during 1905 confirms much of Wolf's picture. In time, landless laborers were able to overcome their initial reluctance to participate, but these steps were nearly always made with the assistance of allotment-holding peasants. Although cohesion was usually achieved, it became necessary to overcome a fundamental tension between the needs and fears not only of landless laborers but of poor peasants as well. Peasants were afraid that agricultural workers could easily be used as strikebreakers, while workers feared that peasant militance could cause their wages to be cut off. The interests of the landless and the poor peasant were, therefore, not identical. The record of their behavior during the strike movement in the southwest suggests that lumping them together into the same leadership group overlooks serious differences in their situations. Even in a region with much wage labor and extensive strike activity, landless laborers played a secondary role that was not the same as that of the peasant.

Peasant Leadership

If it is difficult to specify which groups participated in the disorders, it is even harder to pinpoint what kinds of people became its leaders. The movement in the right bank did not produce any visible regional leaders. Peasants who became instigators and agitators rarely acted beyond the boundaries of their villages. The police paid special attention to identifying and arresting "instigators" in the belief that such actions would strike fear into the peasantry and quiet the rest of the village. This approach proved useless. The forces of order could only guess which individuals

[52]Maslov, 1924, p. 18.
[53]*AD*, 2:108 and 171.

required special attention. When they went so far as to name individuals, they rarely described any of the "instigator's" characteristics. Police and soldiers also found that their attempts to enter villages and arrest so-called leaders were met with violent resistance from the entire community.[54]

The case of Phillip Skirda of Kumeika (Kiev) was typical. On July 1, 1906, 20 soldiers entered the village to arrest the leaders of a recent strike. They quickly found 3 of the men they wanted. Immediately, they were surrounded by a crowd of local peasants. At this point, Skirda was strolling jauntily down the village street; he saw the soldiers just as they saw him. Skirda ran for his life but was chased by the soldiers who quickly captured him. At this point he yelled, "Brothers, don't let them take me. Save me from these scorpions." The village responded and quickly a crowd of 200 peasants surrounded the soldiers and began beating them. The soldiers escaped, only to be confronted by another large group coming from the opposite direction. According to the indictment, the soldiers fired the usual warning shot which had no effect. They then sent a volley toward the crowd, killing 1 and wounding 2. At this point, the peasants prudently dispersed and the soldiers took the arrested to jail.[55]

In the face of government attempts to pinpoint and arrest leaders, peasants responded with solidarity. Quite often, they told police or soldiers that they would have to arrest the entire village, if they took a particular individual.[56] Peasants simply refused to admit there were any significant differences between those who instigated disorders and the rest of the village. From time to time a village elder or a worker from the city might be pointed out by informers as a leader but such incidents were exceptional.[57]

The police may well have thought the people they arrested actually were leaders. Peasants, on the other hand, contended that

---

[54]TsGIAU f. 442, o. 857, d. 195, l. 5. TsGIAU f. 318, o. 1, d. 830, l. 2. *UD*, 6:229.

[55]TsGIAU f. 318, o. 1, d. 1334, l. 2.

[56]TsGIAU f. 442, o. 855, d. 113 ch. 2, ll. 26, 27, and 42. TsGIAU f. 318, o. 1, d. 1346, l. 1.

[57]TsGIAL 1405, o. 116, d. 628, l. 6. TsGIAU f. 442, o. 857, d. 195, l. 6. TsGIAU f. 318, o. 1, 1344, l. 2.

those apprehended were simply ordinary villagers. Limited evidence seems to indicate that the peasants were right. Either there was little to distinguish instigators from other peasants, or the authorities took in unruly villagers largely at random.

It was generally the case that the village youth had played an especially militant role throughout rural Russia. In the right bank, young men were joined by the rest of the village. Information concerning the age of arrested peasants was available on 313 individuals charged in all three provinces in 1905, 1906, and 1907. Their average age was thirty-three, and those arrested ranged from thirteen to sixty-five. Quite a few peasants in their fifties and sixties came to trial. In addition, a considerable portion of the 313 arrested peasants, some 70, were women. Given the importance of women in the labor process and the frequency with which they were mentioned as strike participants, it is not surprising that so many of them were arrested.[58]

By and large, we know little about the thousands of peasants who were arrested in the southwest during the revolutionary period. At the time of their arraignment, peasants answered certain basic questions about themselves and gave preliminary statements. It was possible to find only 135 of these questionnaires in the records of the Kiev court (*Kievskaia sudebnaia palata*).[59] Most of the peasants' statements are of little use. All villagers, even those caught in hand-to-hand combat with the police, denied any involvement in the disorders. Most claimed to have been somewhere else. If they did not deny their own participation, they always claimed to have been coerced by others.

If the 135 statements were unreliable and tell us little, the same cannot be said of the more factual information furnished by the peasants. It is important to be cautious when extrapolating from such a limited sample. Nevertheless, it does appear that the peasants arrested by the authorities in the right bank were very typical of the rest of the population. Nearly all of them were members of

[58]Police filled out a questionnaire when each peasant was arrested. The information cited here comes from these questionnaires. One hundred thirty-five of them were found scattered through the files of the Kiev court (*Kievskaia sudebnaia palata*) in TsGIAU f. 318, o. 1.

[59]Ibid., d. 348.

the peasant estate, locally born, Ukrainian, married with children, and illiterate. Only 5 of them had been arrested previously (see Table 14).

In only one aspect were the arrested peasants atypical. This matter is so tantalizing that the limited character of the data must be stressed. The allotments of peasant households in the right bank were particularly small. In Podol'e the average holding was as low as 3.8 *desiatiny*. Given this fact, it is especially interesting that the 129 peasants on whom we have information concerning land generally came from households with even smaller holdings. Of those interrogated, 26 claimed to be from landless families, and 56 said they owned less than 2 *desiatiny*. The households of 47 peasants possessed more than that amount. One could then argue that peasants militant enough to be arrested came from the ranks of the poor and the landless, perhaps even that the leaders came from these strata. At the same time, there is no evidence that police went out of their way to protect better-off peasants. This finding would seem to support orthodox Soviet conceptions concerning the behavior of the various rural classes. It may not contradict fully the general impression of cohesion, but it does indicate a need for caution before completely embracing this particular culturalist emphasis.

Given the possible significance of this finding, several warnings are in order. First, the sample is quite small, nor is it clear why

Table 14. Characteristics of Peasants Arrested in the Right Bank, 1905–1907

	Yes	No	Total Cases
Member of peasant estate	133	1	134
Locally born	113	21	134
Ukrainian	133	2	135
Married	89	8	97
Have children	76	12	88
Previously arrested	5	130	135
Illiterate	112	17	129

Source: Tsentral'nyi gosudarstvennyi istoricheskii arkhiv Ukrainskoi SSR, fond 318—Kievskaia sudebnaia palata.

some documents were preserved while others destroyed or lost. Second, the argument that those charged were peasant leaders, though plausible, cannot be established, given the arbitrariness of so many of the arrests. Third, police probably did not independently check the information peasants gave on their holdings. Whether to protect themselves from confiscation or to elicit sympathy from their captors, peasants may well have reported smaller holdings than they actually had. Nevertheless, it appears possible that those arrested in the southwest, although generally typical of the village, did in fact come from its poorest elements. By itself, this evidence does not prove that better-off elements of the rural population did not participate. Yet it does confirm an important role for those in the village who were least wealthy. Cohesion may have been the rule, but it is clear that the village's semi-proletarians were at the forefront.

Role of the Village Assembly

The continued vitality of the village assembly of heads of households was the primary reason for the tension between the landless and the rest of the peasantry. The *skhod* divided the propertyless from the poor peasant and reinforced the antagonism between insiders and outsiders. Peasants in the southwest may have chosen tactics (the strike) and made demands (higher wages) that were typical of urban workers, but, ironically, rural proletarians did not share this militance. Agricultural workers, because they were not heads of local households, could not participate in the village assemblies where they worked, and it was in these gatherings that many important decisions were made.[60] This distinction became especially significant during the disorders. Throughout the revolutionary period, peasants met especially often, and their gatherings, regular and irregular, were much better attended than in more placid times.[61]

[60]AD, 2:50. Mirza-Avakiants, p. 33. Moiseevich, p. 21. TsGIAL f. 1278, o. 1, d. 785, l. 47.
[61]Leshchenko, 1955, p. 155. TsGIAU f. 442, o. 855, d. 526, l. 9.

The *skhod* did not operate according to formal rules of procedure. Given the general vagueness of peasant customary law, the legal status, powers, and membership of the *skhod* were always imprecise. In no way was it a participatory and democratic institution of the entire village. Patriarchy alone would have made that impossible. Women were not supposed to participate, nor were unmarried youths without allotments.[62] Still, most assemblies did not take place behind closed doors. Persistent and noisy outsiders could make their views known, even if they were not supposed to vote. The village assembly, much like the commune of which it was the central element, was thoroughly oligarchical. Given the way in which the *skhod* operated, the more powerful members of the community were usually able to exert power over the weak.

Beyond the imprecision concerning the character of the assembly, there was yet another crucial area of confusion. The Russian word *skhod* was applied in the sources to a broad variety of gatherings, not all of which could be called regular meetings of the traditional assembly of heads of households. In many cases, the police or other local officials called villages together to explain the illegality of certain actions and to issue warnings. These meetings, summoned by the authorities and not the peasants, were also called *skhody,* at least according to the reports of the authorities.[63]

Distinctions of this sort were significant. Police and soldiers were somewhat reluctant to intervene in the activities of a legally recognized institution of the village, however unclear its status. This hesitancy provided a certain protective cover and explains why the peasants sought to call any strike deliberation a formal meeting of the *skhod.* Independent strike committees organized by landless laborers or outside agitators enjoyed no such legal protection, however flimsy it might be. If any such groups did surface, they found it necessary to merge quickly with the official assembly.[64]

Eventually, the authorities ceased to respect the sanctity of the

[62]*AD,* 2:140. Moshe Lewin, "Customary Law and Rural Society in the Postreform Era," in *The Making of the Soviet System* (New York, 1985), pp. 72–87.

[63]*Kievlianin,* July 12, 1905. Butsik, 1957, p. 28. TsGIAU f. 442, o. 855, d. 109, l. 96.

[64]Mirza-Avakiants, p. 33.

skhod. By 1906, they exhibited little hesitancy in breaking up any village meeting, regardless of its formal status. When peasants were arrested, they were never charged with taking part in a *skhod.* Instead, their crime was participation in an "illegal public gathering" (*nezakonnoe publichnoe skopishch'e*).[65] The purpose of these meetings, according to later indictments, was to reorganize economic relationships on the estates. In spite of this claim, the police descriptions of these "gatherings" made them sound not unlike supposedly legal meetings of the village assembly. Quite simply, what the peasants called a *skhod* the police called something else. The ambiguity of the terms made it possible for both groups to use different language to describe similar phenomena.

Once the *skhod* ceased to provide protection from repression, peasants began to organize strikes in other ways. Independent groups became more common.[66] A number of strike committees sprouted in Podol'e during 1906.[67] At the same time, illegal meetings took place in all three provinces.[68] At the initiative of sugar factory workers on the Rogovskii estate in Kiev, 3,000 peasants gathered on June 19, 1906.[69] With the *skhod* no longer providing large gatherings certain protection, peasants now had to meet in forests and pastures far more often than earlier.[70] In all, Leshchenko estimated that 284 illegal meetings took place in the right bank during the revolutionary years, primarily in 1906 and 1907.[71] The traditional assembly still was the main arena for peasants to meet and discuss all matters of interest. In the course of the crisis, however, it had lost some of its special importance as a force for cohesion among the right bank's peasantry. Rural cultivators were finding new ways of organizing themselves, and in this process, the *skhod* and the commune began to show some signs of erosion.

[65]TsGIAU f. 318, o. 1, d. 302, l. 3. ZhOGA f. 24, o. 16, d. 621, l. 3. TsGIAL f. 1405, o. 193, d. 2857, l. 9. TsGIAL f. 1363, o. 2, d. 1665, l. 2.
[66]*AD*, 2:59.
[67]Ibid., pp. 200 and 207.
[68]TsGIAU f. 442, o. 856, d. 789, l. 29. Leshchenko, 1955, p. 150. A. Smirnov, *Kak proshli vybory vo 2-uiu gosudarstvennuiu dumu* (St. Petersburg, 1907), p. 3.
[69]Butsik, 1957, p. 63.
[70]TsGIAL f. 1363, o. 3, d. 147, l. 29. TsGIAL f. 1405, o. 119, d. 2636, l. 5.
[71]Leshchenko, 1955, p. 210.

The traditional leaders of the peasantry found it difficult to maintain their positions in the face of growing peasant militance. Some village elders, in deference to their superiors, opposed strikes.[72] Others were thrown out by peasants who felt they lacked militance.[73] In Mezhirechka (Kiev), striking peasants removed their *starosta* (elder) and accused him of acting on behalf of the landlord.[74] At one point in the Voitsovtsy strike, the canton (*volost'*) elder actually went to the neighboring village to recruit strike-breakers.[75] Traditional leaders also informed on their fellow villagers to the police. In fact, many of them had always seen this function as one of their essential roles.[76] During June 1905 in Ometintsy (Podol'e), 100 peasants, meeting in their traditional assembly, ignored the pleas of their elder and went on strike.[77] And 300 peasants in Bolshaia-Ternovka (Podol'e) physically attacked the village *starosta* for collaborating with the police.[78] Events of this sort occurred throughout rural Russia, but above and beyond this tendency, the peasants of the right bank systematically refused to elect their traditional leaders to any position at any level in 1906 and 1907 during the course of the elections to both the first and second Dumas.[79] In the southwest, there was a search for new authorities.

It could not be said these examples of leadership turnover formed the complete picture. Many times, elders led strikes and stood up to the police. Several refused demands by the authorities to turn in leaders and agitators.[80] One *starosta* in Podol'e warned his villagers not to take work as strikebreakers.[81] In Shtakov (Volynia), elders led hay stealing.[82] In moments such as these, peasants were only too willing to accord their leaders respect and authority.

[72]Ibid., p. 157.
[73]*UD*, 2:337.
[74]Los', p. 362.
[75]*AD*, 2:173.
[76]*UD*, 3:207.
[77]TsGIAU f. 442, o. 855, d. 113 ch. 1, l. 250.
[78]TsGIAL f. 1405, o. 193, d. 1553, l. 3.
[79]Emmons, p. 242.
[80]*UD*, 2:224.
[81]TsGIAU f. 442, o. 855, d. 115 ch. 2, l. 96.
[82]TsGIAU f. 442, o. 857, d. 195, l. 8.

On the other hand, when the elders stood in the way of the wishes of the mass of peasants, they were nearly always swept aside. Events of this sort were not limited to the right bank. There, as elsewhere, the Revolution of 1905 changed the political significance of traditional structures of authority. What were thought to be elements of stability had now eroded in the face of massive disruption.

The patriarchal character of the right bank's communes was further undermined by the important role played by women both in the economy of the region and in the peasant movement. Russian peasant women had never been particularly militant at moments of disorder, and women usually have been depicted as a conservative force in peasant societies. This had always been true in Russia and proved to be the case almost everywhere in the countryside during the revolution of 1905. The southwest, however, was an exception. More women participated there than in any other region.[83] They were, after all, a major part, perhaps the majority, of the labor force on the estates of the region.[84] As noted previously, many sugar plantation owners thought women were better workers than men and sought to hire only female day laborers: they were as productive as men and could be paid much less.[85] Women workers were supported by their families, who took care of their own allotments while providing food and shelter.[86] Wage work was not restricted to any particular group of female peasants. Women of all levels of wealth labored on the estates of the region.

Because women composed such a large segment of the right bank's work force and because the movement was characterized by strikes for higher wages, it was unavoidable that women should become active participants in the movement. This appears to have had little to do with the very real differences between Ukrainian and Russian family structures and communes. Women in the left bank and in Novorossiia were not particularly active. The reason

[83]*Istoria selianstva,* 1:471.
[84]*AD,* 2:25.
[85]TsGIAL f. 1405, o. 194, d. 160, l. 9.
[86]*AD,* 2:22.

for the unusual militance of right-bank women seems straightforward. The conditions confronting them in Kiev, Podol'e, and Volynia forced women to work on the estates, and the difficult conditions on those estates led to labor unrest.[87] Female wage workers
did not go out of their way to avoid confrontations. Whenever a
strike occurred on an estate that employed women, women always
participated.[88]

Female peasants in the southwest did not simply limit their activity to joining the men's struggle. In many instances they assumed
leadership roles. This activity went beyond the familiar tactical
ploy of assuming a physical presence in the front lines of demonstrations in order to forestall police violence.[89] Women had their
own protests. In nine villages in Chigirin district (Kiev), only wom-
en took part in strikes during May 1905.[90] One of these strikes
occurred on the Sakhnovskii estate where fifty women demanded a
raise to fifty kopecks a day. When they were refused, they mobilized the rest of the plantation's workers and led a strike that lasted
several days.[91] According to the correspondent of the Free Economic Society, women also played a leading role in the strike at
Smela (Kiev).[92] Four thousand women in Zhitomir district (Volynia) marched on several railroad stations in a series of coordinated strikes.[93] Police also reported that a strike during July, 1905
in Shukaivoda (Kiev) was dominated by women.[94]

Female militance was not limited to strike activity on sugar plantations. They also took part in forest offenses, illegal pasturing,
and arson.[95] Women also played roles in the few political committees established by the various parties in the right bank.[96] The

---

[87]Ibid., pp. 21 and 227.
[88]Butsik, 1957, p. 35. TsGIAU f. 442, o. 855, d. 526, l. 4. TsGIAU f. 318, o. 1,
d. 346, l. 3. TsGAOR f. 102, 1905, d. 2550 ch. 4, l. 86.
[89]AD, 2:104.
[90]AD, 2:179.
[91]TsGIAU f. 318, o. 1, d. 336, l. 57.
[92]AD, 2:180.
[93]Shestakov, 1907, p. 28.
[94]TsGAOR f. 102, 1905, o. 233, d. 2550 ch. 4, l. 14.
[95]TsGIAU f. 318, o. 1, d. 347, l. 51. TsGAOR f. 102, 1907, d. 53 ch. 1, l. 21.
[96]AD, 2:208.

lessons learned carried over into actions that elsewhere were the exclusive province of men.

The partial weakening of patriarchal authority in the right bank was attributable to the importance of women in the labor force of the region. Peasant societies have strictly regulated the roles and functions of women. The communes of Russia and the rest of the Ukraine were not exceptional. The economy of the southwest gave women a new, if not especially fulfilling role. Ironically, the availability of wage work allowed the peasant households of the region to continue existing even as it undermined traditional patterns. Had the sugar plantations not provided employment, many households would have had to abandon the countryside entirely. Yet this kind of activity could not be hidden behind the trappings of custom. It was obvious to the men and could not be denied. The wages earned by women were decisive to the continued survival of the average peasant household in the southwest.

If processes of change had been set in motion, traditional village institutions continued to dominate rural life in Kiev, Podol'e, and Volynia. When strikes were imminent, peasants discussed matters in their *skhody* more often than in any other arena. This fact meant that the tension between insiders and outsiders continued to be a crucial element of life in the southwest. The reasons for the continued vitality of the commune are not elusive. They afforded peasants forms of ongoing social contact and, in the process, made political cohesion eminently realizable in moments of crisis. The reasons for making use of these institutions were sensible, logical, and rational. The *skhod* had always been the arena for consultation. There was no reason to change this practice unless conditions warranted such a course. Peasants did not necessarily need custom and tradition to dictate their actions. In the special conditions of the revolutionary years, old institutions acquired new meanings and functions. Peasant willingness to make use of the *skhod* was politically sensible. This was the institution peasants had created over the centuries. Yet, in the new context, the persistence of the assembly did not represent a blind clinging to the old ways. The village assembly was still the center of peasant life, but by 1907 it had assumed a different and less powerful significance.

Extravillage Forces

The tension between outsiders and insiders controlled many peasant actions. But landlords and soldiers were not the only external forces affecting the peasantry. Other groups came in contact with the village and influenced it in complex and unpredictable ways.

Other villages. If peasants considered landlords, policemen, soldiers, merchants, and landless laborers to be outsiders, the same can be said for peasants from other villages. Most strikes and disturbances were localized and directed against the landlord for whom the peasants labored. The cohesion demonstrated by peasants during 1905 was primarily intravillage. It did not extend to the entire social estate. When strikes occurred, landlords sent to neighboring villages for strikebreakers. Other peasants served in this capacity far more often than landless laborers, largely because landless laborers were such a small fraction of the available labor pool. As a result, violent clashes between peasants from different villages became common. In several locations, peasants began to refuse offers to break strikes. In other places, the people of one village had to explain a situation in order to gain their neighbors' support. Although landlords believed they could always find other hands when their own peasants went on strike, this did not always work out. Invitations might be turned down, or willing strikebreakers might be run off by local peasants. Nevertheless, peasants from one village could be threatened by their neighbors, who in every other way were very much like them.

This isolation was by no means complete. Sometimes peasants from several villages were actually able to coordinate their actions. This occurred in both Kiev and Podol'e during the spring of 1906.[97] Because peasants could know in advance the time of their strikes, it became possible to make mutual plans with surrounding settlements for maximum effect. Some villages, for example Zhidovtsy (Kiev), actually propagandized on neighboring estates.[98] Where a landlord might own several settlements, peasants

[97]TsGIAU f. 272, o. 66, d. 193, l. 34. *AD,* 2:217.
[98]Butsik, 1957, p. 58. *Russkie Vedomosti,* April 28, 1905.

were quick to seek each other out and agree on mutual plans.[99] This occurred in Didovshchina during 1906.[100]

Yet events of this sort were atypical. The peasants of the right bank demonstrated an awareness of developments outside their villages. They acted in ways that differed sharply from peasants elsewhere. Nevertheless, they continued to direct their wrath against local targets. Solidarity from village to village was not typical. If peasants in both central Russia and the right bank acted cohesively, that cohesion did not extend beyond the borders of their settlements. Solidarity with others who shared their relation to the means of production was not extensive. In the fundamental struggle between outsiders and insiders, every peasant was some other peasant's outsider.

Jews. The widespread literary and journalistic picture of the Ukrainian peasant as an arch anti-Semite is not entirely supported by events in the right bank during the revolutionary period. As has been made clear, peasants in the southwest harbored a variety of resentments toward all outsiders, of which Jews were merely one group. There was special animosity toward the few large-scale Jewish renters of sugar plantations.[101] The Brodsky family sugar company had a long-standing reputation as a difficult employer, but, more generally, Jewish merchants were blamed for driving up the price of rented land.[102] Rafal'skii reported extensive rumors of potential pogroms, and in Nesets (Podol'e) on December 28, 1905, peasants destroyed the house and took the property of a Jewish family.[103] There were other isolated incidents of pogromlike activity in the right bank, but violence of this sort was not extensive.[104] The limited number of anti-Semitic attacks in the countryside of the southwest was largely the result of the limited number of Jews in the rural areas. There were some Jewish mer-

---

[99]TsGIAL f. 1405, o. 193, d. 1999, l. 4.

[100]Shestakov, 1930, p. 31.

[101]*AD*, 2:113.

[102]TsGAOR f. 102, 1905, o. 233, d. 2550 ch. 4, l. 5. TsGIAU f. 442. o. 855, d. 7. l. 1. TsGIAL f. 1405, o. 107, d. 7618, l. 82.

[103]TsGIAU f. 442, o. 855, d. 526, l. 15. TsGAOR f. 102, o. 236, d. 700 ch. 54, l. 1.

[104]Maslov, 1908, p. 232.

chants and tavern keepers, along with the large-scale renters, but, for the most part, Jews were urban dwellers. Most of the worst pogroms of the era took place in the cities.

If the absence of overt and widespread anti-Semitic activity had more to do with lack of Jews than with peasant open-mindedness, it should not be forgotten that peasants in the right-bank Ukraine welcomed a variety of political agitators into their midst, and many of these outsiders were Jewish.[105] When peasants agreed with the message of Jewish revolutionaries, they were open and friendly. In June 1907, Jews participated alongside peasants in several acts of arson on the Kiev estate of Countess Brannitskaia.[106] Dozens of youths, a few of them Jewish, engaged in propaganda on the Volynia estate of the Tereshchenko family.[107] During the fall of 1905, peasants in Ol'shanitsa (Kiev) elected a strike committee which included two Jewish members.[108] Clearly then, the picture is mixed. If right-bank peasants saw Jews engaged in activity that threatened their interests, they did not hesitate to resort to violence. On the other hand, if they felt Jewish outsiders shared their sense of anger and injustice, they were only too glad to provide a welcome. Ukrainian peasants in the right bank, therefore, exhibited a wide range of attitudes toward their Jewish neighbors in much the same way that Jews related to peasants in many different ways.

Political parties. It has already been noted that various organized political agitators played a role in spreading the movement in the right bank. Illegal organizing and propaganda had been practiced in the countryside for decades before 1905. After the October Manifesto, however, parties became legal. The populist Socialist Revolutionary party had always been most disposed toward working with the peasantry. For many years the Socialist Revolutionaries had operated underground groups in the Central Black Earth and the Mid-Volga regions. The wings of the Social Democratic party were less concerned with the peasantry. Instead, they focused on the urban proletariat. Of the two wings, the Bolsheviks, and

[105] *AD*, 2:31.
[106] TsGIAU f. 442, o. 857, d. 193, l. 28.
[107] *AD*, 2:187.
[108] Mirza-Avakiants, p. 33. Maslov, 1924, p. 96.

Lenin in particular, showed more interest in peasants, seeing them as a group that merited support despite their uncertain political aims.

Historians of the peasant movement, both Soviet and Western, have not ascribed a controlling role to any of the political forces that appeared in the countryside.[109] The disturbances were too spontaneous, disorganized, and broad for any political group to have controlled.[110] The isolation of most villages and the low level of literacy made the political culture of rural Russia different from that of the cities. In urban Russia, there were specific party labels and a clear awareness of a national struggle. By contrast, political parties had no place in the traditional world of the Russian village. This absence of party affiliation was not limited to the peasants who were not likely to formulate elaborately nuanced political programs. Noble landlords were equally suspicious about parties. Even after independent organizations were legalized, the gentry did not rush to form modern political parties despite the clear necessity for such groups in the newly created semi-parliamentary system.

No party could claim to control or call into action the tidal wave of peasant discontent that was witnessed during the first Russian revolution. This held as true for the right bank, as it did for the rest of Russia. Yet in other ways this region presents a picture different from that of central Russia. In most places, either the Socialist Revolutionaries or the short-lived, amorphous Peasant Union were prominent. In Kiev, Podol'e, and Volynia, various Social Democratic groups were more visible. The right bank was one of the few regions (the Caucasus and the Baltic were others) in which Social Democrats elicited a response from peasants.[111] The significant presence of wage labor may have played a role in this success, but the Social Democrats, like the Socialist Revolutionaries, talked primarily about the land question in their appeals and proclamations. Nevertheless, it is more than interesting that a party with such an

[109]Leshchenko, 1955, p. 82.
[110]Maslov, 1924, p. 45.
[111]TsGIAL f. 1405, o. 108, d. 6824, l. 7. TsGIAU f. 318, o. 1, d. 404, l. 39. TsGIAU f. 442, o. 855, d. 526, l. 8.

urban bias could find an audience in a region of extensive commercial agriculture.[112]

In some cases, peasant awareness of the Social Democrats was quite specific. During June 1905, in the village of Maidenetsk (Kiev), the provincial *prosecutor* reported that peasants left a strike negotiation chanting, "Hail the republic and the eight-hour day. Hail the Social Democratic party." This particular official had elsewhere been an accurate describer of events, and it was usually assumed that so concrete a peasant utterance signified the involvement of agitators with specific party affiliations.[113] On June 28, 1906, 1,000 peasants held a meeting in Kiev province at which calls for political freedom and the eight-hour day were combined with a vote of solidarity with the Social Democratic Duma group. The peasants took this last step despite the fact that the party's boycott of the first Duma elections meant that there was no organized Social Democratic delegation in the new lower chamber.[114]

The most active single group in the right bank was the Ukrainian Social Democratic Union (the *Spilka*) which joined the Russian Social Democratic Labor party in December 1904, as an organization of Ukrainian-speaking workers.[115] By October 1905, the Spilka claimed 7,000 members. Most of them lived in the city of Kiev and in the smaller towns of the left and right banks.[116] Agitators fanned out from the city of Kiev to distribute literature and hold meetings. A regional strike committee was formed in Kiev province, and individual party members helped striking peasants formulate demands.[117] But the successes of the Spilka, like those of all other groups in the right bank, were limited and episodic. In the left bank, the Social Revolutionaries and the Peasant Union were more successful.[118] A well-organized meeting addressed by an ac-

---

[112]Robinson, p. 158. Dubrovskii, 1955, p. 69. Shestakov, 1926, p. 74. Maslov, 1924, p. 53.

[113]TsGIAL, f. 1405, o. 108, d. 6824, l. 7.

[114]*AD*, 2:259.

[115]Ralph Carter Elwood, *Russian Social Democracy in the Underground* (Assen, 1974), p. 16.

[116]Mirza-Avakiants, p. 37.

[117]Moiseevich, p. 34. Maslov, 1924, p. 152.

[118]Mirza-Avakiants, p. 34.

tivist did not signify the presence of an ongoing effective political organization. Quite often activists of all three groups worked together to coordinate strikes, form committees, and distribute each other's literature. So large was the task and so limited the resources that the rural activists of all groups spent little of their time in the countryside engaged in factional fighting.[119]

In the springs of both 1906 and 1907, nationwide elections were held for the lower house (the Duma) of the new semi-parliamentary system. This process might be considered an opportunity to monitor contemporary peasant views, but the complexities of the electoral system, the peculiarities of rural politics, and the inadequacies of the sources make the Duma elections a less than useful guide for understanding peasant political attitudes. It is true that the original framers of the electoral law (of December 1905) thought the peasantry a repository of conservatism and, accordingly, gave allotment holders a near majority of the electors who met in the provincial assemblies that actually chose the Duma deputies. Property restrictions were placed on participation, and the election was a multistage process (peasants went through four stages) which created ambiguities and anomalies at crucial moments. Through a variety of means, the government was able to intervene in the election, limiting certain unreliable groups from the franchise. Because women were not allowed to vote, the election in the southwest was especially unrepresentative, given their crucial role in both the labor process and the strike movement. Finally, the various socialist parties that might have been expected to compete for peasant votes boycotted the first Duma elections. In 1906, peasants throughout Russia then elected the most radical candidates available. Their votes went to the classically liberal Constitutional Democratic party (the Kadets) and an amorphous group that coalesced into the so-called Labor Group (Trudoviki). In 1907, during the second Duma elections, the radicals participated, and peasants gave their support to a variety of individuals who were even further to the left.[120]

In the first Duma elections, twenty-four right-bank peasants

[119]AD, 2:206–8.
[120]M. Boiovich, *Chleny gosudarstvennoi dumy,* pervyi sozyv (Moscow, 1906).

were chosen deputies. Once they got to St. Petersburg, and only then, did they ally with a specific party. Often, they chose not to affiliate. Four of them were simply described as "left," six were Kadets, six were simply "progressives," and eight were nonparty. In the second Duma elections, there were twenty-seven peasants from Kiev, Podol'e and Volynia. Eight were "left," four were Social Democrats, eight were monarchists, six were on the "right," and one was "progressive."

These political labels were even more imprecise at the lower levels of the process. Nearly all the peasant electors chosen to sit in the final provincial assemblies that named the deputies to the first Duma were described by observers from the Kadets as "nonparty." In Volynia, of the sixty-nine peasant electors, sixty-two were unaffiliated; in Podol'e all eighty-two of the peasant electors were unaffiliated; and in Kiev, of the eighty electors, fifty-six were unaffiliated. Specific political labels were not part of peasant politics. Like other parts of the empire, local groupings did not mirror the party divisions on the national level. No one campaigned as a Socialist Revolutionary or as a Social Democrat. Instead, peasants searched out men of talent and honor. The ability to read was obviously desirable, and peasants everywhere sought people with the talent to defend them.[121] This had little to do with the organized political alternatives. Yet the limited success of the Social Democrats in Kiev province (all four peasant Social Democratic deputies were from Kiev) demonstrated that peasant politics in the southwest did differ in some ways from practices elsewhere.

Peasants in the southwest wrote and petitioned their deputies. Many *skhody* actually drew up instructions (*nakazy*) to send to the president of the new Duma. Few of these *nakazy* have survived, and most bear the stamp of outsiders.[122] Eleven such documents are extant from Kiev and Podol'e, and peasants in those two provinces showed they generally shared the concerns of their counterparts in other regions.[123] Right-bank peasants also directly petitioned their deputies. Here too, their demands differed little from

[121] *Vestnik Partii Narodnoi Svobody* 6 (1907), prilozhenie; cited in Emmons, p. 250. Smirnov, p. 175.

[122] Emmons, p. 242. Maslov, 1924, p. 127.

[123] Maslov, 1924, p. 125. TsGAOR f. 102, 4-oe dp., d. 108 ch. 38, ll. 1–32.

those of peasants elsewhere. On June 25, 1906, the villagers of Strizhevka (Kiev) wrote to the Trudovik Duma group calling for a constituent assembly, the establishment of democratic freedoms, and the transfer of all land to the peasantry.[124] Once they began working in the Duma, deputies from the right bank spoke little. For the most part, they limited their remarks to the land question, and they did so in the most general terms.[125]

As has been mentioned, Duma deputies were local heroes who could travel the countryside with parliamentary immunity and agitate comparatively freely. They gave speeches and, in a few instances, fomented actual strikes.[126] Yet it cannot be said that these men represented a clearly defined constituency, organized along modern, political lines. The Duma elections can furnish some indications of peasant views, but they do not reveal all that might be known. The structure of the electoral process made it impossible to gain a clear picture of peasant views. After June 3, 1907, Duma elections became even less representative once Stolypin unilaterally restricted the franchise, penalizing the peasantry for their unexpected rebelliousness. The new third Duma was dominated by the landed gentry who gave their votes to a variety of moderate and extreme conservative groups.

Aftermath of the Revolution of 1905

By the fall of 1907, a tense and guarded peace had come to the Russian countryside. The toll of government repression had been heavy, and peasants were exhausted. They had won some victories, but there were few objective changes. Wages had risen.[127] Sugar prices were up, and despite all the turmoil, the harvest of 1906 was especially good.[128] Otherwise, little had changed. Land prices in the southwest had fallen only slightly. Renting land was no less costly. Large-scale landholding emerged from the turbulence with

[124]UD, 2:214.
[125]Gosudarstvennaia duma, *Stenograficheskie otchety*, soz. 1, zas. 16, cols. 969–702; soz. 1, zas. 21, col. 987.
[126]TsGIAU f. 442, o. 857, d. 193, l. 2.
[127]AD, 2:126.
[128]Ibid., p. 42.

few losses.[129] Moreover, any vestiges of landlord paternalism had evaporated along with the last remnants of peasant monarchism. Stolypin's attempt to reform the village commune was met with great skepticism by right-bank peasants. Plans for the consolidation of peasant holdings meant little when these holdings were too meager to support a family.

As it did elsewhere, the level of disorders dropped sharply in the southwest between 1907 and the outbreak of the war in 1914. In that period, there were 547 incidents. Only 43 were strikes. Most disturbances (119) involved arson.[130] The gentry of the southwest did not see the new peace as anything more than a temporary reprieve. They had become convinced of peasant irresponsibility and began to mobilize politically much more actively than their counterparts in central Russia. After a period of intense political activity during the early years of the third Duma, most Russian landlords returned to their political apathy. By contrast, the gentry of the right bank remained vigilant up to the last moment. They knew that the peasantry of the southwest, although peaceful for the time being, was in no way satisfied. During the prewar years, peasants returned to their fields. They eschewed formal political activity and, instead, waited for a new opportunity.

When revolution finally came to the empire during 1917, the right-bank Ukraine proved to be an especially volatile region.[131] Peasants in the southwest had been cautious in 1905 when it appeared the power of their landlords was still strong. With the collapse of authority in the countryside, the peasants of Kiev, Podol'e, and Volynia joined the nationwide campaign for the seizure of state, gentry, and church lands without compensation. The time for "total repartition" had finally come. Kiev, in particular, was one of the few provinces in which the specially organized committees of poor peasants played an important role.[132]

[129]Ibid., p. 124.

[130]P. Kudlai, "Selianski rukh na pravoberezhnii Ukrainii mikh dvomu revoliutsii," *Arkhiv Ukraini* no. 1 (1970), 58–68.

[131]V. I. Kostrikin, *Zemel'nye komitety v 1917 godu* (Moscow, 1975), p. 280. A. D. Maliavskii, *Krestianskoe dvizhenie v Rossii v 1917 g.* (Moscow, 1981), p. 190.

[132]Graeme Gill, *Peasants and Government in the Russian Revolution* (London, 1975), p. 124.

Overall, the circumstances in 1917 were quite different from those of 1905. The landlords and the authorities that supported them had lost their power. In 1905, when landlords sent telegrams to provincial governors, someone answered. In 1917, there was no reply. Accordingly, peasants in Kiev, Podol'e, and Volynia behaved differently in the course of this new revolutionary moment. Many of the more distinctive features of the earlier movement were not repeated. Few strikes took place. It is, after all, difficult to ask landlords for higher wages, when they are fleeing for their very lives. The events of 1905 may have been a series of strikes and disorders, but it could not be said they constituted a true and successful revolution. In 1917, the peasants of both Russia and the right-bank Ukraine at last got their wish, and the hated landlords were gone.

The conditions confronted by peasants in the southwest had changed drastically. In Kiev, Podol'e, and Volynia, the events of the first Russian revolution did not turn out to be a "dress rehearsal" for 1917. When outside conditions changed, right-bank peasants changed with them. Tactics appropriate in 1905 made less sense in 1917. When revolution finally came, it was necessary to make different choices.

5

The Consequences of
the Prussian Path

At the outset of this book, I raised the two standard questions that must be posed in any examination of rural disturbances. Which factors determined peasant behavior at moments of disorder? Which elements of the peasantry participated in movements of resistance? Each of these questions is, in turn, linked to the other issues that have engaged activists and scholars for the last century and a half. In the course of the first Russian revolution, rural cultivators in the southwest acted in ways that confirmed some of the expectations of both major conceptions of life in the countryside. Conversely, if both sides (neither of which is monolithic) can point to phenomena that affirm their approach, they must also account for situations that do not fit expected patterns.

The events described here present a mixed picture. This, by itself, should be obvious. It is difficult to imagine any concrete historical situation that would not present varied and even contradictory phenomena. My primary concern, however, has been to describe the precise way peasants in the southwest followed multiple patterns of behavior, because this specific structure of combinations suggests ways both schools of thought can rework basic ideas. If Marxists, in the light of this experience, would do well to revise important analytical categories, culturalists should now reconsider the explanatory power of the timeless structures they have described and emphasized.

During the revolutionary years between 1905 and 1907, right-bank peasants acted in ways that confirmed several important culturalist expectations. First, they demonstrated political cohesion in their struggle with the landed gentry; class struggle within the village was not extensive. Second, landless laborers, who were not members of the communes where they worked, were tentative and secondary participants in the strikes and disturbances. Third, the traditional assembly of heads of households continued to play a role at moments of stress. Fourth, disorders were largely localized, with peasants confronting, first and foremost, their own landlords. Fifth, although the movement was widespread, it did not ultimately lead to the creation of ongoing, national political groups that could mobilize and organize the peasantry.

On the other hand, rural cultivators in this region chose tactics (the organized strike) and made demands (higher wages and better working conditions) that were precisely appropriate to the conditions they confronted outside their communities. External forces and structures determined peasants' choices in their battles with the landlords. Rural cultivators were fully able to make reasoned decisions and alter their approach when conditions shifted. They did not cling blindly to custom and superstition, nor did they ignore the changes occurring around them. They had ceased harboring the vision of a long-past and mythical "golden age" when the land belonged to them alone. If anything, right-bank peasants were far from utopian in their aims. Their use of force was judicious, limited, defensive, and almost never random. Finally, peasants in Kiev, Podol'e, and Volynia engaged in formal political activity only episodically, but when they did, they showed greater receptivity to Social Democratic rather than Socialist Revolutionary appeals. The peculiar economic, social, and cultural conditions of the southwest had given rise to a distinctive movement. In these specific ways, the residents of this region affirmed many Marxist and Leninist claims about peasant behavior.

This divided picture is the direct result of the particular form capitalism assumed in the southwest. Landlords, rather than peasants, had been the source of agrarian innovation. The right bank was a clear case of the "Prussian path" to capitalism. Peasant agriculture, meanwhile, remained traditional and primitive. Village dwellers still practiced the three-field system and continued to raise crops that were part of a natural or subsistence economy. Yet, given the special smallness of peasant allotments, subsistence was not easily achieved. Households had to supplement their incomes, and in the southwest, this need was fulfilled through wage work on capitalist estates. This phenomenon was so widespread that it was practiced by families from all but the very wealthiest strata of the village. Therefore, most peasants occupied a similar position vis-à-vis the landlords. This shared dependence on the estate owners was the central fact of peasant life in the southwest. So great was the poverty of all rural cultivators in the right bank that differences of wealth within the village seemed insignificant when compared to the huge chasm between lords and peasants.

The generalized peasant dependence on the large landholders made differences within the village seem comparatively insignificant. In 1905, this fact overwhelmed all others, as peasants acted cohesively against both the proprietors and renters of large estates. For peasants to have been divided against each other, their own agriculture would have had to have been more advanced. For true social classes to have emerged, the right bank would have had to have been the site not of the "Prussian" but of the "American" path to capitalism. If peasants themselves had been part of the market economy, then significant differences of wealth would have emerged in the villages, and those distinctions could have developed into politically and socially meaningful class antagonisms. Because capitalist agriculture in the southwest was exclusively a landlord enterprise, peasants spent little time, during 1905, fighting each other. Soviet scholars have explained this cohesion by describing it as a manifestation of the first of the two "social wars" in the countryside. The first "social war" was a struggle between landlords and the entire peasantry. This clash was to be followed by a second war in which the poor and middle peasants faced the landlords and *kulaks*. For some Soviet historians, the second war came in 1917. Culturalists, of course, doubt that it ever took place. Regardless of later events, it is possible to see 1905 as an early stage of revolution in which one could scarcely expect class struggle within the village to be particularly significant.

The simultaneous appearance of traditional peasant social cohesion and modern proletarian political behavior is, therefore, one of the consequences of the Prussian route to capitalism. Yet in one important way the experience of the right-bank landlord differed from that of his or her Junker counterpart. The noble landlords of East Prussia faced a constant labor shortage throughout the latter half of the nineteenth century. Germany's swiftly expanding industrial sector created a demand for labor, and workers on Junker estates often found it attractive to leave for the cities. By contrast, Russian industry in 1905 was less extensive. Peasants in Kiev, Podol'e, and Volynia did not have all the options of their counterparts in the the German Empire. As a result, there was a huge surplus of labor in the southwest. Landlords were able to keep wages low and avoid improvements in working conditions. This combination of circumstances, as we have seen, made the southwest especially prone to disorder, far more so in this period than East Prussia.

By itself, the relative supply and demand of working hands only partially explains why one place remained passive while the other exploded. Outside political events were obviously very different in Russia and Germany. Crucial for our understanding of peasant behavior here is the fact that the Prussian road to capitalism does not require a complete transformation of the lives of the peasantry. It allows for the simultaneous existence of both primitive and advanced agriculture, even on the same estate. For this reason, the actions of right-bank peasants in 1905 confirm parts of both dominant explanations and deny others. I noted in the introduction that the debate was less about the universal applicability of either approach than it was about the appropriateness of each school to explain the specific situation being analyzed. Leninists and other Marxists have made better sense of capitalist agriculture, whereas culturalists have been best at explaining traditional agriculture. In the right bank, peasants continued primitive practices on their own land, while they participated in a modern labor market when dealing with landlords. Given this set of circumstances, one would expect that the picture would be mixed in this particular way.

The persistence of precapitalist peasant agriculture provides an explanation for the retention of traditional institutions in the villages. The most important of these was the assembly of heads of households. In dividing insiders from outsiders, the *skhod* prevented landless laborers from playing a decisive role and diminished peasant awareness of the divisions in their own midst. The *skhod* did this with no great precision or clarity, however. The assemblies did not operate according to clearly understood legal procedures. They had no rules of order, nor did they have officially designated meeting places. They were more oligarchical than democratic, excluding, in most instances, women and the village youth. In the southwest, these omissions were especially significant, as women and young peasants were militant participants in the movement.

Right-bank peasants were quick to call meetings of the assemblies during the revolution. Yet it is clear that they did not do so out of blind commitment to the ancient ways of the village. The peasant structures that culturalists have considered to be timeless and central changed their meaning in the course of the strike movement. The tactical advantages of peasants' giving their gatherings the title of *skhody* were clear and obvious. It was eminently logical and rational for peasants to seek to imbue their strike planning with some kind of official aura. This step served a protective function, and, initially, made the authorities reluctant to intervene. Eventually, the police recognized these meetings for what they were and sought to break them up. Peasants called any gathering an "assembly of heads of household (*skhod*)." The police called them "illegal public gatherings (*nezakonnye publichnye skopishch'e*)." What had been a traditional institution now became a strike committee. What at first glance seems to have been the persistence of an old structure, turns out to have been something rather different. As outside political conditions changed dramatically in 1905, so did the internal mechanisms of the village.

By 1906, peasants themselves came to recognize this change. It became more common to hold secret meetings in the woods and to elect formal strike committees. This shift was not universal. Yet it was extremely important. The traditional *skhod* was no longer the only appropriate vehicle for bringing together the movement's participants in this region. Women and young men took active roles in the many strikes—yet they were not supposed to participate in the traditional assembly. Clearly the functions, character, and competence of this institution had to change, and they did so in the course of the revolutionary years. If peasants still called meetings of the assembly in moments of disorder, those meetings now assumed very different meanings.

As Mark Harrison and other Marxist writers have noticed, the structures of peasant life may persist, but their character and meaning can change drastically under the influence of outside forces. Under these circumstances the phenomenon of peasant cohesion in 1905 is self-evident. It does not, by itself, explain the experience of rural Russia in 1917, 1930, or, for that matter, 1830. The conditions that made cohesion possible in 1905 may not have existed at other moments. Similarly, the persistence of peasant reliance on the traditional assemblies does not indicate a timeless truth about their lives. The experience of the southwest clearly shows that these structures can wither in their power, adapt to new situations, and change their roles and meanings as times change.

If culturalists have sought to assume the point of view of the peasant, Marxist activists and analysts of rural life have been bedeviled by their roles as outsiders. The Social Democratic movement in both Europe and Russia placed its hopes on the urban proletariat. Marx's analysis derived from the growth of industry in the city. The peasantry, on the other hand, was supposed to be historically doomed. In attempting to make sense of events in the countryside, Marxists have imposed the familiar and comfortable analytical categories of the urban world. The willingness to use a powerful explanatory framework in inappropriate situations was so great that Marx, as well as Lenin, often succumbed to the temptation.

In Russia, urban workers had responded to Social Democratic appeals. Lenin, thinking landless laborers had nothing to lose but their chains, called this group a rural proletariat and ascribed to it the militance of the urban working class. He also included the landless with the allotment-holding poor peasantry in one politically unified group which he called simply "the rural poor." By any rigorous Marxist standard, Lenin's use of this category was decidedly unorthodox. Propertyless rural cultivators and peasants who owned even small amounts of land had a different relationship to the means of production. By this standard, one would not expect them to behave politically in a unified way, and in 1905, they did not, even in the right bank. The narrowly defined rural proletariat, in fact, played the role of an urban *lumpenproletariat*.

If this meant that Lenin's concept of the rural poor was theoretically imprecise, it, nevertheless, made eminent political sense to include the poor peasantry in a category to which one ascribed some form of militance. Lenin called this group either "semi-proletarian" or "proletarianized." At first glance, this choice of words could be seen as an attempt to ascribe a form of urban, working-class behavior to what were, in fact, simply peasants. Yet the experience of the right bank demonstrates that, under certain circumstances, the concept of "semi-proletarian" accurately describes the actions of particular classes of rural cultivators.[1] During 1905, the allotment-holding peasantry of the southwest did not act like peasants elsewhere in the world. They were neither atavistic, millenarian, nor randomly violent. Their actions were straightforward and thoroughly rational, fully consistent with their immediate interests as wage workers on large, capitalistically organized estates. Lenin's "semi-proletarians" played the role usually assigned in the cities to the industrial working class.

Urban workers were brought together on the factory floor and in their neighborhoods. Through these processes, they established the social relations that gave them solidarity and militance. A *lumpenproletariat* of drifters, petty criminals, and the occasionally employed did not experience these lessons. Instead of joining socialist movements, these elements proved susceptible to various fascist and proto-fascist appeals. In the cities, these people were strikebreakers.

In the countryside, the peasantry was the only segment of the population to experience social relations that supported political militance. Agricultural workers did not take part in the life of the village, nor did their work bring them together as it did urban workers. Plantation fields are not factory floors. Organizing a rural proletariat, strictly defined, has never been an easy process.

The very poorest segment of the rural population did not turn out to be the most militant. This finding is consistent with the

[1]Kingston-Mann, 1983, p. 52. Huang, p. 17.

conclusions reached by recent students of the Russian labor movement. The revolution found its staunchest supporters among the most educated and skilled elements of the working class.[2] Before World War I and again in 1917, hereditary proletarians, not recent arrivals to the city, led the strike movement and participated in revolutionary politics. A worker's level of wealth did not turn out to be the crucial consideration. Instead, their political attitudes were the product of their place in the complex social and economic relations of the factory, neighborhood, trade union, and workers' council. The same can be said for the countryside, where only allotment-holding peasants were fully able to participate in processes that generated solidarity and political militance.

The divergent roles of landless laborers and semi-proletarians does, ironically, support Marxist contentions about the heterogeneity of rural cultivators. If landless agrarian workers did not demonstrate the militance Lenin ascribed to them, the wage-earning poor peasantry acted very much in the "proletarianized" manner he expected. The experience of right-bank peasants in 1905, therefore, suggests an adjustment, rather than abandonment, of familiar Marxist and Leninist categories. If urban terms have incorrectly been imposed on rural situations, it is still possible to find meaningful correspondences between events in the cities and the countryside. If one focuses on political role and place in the relations of production as the basis for one's categories, rural social classes in the southwest translate in the following way into urban groups:

Rural	Urban
landless proletarians	lumpenproletariat
semi-proletarians	industrial workers
kulaks	petty bourgeoisie
landed gentry	grand bourgeoisie

Certainly, disagreements may arise about the size of the various subgroups. It also need scarcely be said that the *kulak* has been the

[2]See Steven Smith, *Red Petrograd* (Cambridge, 1984). Victoria Bonnell, *Roots of Rebellion* (Berkeley, 1983). Diane Koenker, *Moscow Workers and the 1917 Revolution* (Princeton, 1981).

subject of the most intense debate over the decades. Yet it should be stressed that the basis for these correspondences is not ownership or nonownership of property. Relations rather than forces of production are central to this process of translating urban categories in order to comprehend rural situations. When modified in these ways, Marxist approaches, including those faithful to Lenin, can make sense of peasant behavior, not only in special places like the right-bank Ukraine, but elsewhere as well. The Prussian example may seem an especially appropriate case in which Marxist approaches are likely to be especially fruitful. A wide variety of situations can be comprehended, if one understands the ways different categories can have similar meanings in differing situations.

Landless laborers did not control the peasant movement in the southwest during 1905. As often as not, they were strikebreakers. Instead, wage-earning peasants led the strikes and disorders. They acted as would any employees in large, capitalist enterprises. Without leaving the land or abandoning all their traditions, peasants in the southwest transformed the ways they confronted the estate owners. Despite all the ambiguities of the phrase, the women and men who worked the fields of Kiev, Podol'e, and Volynia can properly be called proletarian peasants.

Glossary

batrak: peasant without land; either a wage laborer or a young peasant who had not yet succeeded to an allotment

bedniak: poor peasant

borshch: any thick soup with vegetables and/or meat

desiatin: 2.7 acres

dvorianstvo: the nobility

ekonomiia: subunit of an estate

gromada: Ukrainian commune

guberniia (gubernii): province(s)

izba: peasant house or hut

kulak: literally a "fist"; a wealthy peasant or a moneylender

kupets (kuptsy): well-to-do merchant(s)

malozemel'e: lack of land, land hunger

meshchanstvo: the social estate of the petty bourgeoisie

mir: village community or its government

otkhodnik: migrant day laborer

plug: a slightly advanced type of wooden plow

podvornoe vladenie: hereditary land tenure

podzhog: arson

pud: 36.11 pounds

seredniak: middle peasant

servitutnye prava: customary rights accorded peasants before the emancipation of 1861

Glossary

skhod (skhody): village assembly(ies) of heads of households

sokha: the primitive type of wooden plow

soslovie: social estate, *stand* (Ger.) or *état* (Fr.)

starosta: elder

uezd(y): district(s)

usad'ba: the garden area of an estate or a peasant's personal land for his/her own use

verst: 1.06 kilometers

volost': a peasant administrative subunit of the district *(uezd)* usually including several villages

zavod: literally, a factory; any industrial establishment on an estate including refineries, distilleries, and breweries

zazhitochnyi: powerful or well-off

zemstvo: semi-autonomous, elective local government bodies created in 1864, dominated by the gentry but providers of social services to peasants; did not exist in the southwest until 1911

Bibliographical Note

Many of the major contributions to the debate on peasant revolutions are available in English. The central works of Lenin and Chaianov have been translated. See V. I. Lenin, *The Development of Capitalism in Russia* (Moscow, 1972), and A. V. Chaianov, *The Theory of the Peasant Economy* (Homewood, Ill., 1966). Marx's earliest discussion of peasant politics can be found in the conclusion of *The Eighteenth Brumaire of Louis Bonaparte* (New York, 1963). Marx's discussion of rural economics can be found in *Capital,* vol. 3 (New York, 1967). Engels's best-known work on the rural world is *The Peasant War in Germany* (Moscow, 1974).

The leading protagonists in the "moral economy" versus "political economy" debate are James Scott, *The Moral Economy of the Peasant: Rebellion and Subsistence in Southeast Asia* (New Haven, Conn., 1976), and Samuel Popkin, *The Rational Peasant* (Berkeley, 1979). Jeffrey Paige's work, *Agrarian Revolution: Social Movements and Export Agriculture* (New York, 1975), discusses the roles of rural cultivators in a broad range of Third World countries. The concepts of Chaianov were extended by the Polish rural sociologist Boguslaw Galeski, *Basic Concepts of Rural Sociology* (Manchester, England, 1972).

The predominant role of the middle peasant was first systematically asserted by Hamza Alavi. See "Peasants and Revolution," *The Socialist Register* for 1965. The idea was more fully elaborated by Eric

Bibliographical Note

Wolf in *Peasant Wars of the Twentieth Century* (New York, 1969). Differing approaches can be found in Barrington Moore, *The Social Origins of Dictatorship and Democracy* (Boston, 1966), Eric Hobsbawm, *Primitive Rebels* (New York, 1959), and Henry Landsberger, ed., *Rural Protest* (London, 1974). Throughout the 1970s and 1980s, the debate raged in the pages of the *Journal of Peasant Studies.* Important contributions were made by Sidney Mintz (October 1974), Terry Cox (January 1984), Judith Enew (July 1977), Mark Harrison (January 1977), Teodor Shanin (October 1973), Claude Meillasoux (October 1973 and April 1983), and Eric Hobsbawm (October 1973).

The prevailing consensus on the Russian peasant was thoroughly challenged by Moshe Lewin, *Russian Peasants and Soviet Power* (London, 1968), and Teodor Shanin, *The Awkward Class* (Oxford, 1972). Their studies provoked new work on the Russian peasant, much of it still in progress. Three important works from the next wave of research are Esther Kingston-Mann, *Lenin and the Problem of Peasant Revolution* (Oxford, 1983), Dorothy Atkinson, *The End of the Russian Land Commune* (Stanford, 1983), and Maureen Perrie, *The Agrarian Policy of the Russian Socialist-Revolutionary Party* (Cambridge, 1976). Although it has been challenged on several important points, Geroid Robinson's *Rural Russia under the Old Regime* (Berkeley, 1932) remains a classic general account. Roberta Manning's *The Crisis of the Old Order in Russia: Gentry and Government* (Princeton, 1982), contains a chapter on peasants in 1905.

This book is based largely on primary sources. These include police archives in the Central State Archive of the October Revolution (TsGAOR) in Moscow (fond 102) Ministry of Justice records (fond 1405) and State Duma materials (fond 1278) in the Central State Historical Archive in Leningrad (TsGIAL). The bulk of the material comes from local archives in Kiev and Zhitomir. These include the papers of the governor-general of the southwest (fond 442) and the Kiev court (fond 318) in the Central State Historical Archive of the Ukrainian SSR (TsGIAU) in Kiev and the provincial administration for peasants (fond 115) in the Zhitomir Region State Archive (ZhOGA).

Published primary sources include the famous contemporary sociological survey of the disorders carried out by the Imperial Free Economic Society. See *Agrarnoe dvizhenie v Rossii v 1905–1906 gg. (AD)*, 2 vols. (St. Petersburg, 1908). See also the massive collection of documents published by Soviet scholars on the fiftieth anniversary of the revolution, F. E. Los', ed., *Revoliutsiia 1905–1907 gg. na Ukraine (UD)*, 3 vols. (Kiev, 1955). Extensive Ukrainian-language research by

Soviet scholars provided broad information on economic conditions and on the disorders themselves. The leading Soviet authority on peasants in the right bank is M. N. Leshchenko. See his *Selianskii rukh na pravoberezhnii ukraini v period revoliutsii 1905–1907 rr.* (Kiev, 1955), and *Ukrainsk'e selo v revoliutsii 1905–1907 rr.* (Kiev, 1977).

Soviet historiography on the peasant movement and the agricultural revolution is highly developed. For years the field was dominated by S. M. Dubrovskii, *Krestianskoe dvizhenie v revoliutsii 1905–1907 gg.* (Moscow, 1956), and P. N. Pershin, *Agrarnaia revoliutsiia v Rossii,* 2 vols. (Moscow, 1966). Their work has been challenged in different ways by A. M. Anfimov, *Ekonomicheskoe polozhenie i klassovaia borba krestian evropeiskoi Rossii, 1881–1904 gg.* (Moscow, 1984), and I. D. Kovalchenko and his collaborators. See Kovalchenko and L. Milov, *Vserossiiskii agrarnyi rynok* (Moscow, 1974), and I. D. Kovalchenko, N. B. Selunskaia and B. M. Litvakov, *Sotsial'no-ekonomicheskii stroi pomeshchich'ego khoziaistva evropeiskoi Rossii v epokhu kapitalizma* (Moscow, 1982).

In the absence of detailed statistical material that might have been compiled by *zemstvos,* had there been *zemstvos* in the southwest, it was necessary to reconstruct the economy of the region from the extensive contemporary professional and scientific literature on agriculture in the region. The bulletin of the sugar industry *(Vestnik sakharnoi promyshlennosti)* and the monthly journal of the Kiev Agronomic Society *(Zemledelie)* were especially useful.

Index of Sources

To assist the reader in following up references, an index to the complete citations of the works used in this book has been compiled. Short titles following an author's name indicate more than one work published in a single year.

Index of Sources

General Index

Abamelek-Lazarev, Prince, 112–13, 127
Activists. *See* Political activists; *name of specific group (e.g., Agricultural workers)*
Adamovka [Kiev], 115
Agricultural workers, 71–80, 81, 145–48, 152, 156–57. See also *Batraks*
Agulhon, Maurice, 12
Alavi, Hamza, 11, 29, 31
Alexander II, 41, 47
Allotments to peasant households, 151–52
American path to capitalism, 45, 133, 171
Anfimov, A. M., 28
Anti-Semitism, 40, 119, 160–61
Arson. *See* Disorders: forms of

Balashev family, 54–55, 56–57, 114
Balt district [Podol'e], 91
Baltic provinces, 76, 80
Batraks, 142–43, 147
Bazaars and fairs, 112–13
Berger, John, 17, 24
Bezrobodko family, 50
Bloody Sunday, 84–85, 93
Bobrinskii family, 50, 54–55, 90, 114, 130
Bogdanovka [Volynia], 113
Bolshaia-Ternovka [Podol'e], 155

Bolsheviks, 117, 145, 161–62. *See also* Social Democrats
Bourgeoisie, 38, 46. *See also* Merchants
Brannitskii family, 50, 54–55, 127, 161
Bratslav [Podol'e], 144
Brodskii family, 100–101, 118, 160

Capitalism: American path to, 45, 133, 171; and peasants, 20, 22–23, 27–28, 29, 131–32; Prussian path to, 44–45, 71, 80–81, 132, 170–77; and rural proletariat, 8, 9–10, 15, 71
Central Black Earth region, 35, 37, 70, 101, 105, 161. *See also name of estate, province, and village*
Chaianov, Alexander V., 4, 14, 16–18, 20, 24
Character of peasants, 2–7
Chernigov [province], 41
Chigirin [Kiev], 144–45, 157
Chikhachev, Admiral, 144
Children, 56, 58, 77
Clerical activism, 118
Closed shop, 128–29, 135
Collectivization program, 4, 10, 142
Commercial agriculture, 38–39, 40–61, 97, 132. *See also* Sugar industry
Communes, 3–4, 8, 13–14, 16–17, 24, 61–63. *See also* Villages

General Index

Confino, Michael, 29
Conservatives' views of peasants, 2
Constitutional Democratic party
[Kadets], 164–65
Contracts, 74–75
Crop stealing. *See* Disorders: forms of
Culturalists' views of peasants, 13–14,
16–33, 170, 171, 172, 174
Culture, 5, 63–64, 96–97. *See also* Culturalists' views of peasants
Czechs in Southwest Russia, 39–40

Dairy farming, 43
Demands of peasant movement, 121–
32, 135–36, 165–66
Demidova, Elena Petrovna, 53–54
Didovshchina [Kiev], 130, 159–60
Disorders: after 1907, 167; attitudes of
police/soldiers toward, 140–41,
153–54; causes of, 84; forms of,
85–86, 90–91; and government repression, 138–41; and nonstrike
scenarios, 137–38; number of, 85,
87, 89, 92–93, 98; prior to 1905,
84; spread of, 87, 88; timing of, 94,
97–99; urban, 84, 87. *See also*
Strikes; Violence
Distilleries, 43, 48–49
Doctors, rural, 118–19
Donskoi, Doctor, 119
Dovgiallo, Anna, 107
Drozdov, G., 76, 78–79, 125–26
Dubrovskii, S. M., 27, 79, 85, 86, 92,
98, 116, 125–26, 142
Duma, 87, 100, 107, 110, 120, 125,
127, 163–65, 166
Durrenberger, Paul, 24
Dziunkovskii sugar plantation, 115

Eiler, A. A., 105, 116–17, 141
Ekaterinoslav [province], 41, 47, 62
Elders, village, 155–56
Emancipation of 1861, 36, 41–46, 45,
50, 65, 82, 127
Enew, Judith, 19
Engels, Frederick, 9
England, 17, 25, 28, 103

Family, importance of, 19, 20–21, 22,
26–27, 38–39
Ferro, Marc, 31
Fillipovich, Nestor, 113, 115
Forest offenses. *See* Disorders: forms of
France, 2, 5, 12, 16, 28–29, 110–11

Free Economic Society, reports of: Kiev
disorders, 1–2; land hunger, 100;
participation in disorders, 114,
143–45, 148, 157; repression of
disorders, 140; wages, 123, 126;
working conditions, 130

Gaisin [Podol'e], 110, 144
Galeski, Boguslaw, 18–19
Galiatinskii, S. S., 108
Geiden, Alexander Feodorovich, 49
Gel'man, Samuel, 119
Germanovskaia Slobodka [Kiev], 136
Germans/Germany, 9, 12, 39–40, 50,
172. *See also* Prussian Junkers;
Prussian path to capitalism
Gill, Graeme, 31, 32
Goodman, David, 24
Government: disorders against, 84–85,
86; petitions to, 107–8; repression
by, 87, 136, 138–41
Grain, 41–43, 47, 48–49, 51–52, 70,
83, 101
Great Russians, 39–40
Gudim-Levkovich, Prince, 141

Harrison, Mark, 19, 20–21, 174
Harvests, 101–2
Heads of households. *See* Villages: assemblies in
Hereditary tenure, 61–63
Hilton, Rodney, 23, 28–29
Hobsbawm, Eric, 14, 19, 23
Hops farming, 43
Huang, Phillip, 16

Iampolsk [Podol'e], 144
Iaroshevich, A. I., 67
Industry, 72–73, 83, 93, 109, 125, 172.
See also Sugar industry
Intellectuals/rural intelligentsia, 2, 118

Jews, 39–40, 58, 100–101, 160–61
Johnson, Robert, 38

Kachanovka [Podol'e], 137–38
Kamenets [Podol'e], 122
Kashperovka [Kiev], 123
Keep, John, 31
Kharkov [province], 41, 62, 68, 84, 89
Kherson [province], 41, 47, 62, 68
Kholonevskii, Stanislav, 137
Kiev: disorders in, 92, 94, 95, 111–12,
114, 120, 147, 150; landholding

General Index

Novorossia (*continued*)
  125; migrant labor in, 38; peasant movement in, 96; population in, 37; poverty in, 68; women in, 156; working conditions in, 76
Novo-Ushits [Podol'e], 112
Novyi Chartori [Volynia], 130

October Manifesto [1905], 87, 93, 98, 111, 115, 129, 161
Okninaia [Kiev], 129
Ol'shanitsa [Kiev], 115, 119, 140, 161
Ol'shevskii [Podol'e], 112, 130
Ometintsy [Podol'e], 155
Orel [province], 85
Osadchii, T. I., 61–62
Ownership of land, 12–15, 22, 73–74, 77. *See also* Nobles; Peasant landholding

Paige, Jeffrey, 22
Patriarchal structure, 80, 123, 153, 156, 158. *See also* Family, importance of; Villages
Pavel' Vikul', Father, 118
Peasant agriculture, 61–64, 67–71, 81, 84, 101, 133. *See also* Peasant landholding; Russian peasants
Peasant landholding, 46, 61–71, 82, 144, 145
Peasant movement: aftermath of, 166–68; and capitalism, 131–32, 170–77; causes of, 99–108; character of, 92, 93, 96–97, 99; conditions leading to, 82–84, 85–91; demands of, 121–32, 165–66; external influences on, 107, 109–21, 159–66; forms of, 94–97; and mobilization of peasants, 146; patterns of participation in, 141–48; peasant leadership in, 141, 144, 148–52; and politics, 115–20, 121, 131, 161–66, 170; results of, 166–68; and revolution of 1917, 167–68; spread of, 108–21, 161–66; statistical extent of agitation during, 85, 87, 89, 92–94, 98; summary of, 170; and timing of disorders, 97–99; and tradition, 158, 170; and urban proletariat, 107, 113–14, 131–32. *See also* Disorders; Land hunger; Wages; *name of estate, family, province, and village*
Peasant Union, 115, 116, 119, 162, 163

Peasants: character of, 2–7; conservative behavior of, 2; and culture, 5, 63–64; definition of, 13, 14, 15–16, 19–20; intellectuals' views of, 2; liberal views of, 2–3; populists' views of, 3, 5, 6, 7; revolutionary potential of, 4–5, 6, 8–9, 10–12; schools of thought about, 13–25; Slavophile concept of, 2, 5; and socialist movement, 4; and Third World countries, 22–23. *See also* Rural proletariat; Russian peasants; *name of specific country*
Perkins, J. A., 12
Perrie, Maureen, 31–33
Pershin, P. N., 27
Personal dignity, 129–31
Pikova [Podol'e], 130
Pilipy-Aleksandrovi [Podol'e], 112
Podgarskii, Valdislav, 139
Podol'e: allotments of peasant households in, 151; disorders in, 92, 94, 95, 111–12, 154; farming in, 43; landholding around, 46, 64, 99, 122, 126, literacy in, 110; peasant movement in, 108, 109, 148; political activists in, 116–17; population of, 38; prices in, 105; village cohesion in, 159; wages in, 103, 122–23, 123, 124, 124, 128; working conditions in, 129, 130. *See also* Southwest Russia; *name of specific district, estate, family, and village*
Pogrobishche [Kiev], 115
Poida, D. P., 89
Poland, 35, 62
Police/soldiers: attitudes toward disorders, 140–41, 153–54
Polish in Southwest Russia, 39–41, 44, 45, 48, 89
Political activists, 115–20, 121, 131, 161–66
Politics, 27, 28–33, 87, 131, 161–66, 170
Poltava [province], 41, 84, 89
Popkin, Samuel, 22–23
Popovaia [Podol'e], 127, 136
Populists, 3, 5, 6, 7
Potato farming, 43, 48–49
Pototskii family, 50, 54–55, 74–75, 110, 111
Poverty of peasants, 61, 67–60, 84, 99, 171
Prices, 66, 105–6

General Index

Working conditions, 74–76, 122, 129–31
Wrangel', Baroness, 139

Zagrebel'nyi family, 51
Zasulich, Vera, 24

Zavadovka [Kiev], 124
Zemlitsy [Volynia], 68
Zemstvos, 47–48
Zhidovets [Kiev], 130
Zhidovtsy [Kiev], 156
Zhitomir [Volynia], 157
Zvenigorod [Kiev], 143